Word Attack
p. 144

Betty
@ 19

Sounds of Language p. 50

Advance Organizers p. 76
Sounds of Language p. 50
Affixes p. 158-59
Reading Formats p. 195-7

p. 236

p. 237

p. 144
103
168-69

Get Little Ann
to make transparencies
p. 66
69

p. 228
113
109-11
137
203

206
60
75
114

p. 205
Strategies
Syn.
Ant.

Wordless Story books
p. 323-4

Teaching and Learning Reading

A PRAGMATIC APPROACH

Teaching and Learning Reading

A PRAGMATIC APPROACH

Barbara E. R. Swaby
University of Colorado at Colorado Springs

Little, Brown and Company
Boston   Toronto

To my parents

Library of Congress Cataloging in Publication Data

Swaby, Barbara.
  Teaching and learning reading.

  Includes bibliographical references.
  1. Reading. I. Title.
LB1050.S955 1984   428.4'07   83-19930
ISBN 0-316-82440-2

Library of Congress Catalog Card No. 83-19930

ISBN 0-316-82440-2

9 8 7 6 5 4 3 2 1

HAL

Published simultaneously in Canada
by Little, Brown & Company (Canada) Limited

Printed in the United States of America

TEXT CREDITS

Chapter 1, page 8:   "Brown Bear, Brown Bear, What Do You See?" From *Bill Martin Instant Readers* by Bill Martin, Jr. Copyright © 1970 by Holt, Rinehart and Winston, Publishers. Reprinted by permission of the publisher.
Chapter 2, page 25:   From *The Bus Ride,* Reading Unlimited, Scott Foresman Systems, revised, Level 2, 2–11. Copyright © 1971 by Scott, Foresman and Company, Glenview, Ill. Reprinted by permission.

(continued on page 334)

Preface

The acquisition of reading may be considered the most valuable gift that schools can give to children. Indeed, reading is such an important skill that it is a mistake to think of it as a subject; rather, it is an introduction to living and an extension of knowledge.

This text is built on the premise that there are two basic philosophies underlying reading instruction. The first is the "curriculum-driven" philosophy, which views the reading curriculum as the primary focus. That curriculum is seen as relatively inviolate and children are taught and retaught the information until they learn it appropriately and learn it in the way it is presented.

The second view — the "alternatives-driven" philosophy — sees the child as the primary focus. It accepts the notion that the best and most effective route into reading may be different for many groups of children. All reading curricula, then, must be modified to meet the needs of children.

This text totally endorses the second philosophy. I view the teaching of reading as a spiral of modifications of any given curriculum based on the strengths and weaknesses of children. I am fully aware, however, that in order to be able to modify curriculum, to teach *reading* rather than to teach a *text,* teachers must have a thorough knowledge of the reading process, children's learning styles, and strategies of reading instruction. To this end, this text provides clear, practical, and realistic information relevant to these three topics.

In the area of the reading process, the text provides a thorough analysis of the six major methodological perspectives in the field of reading instruction. It also gives a clear explanation of the process of comprehension.

In the area of learning styles, the text explains the major characteristics of inductive and noninductive learners and shows the ways in which learning styles affect the processing of information and dictate specific instructional procedures.

In the area of instructional strategies, the text provides a myriad of procedures designed to effectively teach reading to the average reader, the gifted reader, the remedial reader, and the child with oral language difficulties. Valuable suggestions for motivating children to read and for involving parents in the learning-to-read task are included.

The entire text adheres to psycholinguistic theory, which places primary emphasis on the importance of prior knowledge in reading. Reading is viewed as an active information-seeking activity in which a reader brings prior knowledge to bear and links that knowledge to the information presented by the writer. This active connection is responsible for the richness of comprehension. The teacher's responsibility is to assist children in reaching this vital level of interaction with print. Major stress, therefore, is placed on interactive teaching.

Throughout the text a conscious and continuous effort has been made to merge theory and teaching practice. By helping teachers *use* theory to heighten the effectiveness of instruction, it is hoped that the information in this book will assist teachers in becoming not only skilled technicians of reading, but also effective artists in the teaching of reading.

After dealing with basic issues like definitions of reading and approaches to reading in the initial two chapters, we go on to take an in-depth look at the basal reader approach in the third chapter. This is followed by a detailed chapter on comprehension. In Chapters 5, 6, and 7 the topics of readiness, word recognition and word analysis, and basal reading instruction are covered. Teaching the remedial reader and the gifted are the topics of Chapters 8 and 9. Oral language development is the subject of Chapter 10, and the final chapter focuses on developing interest and motivation. The book concludes with four appendices.

In preparing the text, a number of people were instrumental in providing me with invaluable assistance. I would like to acknowledge the editorial staff of Little, Brown and Company, particularly Mylan Jaixen, Cynthia Mayer, and Sally Stickney, who not only got the project started, but who offered capable leadership. I would also like to thank my reviewers, many of whom provided valuable and constructive guidance. They were: Gerald H. Maring, Washington State University; Marvin E. Oliver, Eastern Washington University; Peggy E. Ransom, Ball State University; Don Richardson, The University of Kansas; and Diane Ris, Morehead State University. Most sincere appreciation is offered to my typist, Judy Jones, who spent hundreds of hours typing, retyping, and revising the entire text; and to Ann Higgins and Margaret Bacon for their assistance in initial typing, editing, and analysis of the content.

Barbara E. R. Swaby

Brief Contents

Reading Process
6 major methodological perspectives / 1. Phonic
2. Linguistic
Basal — 3. Language Immersion
4. Symbol Augmentation
5. Individualized
6. Basal

Learning Styles
Major characteristics of inductive and non-inductive learners

Instructional Strategies for:
average
remedial
gifted
Child with oral language difficulties

Readiness

Word Recognition

Psycholinguistic theory
Interactive teaching

Developing Interest
and Motivation

Contents

⊕ Merge of theory & Teaching Practice

ch 2 Approaches
Basal

(Ch 4.) Comprehension

Chs 5, 6, 7 Readiness

3
The Basal Reader: Insights   46

4
Understanding Comprehension as a Process 62

5
Reading Readiness 118

6
Word Recognition and
Word Analysis Skill Instruction   *140*

7
The Basal Reading Lesson   *186*

8
Diagnosis and Remediation
of the Remedial Reader   *210*

9
Reading and the Gifted and Creative Reader   *244*

10
Oral Language and Reading Development   *278*

Teaching and Learning Reading

A PRAGMATIC APPROACH

1

Reading: Definitions and Perspectives

The field of reading is one of the most intriguing, complex, and seemingly overwhelming areas in all education. But what is reading? What is the definition of reading? Is there one definition of reading? These are questions that should be and often are asked by professionals involved in education, particularly elementary education. Regardless of how we answer each question, there are two general premises about reading that many mature readers would accept. Conscious attention to these premises makes it easier to arrive at a personal definition of reading.

☐ How does a teacher's definition of reading affect the way in which that teacher teaches reading?

☐ What are some of the major definitions represented in the field of reading?

☐ What are the main implications that result from a particular definition of reading?

☐ How does the teacher make his or her definition obvious to the children he or she teaches?

Basic Premises

Reading and Language

Reading has something to do with spoken language. We may not be sure about the exact nature of this relationship, but we intuitively feel that there are strong connections. Our ability to speak — to manipulate sounds — assists us in some way in reading print. Spoken language is affected by three major systems, which linguists call syntax or word order; semantics or word meaning; and phonology or sound. Each system allows us as speakers of the language to use natural prediction skills to process and understand spoken language quickly and successfully.

Syntax helps us predict the sequence of spoken words. Our knowledge of syntax tells us that certain parts of speech fit into specific slots in a sentence. At the simplest level, the phrase "The farmer _____" will likely be followed by either a single verb or an adverb followed by a verb. It is very unlikely to be followed by a noun. In contrast, the phrase "The farmer's _____" will most likely be followed by a single noun or an adjective followed by a noun. Syntax gives us certain expectations about word order and sequence in spoken language.

Semantics in language has to do with meaning; it allows us to make predictions based on content. Suppose we are involved in a discussion about a farm, and the following statement is made: "I want to help the farmer cut the _____." Our knowledge of syntax leads us to expect a noun, and our knowledge of semantics helps us predict that the noun will be something like *wheat*, *corn*, or *hay* rather than *wave*, *shell*, or *cloud*.

Phonology in language refers to sound. If in the previous sentence, "I want to help the farmer cut the _____," we are told that the omitted noun begins with the sound /h/, we strongly expect the word *hay*.

Syntax, semantics, and phonology work together to help us predict spoken language, and in varying degrees they also help us read printed language.

Reading and Early Experience

Familiarity with, attention to, and prediction of printed language are aspects of reading that should begin to be developed prior to formal reading instruction. We know intuitively that familiarity with print assists the acquisition and development of reading skills. We know

Children's early experiences with print prior to formal reading instruction assist them in the acquisition and development of their reading skills.

that books should be a stable part of young children's home environment. If from a very young age children are read to, they become familiar with books and learn early the importance and the pleasure of print. They learn to attend to print. They learn that print carries meaning, and so they expect meaning from it. They learn that the pictures in books relate to the content and are thus an aid to prediction. They learn that print starts at the left and moves to the right. They learn that words are spelled the same way from book to book regardless of factors such as color or size of print. They also learn that, despite the similarities, printed language differs from spoken language. They learn a basic, meaningful sight vocabulary and then they begin to use their own inductive strategies to abstract letter-sound relations from that vocabulary. They learn that their opinions about print are important and that reading is to be discussed. Many of these skills and attitudes should emerge by the time children enter school. This expectation points to the important part parents play in fostering reading in children.

The two premises — that reading is related to spoken language and that reading skills are related to early experience with printed language — can help us begin to formulate our definitions and perspectives of reading.

Toward a Definition of Reading

One of the most pressing needs of teachers of reading is articulating their own definition of reading and recognizing the instructional implications of that definition. To arrive at their own definition, teachers must sort out the many definitions of reading that have been formulated by educators. Each definition emphasizes certain aspects of the reading process. We will examine three definitions of reading and then go on to analyze which aspects of the reading process each emphasizes.

Three Definitions of Reading

Leonard Bloomfield (1942) defines reading as the act of turning letters of the alphabet into speech. He sees reading primarily as a decoding process that results in the production of appropriate sounds from specific combinations of letters. Bloomfield clearly emphasizes the decoding or sound elements of reading. This position is still popular. There is no question that reading involves decoding; Bloomfield simply focuses on this aspect. His rationale for his definition is that young children are language users who have a good grasp of oral language production and comprehension but who cannot turn combinations of written letters into sound. Children's ability to use their oral comprehension skills is very important once they have mastered reading, but the first skill to be learned is decoding or saying the sounds of combinations of letters.

Kenneth Goodman (1976) defines reading as a process in which a person reconstructs a message encoded by a writer in printed language. Goodman emphasizes the meaning of reading. He sees reading as an active language process that is highly dependent on prediction. Goodman feels that because reading is a language process, it is affected largely by the same factors that affect oral language: the systems of syntax, semantics, and phonology. (In reading, the last system, phonology, is referred to as *grapho-phonology* or *symbol-sound relationships*.) Whereas Bloomfield places almost total emphasis on grapho-phonology, Goodman sees each system as extremely vital and places more emphasis on syntax and semantics than on phonology. To Goodman, reading is the ability to use all the systems in language to make predictions constantly from print. Goodman believes that all grammatical sentences contain semantic, syntactic, and grapho-phonological information that, if used together, makes the act of reading a basic problem-solving or information-gathering activity. In reading the sentence "John went downtown to buy a new shirt," our first clue is the word *John*. Syntactically, we can predict that the next word will most likely be a verb. Semantically, we know that *John* is a person, so the verb will be related to human activity (*ran, walked, called*) as opposed to nonhuman activity (*barked, quacked, rained*). Grapho-phonologically, we know that the word begins with the sound /w/, which eliminates words like *ran* or *called* and allows us to predict words like *went, walked,* or *washed*. Further graphic information (/e/, /n/, /t/) leads us to expect the word *went*.

Similarly, the word *went* leads us to predict a prepositional phrase or an adverb (syntax), specifying a place (semantics) beginning with the sound /d/. Thus Goodman sees reading as a series of prediction activities assisted by the syntactic, semantic, and grapho-phonological information present in printed language. To focus predominantly on the graphic clues, as Bloomfield does, means to disregard context clues; this approach makes reading significantly more difficult and inefficient.

A third definition of the reading process comes from Sylvia Ashton-Warner (1963), who views reading as a natural extension of the oral language process. Ashton-Warner sees reading as an intensely personal act in which the individual attends to, assimilates, interprets, and reacts to verbal expression encoded in print. Her definition emphasizes the emotional aspects of reading and considers reading a personal investment in verbal graphic communication. Reading is language and has a striking similarity to speech. Therefore, the clues that make interpreting speech easy also make reading easy. Young readers must learn immediately that speech can be written down as print and should be just as understandable in written form as it is in oral form. As speakers, children are active participants in oral conversations; similarly, as readers, they must learn to be active participants in graphic conversations.

The three different views of reading emphasize particular aspects of the reading process. But what is the purpose of a definition of reading? Are definitions the domain of reading theorists, or do they have practical applications for the actual job of teaching reading to children?

Relating Definitions to Teaching

Our definition of reading dictates the instructional methods we will endorse. Our answer to the question "What is reading?" will lead directly to the answer to another question: "How should we teach reading?" We can see the connection between definitions and instructional methods by considering the preceding three definitions and their instructional implications.

Bloomfield defines reading as the process of decoding or producing appropriate sounds from specific combinations of letters (Bloomfield, 1942). If we accept this definition, how would we instruct children in reading? Initially, we would place heavy emphasis on the sound system of the language. We would teach children to focus on and recognize the patterns in print and to use the patterns in decoding. We would teach patterns such as consonant-vowel-consonant (c-v-c), as in *cat, rat, mat, pat* or *pin, tin, sin, kin*. Because the primary emphasis is on the symbol-sound system, children's first reading material would be determined by that system. Material would consist of sentences like "The cat is fat" rather than "The little girl ran to her mother."

Comprehension would not be a major concern in initial reading instruction because the main emphasis is on word analysis. Comprehension would be limited primarily to literal recall. More inferential strategies would be included as children become more proficient in handling decoding.

Goodman's definition of reading is the reconstruction of meaning using all three cue systems in language (Goodman, 1976). What are the instructional implications of this definition? Obviously, the definition includes symbol-sound knowledge, but the most important skill according to Goodman is prediction. For prediction to work naturally, however, the language of print must be quite similar to the language of speech. The more predictable the printed language, the more accurate predictions are likely to be. The reading material used to satisfy the first definition — sentences such as "The cat is fat" — would be unacceptable under Goodman's definition because of limited language clues and lack of predictability. Reading instruction based on Goodman's definition would need to begin with meaningful, predictable language such as "Brown Bear, Brown Bear, what do you see? I see Yellow Duck looking at me. Yellow Duck, Yellow Duck, what do you see? I see Green Frog looking at me" (*Brown Bear*, 1974). Because of the natural flow of the language, children are easily able to predict and memorize such printed material. Once they understand the meaning, they can be taught meaningful sight words; then phonics would be presented as an aid to meaning. Children would be taught immediately to use context (syntax and semantics) in decoding and to depend on context clues at least as much as they depend on phonic clues. Comprehension would be a requirement as soon as reading instruction begins because reading is defined as the reconstruction of meaning.

Ashton-Warner defines reading as a personal investment in graphic conversation (Ashton-Warner, 1963). To teach reading according to this definition, we would allow children to converse with the most meaningful and intimate people they know: themselves. Children would be encouraged to speak, to give their opinions about any topic of interest. Their speech would be written down, and it would become their first reading material. Because the content is so meaningful, personal, and predictable, successful understanding of the printed material would be inevitable. Once the personal, interactive link has been made, children would be taught a sight vocabulary and phonic skills that would help them understand not only their own written material but also the written material of others.

It is clear that there are numerous definitions of reading, although we have considered only three, and that instruction in reading is a direct outgrowth of a particular definition. In addition, children will internalize their own definition of reading based on our instructional methods. Children taught according to the "reading is decoding" approach, for example, will emerge from their reading experience with the personal definition that reading is sounding out or calling words. Our first task, then, as teachers of reading is to formulate our own definition and to understand how our instructional methods will be determined by that definition.

A Personal Definition of Reading

This book is an outgrowth of my personal and professional definition of reading: Reading is an active language process in which the reader uses the familiar language clues of syntax, semantics, and phonology to aggressively and purposefully anticipate and access meaning in printed language. The strategies I recommend in this book are aimed at helping teachers assist children in making conscious and effective use of all three cue systems in graphic language.

The rationale for this text is built on seven major premises.

1. *Reading is closely related to language.* The ability to use spoken language is of great significance and assistance in learning to read. Children need to be shown from early childhood that print represents language; that it has a predictable pattern; that it can reflect pitch,

pause, and stress; that it represents the human emotions; and that oral reading is done with the normal expression of spoken language.

2. *Language development assists reading development.* Because reading is a form of language, we can assume that growth in oral language will affect reading skill. Similarly, growth in reading will typically affect speech and comprehension of speech. As children develop complex language skills and a complex vocabulary, they can make more sophisticated predictions in reading. As they develop strength in the comprehension of oral language, in the ability to think critically and creatively, and in the ability to respond flexibly in problem-solving situations, these strengths should also be evident in their reading.

3. *Reading is an active process.* Reading is not passive. It involves a large degree of personal interaction. To gain meaning from print, readers must actively bring their own knowledge and skills to the task of reading. Reading is most successful when the knowledge and skills of the reader interact with the information provided by the writer. This interaction results in the meaningful interchange crucial to comprehension.

4. *Reading is anticipation.* Reading is an active process partly because the natural anticipation of meaning causes readers to constantly predict printed language. Children learn intuitively to anticipate meaning from their oral linguistic environment. They know that language is supposed to be meaningful, and they learn to use all cues in language to anticipate meaning. This anticipation allows speakers to understand speech that is too fast or too garbled to be decoded word by word. This anticipation also allows readers to decipher print quickly and efficiently.

5. *Reading depends on prior knowledge.* If reading depends on anticipation, then it must to a large degree depend on the knowledge that makes anticipation and prediction successful. Comprehension in reading depends on the reader's prior knowledge, on information the reader brings to the task of reading. If the reading material tells a story that takes place on an Indian reservation, the reader's understanding of the story depends to a large degree on what the reader knows about an Indian reservation. This dependence on prior knowledge does not mean that readers' understanding is limited only to their existing knowledge. It simply means that new information must be made relevant to their knowledge.

6. *Reading depends on interest.* Since reading is an active process, it requires that the reader be at least as involved as the writer. One of the factors that makes the interchange between writer and reader successful is the reader's interest in the information the writer com-

Instructional materials that interest children will make them more eager to spend time and energy learning to read.

municates. The greater the reader's interest, the more willing the reader will be to invest the time and energy necessary for comprehension. Material used to teach children to read, therefore, should be constructed so that it not only stimulates prediction but also captures children's interest.

7. *Reading instruction depends on the ability of the teacher to modify instructional materials.* Teachers often have no control over the materials they use to teach reading. Any material directly reflects an author's (or authors') definition of reading. It is imperative that teachers identify the definition of reading implied or stated in the texts they use and compare it to their own definition of reading. The success of teaching reading rests on the teacher's knowledge of materials, of children, and of strategies that can be used both to build on the strengths of and to compensate for the weaknesses of any reading materials.

Summary

There are many definitions of reading, three of which are considered in the chapter. The definition of reading accepted by a teacher affects both the strategies of instruction and the materials the teacher uses to teach reading. In addition, the strategies and materials used with children lead them to formulate their own definitions of reading. Each reading series or set of reading materials reflects a definition of reading, either stated or implied. When teachers use instructional materials, they consciously or unconsciously are influenced by that definition. Thus, the teacher's and the materials' definitions of reading affect the instructional strategies the teacher uses and these in turn affect children's definitions and impressions of reading.

It is very important that teachers formulate their own definitions of reading, develop the ability to identify the definition implied in the materials they use, and be constantly aware of how their instructional methods create and reinforce children's own definitions of reading.

References

Ashton-Warner, S. *Teacher*. New York: Simon & Schuster, 1963.

Bloomfield, L. "Linguistics and Reading." *Elementary English Review*, no. 19 (April–May 1942).

Brown Bear, Brown Bear, What Can You See? Bill Martin Instant Readers. New York: Holt, Rinehart and Winston, 1974.

Goodman, K. "What We Know About Reading." In *Findings of Research in Miscue Analysis: Classroom Implications*, edited by P. David Allen and Dorothy J. Watson. Urbana, Ill.: E.R.I.C. Clearinghouse on Reading and Communication Skills and National Council of Teachers of English, 1976.

2

Current Approaches to Reading Instruction

This chapter examines the six predominant methodologies presently used in teaching reading: phonics, linguistics, language immersion, symbol augmentation, individualization, and basal readers. Each approach is based on a specific definition of reading, which in turn determines the instructional method. Each approach has its own strengths and weaknesses and no one approach is effective for all children. Success in teaching reading lies in the ability of the teacher to modify any approach to meet the needs of individual children.

☐   What are six major methodologies of teaching reading?

☐   What is the philosophy of each methodology?

☐   What are the most important characteristics of the major methodologies?

☐   Are there any methodologies that are particularly effective for specific groups of children?

☐   Is there any methodology that has been identified by research as the best method of reading instruction?

Evaluating Methodologies

To facilitate our study of current approaches to teaching reading, we must make a distinction between a reading methodology and a reading program. *Methodology* is a general, "umbrella" philosophical position. *Reading program* denotes a specific instructional package that reflects to some degree the philosophical position of a methodology. You can view methodology as the overriding theory and a program as the instructional exemplification of that theory. It is important to acknowledge that different reading programs can reflect the same methodology. A program can exhibit some, most, or all of the basic philosophical positions of a particular methodology; or a program can incorporate portions of several philosophies.

The following six indexes can help us evaluate the predominant methodologies.

1. *Definition of reading and the resulting philosophy of how reading should be taught.* Each methodology is based on a stated or implied definition of reading, and, as we saw in Chapter 1, the definition determines the instructional strategies endorsed by each method.
2. *Historical perspective.* Each methodology evolved out of a specific set of historical realities that gives each methodology a purpose and creates a rationale for its instructional decisions.
3. *Content.* The content of each methodology suggests both a scope (the individual skills to be taught) and a sequence (the sequence in which those skills should be taught) of reading instruction.
4. *Prerequisites of the child and the teacher.* All methodologies will be successful with *some* children. All methodologies will fail with *some* children. Success or failure depends on the degree to which both the teacher and the children possess the prerequisite skills for success in a particular methodology. Knowledge of what the prerequisites are will help teachers make programmatic modifications necessary for the success of children who do not possess the prerequisite skills.
5. *Criticisms or weaknesses.* All methodologies have certain weaknesses. The effectiveness of each methodology rests on the ability of the teacher to identify the weaknesses and compensate for them instructionally.
6. *Strengths.* All methodologies have certain strengths. The effectiveness of each methodology rests on the ability of the teacher to identify the strengths and build on them.

The Phonic Methodology

The phonic methodology places heavy initial emphasis on symbol-sound or letter-sound relationships. It emphasizes the rules that are necessary to help the child make the transition from symbols or letters to sound.

Basic Features

Philosophy   The phonic methodology defines reading as the decoding of graphemes, or letters, into phonemes, or sounds, and the understanding of the rules governing decoding. The underlying philosophy is that reading is a code system; it is speech coded by letters. The key to reading is learning how to break the code that is bound in the letters. Once the code is broken, meaning is released. Because reading is defined as decoding, instruction in reading concentrates on teaching children as quickly as possible to break the code. Instruction thus focuses on teaching the forms and names of letters, associating the letters with their sounds, blending the individual letter pairs, blending strings of letters into words, and learning the rules of more complex pronunciation and syllabication. In initial instruction, secondary attention is placed on sight vocabulary and on processing literal information.

Because the basic philosophy is committed to code breaking, initial instruction in nonliteral comprehension is not a priority. Once children have adequately learned to break the code, they can use their comprehension abilities to consider the actual content of the reading material.

Origin   The phonic methodology of reading dates to the mid-1800s. It grew out of the alphabetic method, which emphasized letter names and spelling, but the phonic methodology stressed letter sounds rather than letter names (Moe and Johnson, 1980). The method enjoyed widespread use from the mid-1800s to the early 1900s, when the use of basal texts was on the rise and phonic programs were viewed as supplementary rather than as total reading programs. The next twenty to thirty years saw a decline in emphasis on phonics and an increasing emphasis on meaning. Around the 1950s, emphasis on phonics in basal programs began to increase, and the trend today is toward a strong phonic strand in basal readers. Intensive phonic programs usually are viewed as ancillary or remedial. Few strict phonic programs are adopted for use in regular classroom settings.

Content   The content of the phonic method consists of instruction in letters, sounds, and blending, and in the rules that explain how phonemes (sounds) are represented by graphemes (letters). This content is communicated to children by two basic strategies: the inductive, or analytic, strategy and the deductive, or synthetic, strategy.

The inductive strategy involves reasoning from particular words to the rules or conclusions about them. For example, children would be presented with words such as *boy, book, bed,* and *ball* as sight words. They would be led to induce or see (1) that the words begin with the same sound, (2) that the words begin with the same letter, (3) that the letter is *b* and the sound is /b/, and (4) that all words that begin with the letter *b* begin with the /b/ sound.

The deductive strategy involves reasoning from the rule to specific applications. For example, children would be presented with the letter *b* and with the rule that the letter *b* represents the sound /b/. This information would be drilled, practiced, and reinforced. Letters such as *a* and *t* would be presented in the same way. Then children would be helped to blend /b/ + /a/ + /t/ to make the word *bat.*

Prerequisites for Children   For the most successful use of phonics programs, children should have good auditory and visual discrimination. Because phonic programs emphasize the sound system of written language, learners must be able to differentiate easily among letter sounds. This is no simple task, as so many sounds are closely related — /b/, /d/, /p/, and /q/, short /i/ and short /e/. In addition, many words in isolation are closely related — *pin* and *pen, big* and *fig, bat* and *bet.* Phonic programs demand that children discriminate auditorily between and among very similar isolated sounds and words. Children are also required to discriminate between and among visually similar stimuli — *b, d, p,* and *q, a, o,* and *e, bag, big, bug,* and *beg.*

If phonics is presented by analytic means, children will need to have inductive skills, that is, to be able to recognize the parts (/b/, /a/, /ll/) in the whole (*ball, bed*). If phonics is represented by synthetic means, children must be able to learn relatively meaningless parts (/b/, /a/, /ll/) and remember the parts over a period of time until they learn meaningful words (*ball*).

Children must have a high learning rate and a good memory. They must be able to learn isolated bits of information quickly and hold them in memory. This is mandatory because phonics consists of bits and pieces of isolated sounds that often do not hold much meaning for children.

Prerequisites for Teachers Teachers must know when it is worthwhile to teach a rule. They must know the prerequisites for children and must be able to modify programs appropriately to meet the needs of children who do not have the adequate prerequisites.

Teachers need to be aware that children who have difficulty processing phonic instruction need to use other strategies of word recognition. Teachers should help children use all clues in language. They should also be able to teach reading to those children who are unable to learn to read using the phonic method.

Teachers must be committed to providing children with many experiences in realistic, meaningful language and to developing high-level comprehension skills through listening. The dull content of initial reading material demands this.

Criticisms and Weaknesses

Critics of the phonic methodology point to some specific programmatic weaknesses. Phonic methods teach reading as though there is a one-to-one correspondence between letters and sounds. But because there are 26 letters and approximately 44 sounds in English, phonics cannot be thought of as the only or even the major strategy of word recognition.

Much unnecessary information is taught in the phonic method — for example, dividing words into syllables or placing accents over syllables. Critics see such strategies as useless, reasoning that if children can read a word, they have successfully syllabicated and accented it, and if children can't read a word, the strategies do not necessarily help them.

Many teachers confuse the teaching of phonics with the teaching of reading. Phonics is a word analysis strategy, but reading is accomplished in connected discourse and involves interaction between the writer and the reader. Much of the mastery of phonics is achieved through paper-and-pencil tasks (workbooks, tests, skill pages, and so on), and often transfer is not made to real reading situations. The heavy emphasis on code results in initial material that is often neither interesting nor realistic. Similarly, the language of the texts is restricted, and inferential comprehension skills are not developed early enough.

Because of the heavy emphasis on decoding, some children may internalize a definition of reading as sounding out words rather than seeking meaning.

Strengths

Programs reflecting the phonic methodology give children very systematic instruction in word analysis skills.

Children who have the prerequisites develop independent reading ability quickly. Children receive a strong background in letter-sound knowledge, which provides them with orderly, productive strategies for decoding new words.

Children are able to read for enjoyment early because of their ability to "sound out" new words independently.

The major characteristics of the phonic methodology can be summarized as shown in Figure 2–1.

Phonic Materials

Keys to Reading Series
Economy Company

Merrill Phonics Skill Texts
Charles Merrill

Phonics Is Fun Series
Modern Curriculum Press

Phonics Plus
Prentice-Hall

Phonics We Use Series
Rand McNally

The Linguistic Methodology

The linguistic methodology capitalizes on the regularity of English spelling. It emphasizes the patterns that exist in the alphabetic spelling system and uses those patterns to teach children the relationships between combinations of letters and sounds.

Basic Features

Philosophy   The linguistic methodology defines reading as a decoding activity in which readers use the patterns implicit in the spelling system to make sounds from letter combinations. The key to learning to read is breaking the code of writing, which is captured in the spelling patterns of written language.

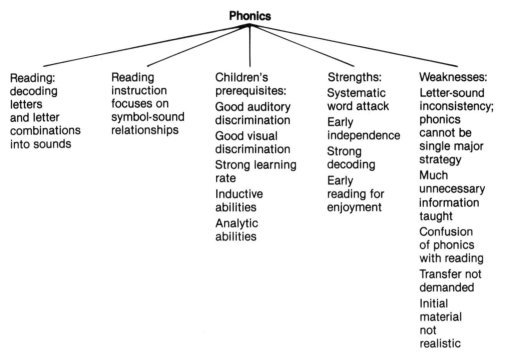

FIGURE 2–1
Major characteristics of the phonic methodology

Since reading is decoding spelling patterns, instruction in reading concentrates on teaching children to recognize the spelling patterns of printed language. Instruction begins with groups of words that conform to spelling patterns — *an, man, fan, tan, can.* Children should be encouraged to discover for themselves the relationship between individual letters and their sounds. First they are taught the spelling patterns. Once children have learned a pattern, another pattern is introduced and is contrasted against the first pattern. For example, pattern 1 = *an*: *pan, man, tan*; pattern 2 = *in*: *pin, min, tin.* Contrast patterns 1 and 2:

      an   in
    pan   pin
   man min
    tan   tin

Notice that nonsense syllables are permissible because the major emphasis is on decoding, not meaning, and because nonsense words will assist eventually in decoding larger words, such as *minister, minstrel.*

Regular spelling patterns should be taught first, and then less regular patterns should be introduced (*fine, week, lead*). Irregularly spelled words (*the, enough, though, through, said*) should be taught as sight words and presented infrequently during initial reading so as not to disturb pattern learning. Breaking the code is the primary objective of reading instruction, so initial attention to developing comprehension skills is not a priority.

Origin   In the late 1930s, the linguist Leonard Bloomfield became interested in the field of reading instruction, motivated by his young son's difficulty with decoding in his early reading experience. Bloomfield began analyzing the existing reading methods and rejected the three major methods used at that time: the phonic, whole word, and ideational methods.

He rejected the phonic method because it taught children to pronounce isolated sounds and thus ignored the basic patterns in writing. He rejected the whole-word method because it treated English writing as though it were a logographic system like Chinese in which each word was viewed as a unique picture that had no real relationship with similar words. He rejected the ideational or "meaning first" method because he felt that children should not struggle with meaning until they had broken the code.

Bloomfield viewed written English as a predictable system that consists of specific spelling patterns. He hypothesized that knowledge of the patterns helps the reader gain meaning from print. As a result of his rejection of existing methods of reading instruction, Bloomfield created the reading program *Let's Read*, which he based on spelling patterns. Because its creator was a linguist, the spelling pattern approach came to be known as the linguistic method of teaching reading. Although some linguists do support the method (Fries, 1962; Lefevre, 1964), the name of the method in no way assumes that it is accepted by all linguistics.

Content   Programs that reflect linguistic methodology contain regularly spelled patterns (*man*), irregularly spelled patterns (*line*), and sight vocabulary (*the*). Because attention is drawn to whole patterns, there is no sounding out of individual letters and no verbalizing of phonic rules. Nonsense syllables can be used because the pattern, not the meaning, is important. Few or no illustrations are used because the total attention of children should be focused on the patterns in words, not on understanding meaning.

Prerequisites for Children   To be successful with linguistic methods, children must have automatic recognition of letters and their names.

They must have visual discrimination skills to help them discriminate among very similar groups of words, such as *bat, tat, lat, pat.*

In addition, children must induce or abstract the phonic information in the linguistic method because letter-sound relationships are not usually taught directly. Thus, an inductive learning style is a prerequisite.

Prerequisites for Teachers Teachers should have a firm understanding of inductive instruction and the ability to modify such instruction to meet the needs of noninductive children. They should be able to familiarize children with a variety of meaningful literature because the material presented to children has very restrictive content ("Nan can fan Dan," "Nat is a fat cat").

Teachers should be able to develop children's comprehension skills through the use of meaningful graphic material that they read to the children, and they must be able to teach reading to those children unable to learn to read using the linguistic method.

Criticisms and Weaknesses

Critics of the linguistic method point to the lack of realistic content because of the restrictive vocabulary. The language used in the beginning books of linguistic programs is very unlike children's language.

In this methodology little immediate attention is given to the development of higher-level comprehension skills. Because of the relatively dull content, linguistic programs require a creative teacher to convince children that reading is enjoyable and that reading has meaning.

Strengths

Programs that reflect the linguistic methodology provide strong instruction in a specific decoding strategy. The focus on spelling patterns makes children aware of those patterns and may help their spelling. Because of the emphasis on spelling patterns, children are exposed to a large number of words in a short amount of time. Because the focus of decoding is not on isolated letters but on words conforming to patterns, children are almost immediately confronted with connected print.

Figure 2–2 presents a summary of the major characteristics of the linguistic methodology.

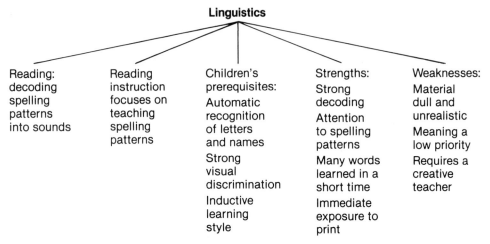

FIGURE 2–2
Major characteristics of the linguistic methodology

Linguistic Materials

Merrill Linguistic Reading Program
Charles Merrill

Miami Linguistic Readers
D. C. Heath

Programmed Reading: Buchanan-Sullivan
McGraw-Hill

The Language Immersion Methodology

The language immersion methodology capitalizes on the common language patterns and vocabulary of children and uses them as the initial graphic material to teach children to read. This methodology emphasizes the strong relationships between oral language and written language and shows that the processes of understanding speech and understanding print are very closely related.

Basic Features

Philosophy   The language immersion methodology defines reading as a process by which readers use all possible language cues to obtain meaning from print. Learning to read involves viewing written language as spoken language and applying skills of interpreting speech to the process of interpreting print.

Since the goal of reading is to extract meaning, the primary objective in instruction is to teach children to anticipate and expect meaning from print. This is achieved by presenting the child with interesting, meaningful, predictable print through constant listening activities (immersion). As children listen to the words, they also follow the print; they can make predictions as they do so, and begin to memorize the print. The first step in reading thus is recognizing that print is meaningful. Once that recognition has been established, sight words are identified, taught, and practiced. Finally, phonic information is pulled out from the sight words and taught. Consider the following example:

> A girl got on the bus.
> Then the bus went fast.
> A boy got on the bus.
> Then the bus went fast.
> A fox got on the bus.
> Then the bus went fast.
> A hippopotamus got on the bus.
> Then the bus went fast.
> A goat got on the bus.
> Then the bus went fast . . . .

First such a story is read often to children. The content is discussed and many literal and inferential questions are asked. Next the children are encouraged to "read along" by following the printed version of the story. Memorization comes easily because of the predictability of the print. When the children understand the story thoroughly and repeat it fluently, words such as *boy* and *bus* are isolated and taught as sight words. Much practice with the words is provided. Children are encouraged to find the sight words in the story and in other printed material.

Finally, letters such as *b* are isolated from words (*boy, bus*), and the sound /b/ is presented. All instruction in phonics is done after phonic skills have been demonstrated in highly meaningful material. Both inferential comprehension and meaningful sight vocabulary are of primary importance.

Origin   Historically, reading instruction has been predominantly code-centered. Reading was always seen primarily as a decoding act and emphasis was placed on breaking the code. As early as the 1940s, however, some educators, such as William S. Gray, called for more emphasis on meaning in initial reading instruction. Though reading instruction remained code-centered, some changes were made. For example, to test children's comprehension, questions were included in reading texts and an effort was made to bring the content of texts closer to the actual experiences of children.

In the mid-1940s, Roach and Claryce Van Allen created the language experience approach, which had a major impact on the instructional practices of that period. The Van Allens created their approach in reaction to the existing code-oriented methods, which they felt promoted word by word reading and de-emphasized comprehension. The language experience approach was based on the premise that there is a strong relationship between oral and graphic language and that this relationship should be evident in reading instruction. Consequently, reading instruction was built around four major propositions:

1. Initial reading material should represent children's speech patterns and vocabulary.
2. Reading instruction should build on the relationship between oral and graphic language.
3. Instruction should focus on helping children realize that reading is communication between a writer and themselves.
4. Reading should be viewed as part of the language arts system, which includes writing, reading, listening, and speaking (Hall, 1976).

Reading instruction, therefore, begins with children dictating sentences or short stories, which their teachers write down for them. Children are guided to read their own statements; they illustrate their own stories, which become their first reading material. From this material, vocabulary items are isolated and taught, and finally sound-symbol relationships are taught. Because children are reading their own language, they begin to realize that many of the clues that operate in oral language also operate in graphic language and that they should actively anticipate meaning from print (Allen and Laminack, 1982; Stauffer, 1980).

The decade following the creation of the language experience approach saw its popularity as an initial teaching method grow steadily. By the 1960s, the approach was known and used across the country. Following the wide use of the language experience approach, several basal texts adopted portions of its philosophy. Gradually, it was modified to include the use of very familiar, popular, predictable, simplified children's literature as initial reading material. The term *language immersion methodology* derives from children's immersion in meaningful literature that was used in initial texts.

Content   The content of programs that reflect the language immersion methodology includes a varied, familiar strand of literature used for listening. Predictable, simplified literature is also used for initial reading instruction, and a strong sight vocabulary is included. Phonic instruction is based on the sight vocabulary. Material to be read is representative of vocabulary, experiences, and language patterns common to a large number of children, so many of the reading selections are familiar to children. Heavy emphasis is placed on oral discussion and a strong literal and inferential comprehension strand is incorporated from the beginning.

Prerequisites for Children   The language immersion method does not have many prerequisites for children, but it requires much of teachers. Children must be able to use oral language and to process language auditorily. They must have a certain interest in literature, some motivation toward reading, and a reasonable memory.

Prerequisites for Teachers   Programs that reflect the language immersion methodology are highly teacher-dependent: they are often somewhat nondirective and expect a high level of flexibility and knowledge from the teacher. Teachers must be skilled in asking questions that develop broad levels of comprehension since this is the major purpose of reading instruction. They must be able to help children use all language systems (syntax, semantics, and phonics) in decoding print.

They must be flexible in dealing with a range of abilities and temperaments in children; they must also be able to present phonic information in a variety of ways to a variety of children; to provide constant oral language reinforcement for children with slower, ineffective language development; and to recognize children who need a more systematic or synthetic presentation of phonic skills and to provide such instruction.

Criticisms and Weaknesses

In general, language immersion programs are extremely teacher-dependent and nondirective, requiring knowledgeable, flexible teachers. Often the skills strand is not as extensive or sequential as some critics prefer.

Language immersion programs lack the internal structural restriction of code programs. Some critics feel that children who are basically nonstructured and noninductive need more structure than language immersion programs provide.

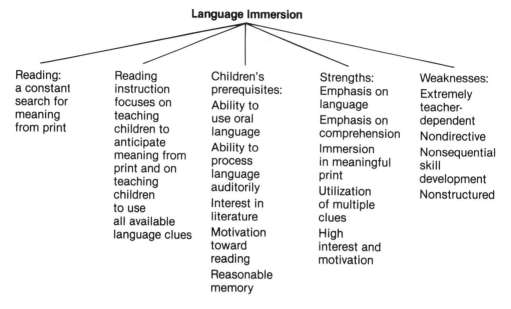

FIGURE 2–3
Major characteristics of the language immersion methodology

Strengths

Language immersion programs emphasize language and comprehension from the beginning stages of reading, and immersion in meaningful language occurs from the beginning. In this methodology multiple clues are used in teaching reading (sight, phonics, syntax, semantics, and so on). This method promotes interest in and motivation toward reading.

Figure 2–3 presents a summary of the major characteristics of the language immersion methodology.

Language Immersion Materials

Instant Readers
Bill Martin and Peggy Brogan
Holt, Rinehart and Winston

Language Experience Activities
Roach and Claryce Van Allen
Houghton Mifflin

Scott, Foresman Reading Systems
Scott, Foresman

Scott, Foresman Reading Unlimited
Scott, Foresman

Sounds of Language Series
Bill Martin and Peggy Brogan
Holt, Rinehart and Winston

The Symbol Augmentation Methodology

The symbol augmentation methodology places heavy initial emphasis
on the symbol-sound relationships in graphic language. To this point
this methodology sounds very much like the phonic methodology.
However, there is a major difference. The symbol augmentation
methodology identifies a huge stumbling block to efficient code
breaking — the fact that single letters in English represent more than
one sound and thus create ambiguity. The solution to this problem
is to augment the alphabet to achieve symbol-sound consistency. The
symbol augmentation methodology presents a 44-character alphabet
rather than the existing 26-letter alphabet.

Basic Features

Philosophy   The symbol augmentation methodology defines reading as the decoding of graphemes, or letters, into phonemes, or
sounds. The underlying philosophy is that reading is code breaking.
Code breaking is a simple process once the ambiguity in graphic
language is eliminated by the augmentation of the existing alphabet.
The graphic code is broken easily and quickly and immediate attention is given to the meaning in print.

Since reading initially involves decoding, instruction in reading
begins with the code. The augmented alphabet consists of letters or
symbols that closely match the sounds in the language (see Figure
2.4). The first step in the methodology is to teach the letters and
their sounds. Children are expected to know and to use the sound
for each letter, and they are taught to blend sounds: /b/ + /a/ + /t/ =
bat. Reading and writing of the sounds and letters are practiced and
reinforced constantly. Once the letters and their sounds have been
learned, reading, writing, and spelling are practiced and extended

FIGURE 2–4
Initial teaching alphabet

quickly. The processes are simplified because there is no ambiguity. When children have learned blending, they practice reading meaningful children's literature, and the emphasis shifts immediately to in-depth comprehension analysis and reading over a wide range of material.

Origin   The symbol augmentation methodology grew out of an effort to simplify spelling rather than reading. Its roots are in the seventeenth century, when an English teacher named Richard Hodges published a program called *Simplified Spelling*, which placed pronunciation marks immediately above or below certain letters to indicate systematic sounds ($\bar{\imath}$ = long /i/). By the 1800s, Benjamin

Pitman proposed an alphabet that combined Simplified Spelling symbols with new symbols. Out of this grew Isaac Pitman's system of Fonotype in the late 1800s. Fonotype used all capital letters, several of which bore little resemblance to English letters. Fonotype was not very popular because the strangeness of the letters made transition to English print difficult.

During the late 1800s and early 1900s, Fonotype underwent several changes. In the 1950s, Sir James Pitman created the initial teaching alphabet (i/t/a) primarily as a reading reform. The letters were simple enough and close enough to English letters to permit easier transition to English print.

In the 1960s, the i/t/a was introduced in the United States and was used experimentally in U.S. schools. Although many schools tried i/t/a in the 1960s and 1970s, very few schools presently use the program.

Content   Programs that reflect the symbol augmentation methodology often initially employ a code-oriented philosophy. In most cases, early emphasis is on code breaking. These programs begin by teaching the letters and sounds of an augmented alphabet. The most popular augmented alphabet is the initial teaching alphabet, which is shown in Figure 2–4.

Children are shown each letter of the augmented alphabet and are told the sound it represents. They practice writing and reading with the augmented alphabet. They then learn blending and, once all letters and sounds have been learned and blended, are ready to read widely. Writing creatively is an integral part of the program, and attention is given to inferential comprehension. The reading material is representative of a wide variety of children's literature. After the first year of instruction, children begin working on the transition to traditional writing and reading.

Prerequisites for Children   This methodology usually employs code breaking, so many of the prerequisites are the same as those of phonic programs. Visual discrimination is necessary because many letters have similar form; for example, /ţh/ = /th/ as in *three*, ţh/ = /th/ as in *the*.

The sound system of language contains very many similar features that require good auditory discrimination; for example, /b/, /d/, /p/, or /q/, and /th/ as in *the* or /th/ as in *three*.

Children must have a fair level of manual dexterity because many of the letters are complicated in form. They must be able to learn phonics either inductively or deductively and must have a reasonable memory for isolated letter-sound relationships.

Prerequisites for Teachers   Teachers must recognize the prerequisites for children so they can modify the program to meet children's needs. They must be flexible in teaching children who find code learning difficult and in using various strategies of teaching code to children. Teachers should be prepared to move children through the transition phase.

Criticisms and Weaknesses

Critics of the symbol augmentation methodology point to the fact that learners must process two alphabets; for children who have difficulty learning code, this program presents more code to be learned and hence may be more difficult. Materials using the augmented alphabet are not readily available, and there is not adequate proof that the transfer to traditional spelling and reading is made with ease.

Strengths

Once children learn to break the code, they learn quickly to spell, read, and write, and they are exposed to a great number of words in a short period of time. Vocabulary is chosen on the basis of child language rather than by phonic rules or by linguistic patterns. Once children learn the letters of the augmented alphabet, they can spell with ease; thus, creative writing is not restricted by inability to spell.

Heavy emphasis is placed on comprehension early in the reading process. Once children break the code, meaningful, interesting literature is presented to them.

Figure 2–5 summarizes the major characteristics of the symbol augmentation methodology.

Symbol Augmentation Materials

Easy-to-Read i/t/a Program
Fearon Pitman

i/t/a Edition
Scholastic Book Services

The Individualized Methodology

The individualized methodology views reading as a personal, meaningful interaction between the writer and the reader. It is the result of a graphic conversation between two individuals and as such its

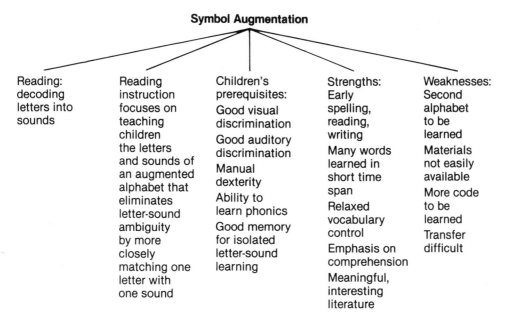

Symbol Augmentation

| Reading: decoding letters into sounds | Reading instruction focuses on teaching children the letters and sounds of an augmented alphabet that eliminates letter-sound ambiguity by more closely matching one letter with one sound | Children's prerequisites: Good visual discrimination Good auditory discrimination Manual dexterity Ability to learn phonics Good memory for isolated letter-sound learning | Strengths: Early spelling, reading, writing Many words learned in short time span Relaxed vocabulary control Emphasis on comprehension Meaningful, interesting literature | Weaknesses: Second alphabet to be learned Materials not easily available More code to be learned Transfer difficult |

FIGURE 2–5
Major characteristics of the symbol augmentation methodology

success depends largely on the experiences and interests that the reader and writer share.

Basic Features

Philosophy The individualized methodology defines reading as an individual's graphic conversation with a writer. The reader invests time and energy in print to understand the intended message of the writer. In addition, the reader's responses to the material result in two-way conversations: questions are asked and answered, information is presented and gained, humor is created and responded to, and emotions are generated and projected.

Because reading is personal communication, the reader must choose the material to be read. Instruction in reading must be provided with the needs and interests of the reader in mind. Children are allowed to choose the material they will read, and they will learn at a pace that is consistent with their needs, abilities, and motivation. Because reading is an individual activity, this methodology rejects the notion of prepackaged reading material found in traditional reading series. Proponents of the individualized methodology feel that such series reflect the interests of very few children and thus fail to motivate most children to interact and converse with print. As children develop their reading ability, they are taught those skills that they demonstrate they need, allowing the reading process to develop effectively for each child.

Origin If we think carefully about the concept of individualized reading — based on personal interest, rate, and motivation — we can see that this concept is relatively old. Some children have used their own individualized approaches and have learned to read prior to school. They have been read to, they have requested books that interest and amuse them to be read to them over and over, they have started to memorize individual words and to ask the identification of unknown words, and they have begun to make their own generalizations about symbol-sound relationships. Their motivation to read was high because learning came from need and desire, not from external imposition.

In the 1950s, the basal series (described in the next section) flourished, and the widespread adoption of basal readers actually contributed to a more formal interpretation of the old concept of individualized reading. Groups of children were taught with one basal text, which meant that children whose abilities were significantly higher or lower than the group norm often did not have their needs met. The reality of individual differences was dealt with by the formalized adoption of the old concept of individualized reading: the instruction of children who were unable to keep up with the group or who were significantly ahead of the group was individualized, and they were allowed to use material that enabled them to learn at their own pace.

In the 1950s, therefore, individualized reading had become an important concept in reading instruction, side by side with basal readers. New York City is considered the center of individualized reading in its earliest stages; from there it spread throughout the country.

Content Since the major emphasis of the individualized methodology is on generating and maintaining interest in reading, the content consists of a wide variety of reading material chosen on the basis of children's interests and needs. Since each group of children is different, no prepackaged collection of materials would be appropriate for all groups. Reading material must be selected according to the individual interests and needs within each group.

The individualized methodology cannot be started until children have begun to develop reading skills. Beginning readers must first learn decoding skills and sight vocabulary that will enable them to read and enjoy print. Initial instruction can use any method. For example, language experience can be used at first to build a strong sight vocabulary. Phonic skills can then be used to teach word analysis and to further extend reading ability and range. Another option is to use the beginning pre-primer books from a basal series and to concentrate on letter-sound relationships and sight vocabulary. Once children have a workable sight vocabulary and a beginning understanding of word analysis, they are ready to read beginning reading books, and individualized reading can begin.

The content of this methodology consists of two important strands: the reading strand and the skill strand. The reading strand consists of a large number of books from which children can choose. Reading is primarily on an individual basis with time allowed for sharing material. Often, however, if groups of children demonstrate similar abilities, interests, and/or needs reading instruction can be done in small groups. The skill strand consists of instruction in specific phonic and comprehension skills to help children develop and extend their reading abilities. The teacher listens to each child read, keeps a record of the analysis skills each child needs, asks questions to ensure that the child has literal and inferential comprehension of the material, records any deficits in comprehension, and possibly gives the child help in choosing additional books. Phonic and comprehension skills are taught according to the skill needs of the children, either individually or in small groups formed on the basis of common needs.

Prerequisites for Children   This methodology requires children to spend much time reading and learning independently; therefore, children must be internally structured so they can concentrate on one task without direction, persist until the task is completed, and exhibit appropriate motivation toward independent learning.

Children must independently glean much information from their reading. They need to have good inductive abilities to comprehend inferences, generalizations, and so on.

Part of the philosophy of the individualized methodology is that children have a right to progress at their own pace. For learning to be consistent with grade-level progression, however, the pace needs to be relatively fast. Children with a slow learning pace will not make enough progress independently to maintain their grade level.

Prerequisites for Teachers   Teachers need to have a good knowledge of children's literature. They have the responsibility to provide a constant flow of many children's books on a variety of grade levels, interest levels, and subject areas.

At the heart of individualized programs is the necessity of keeping track of the books children read, the skills they master, and the skills they need. This requires both record-keeping and organizational skills.

Teachers must be able to use a variety of questions to stimulate a range of thinking patterns and to develop literal and interpretive comprehension, critical and creative thinking, and problem-solving abilities.

Teachers need to be aware of slower-paced children who, if left to pace themselves, would make inadequate progress through school. Teachers should motivate such children to more appropriate pacing.

Criticisms and Weaknesses

The individualized method is very teacher-dependent. To be successful, teachers must possess the prerequisites given in the previous section and must have a sound knowledge of children and of the process of reading itself. Beginning teachers would have a difficult time using this methodology.

The methodology is dependent on children's internal structure. Children must be internally motivated and independent in learning tasks.

The individualized method does not provide a specific, sequential, and consistent skill program. It must be greatly modified to suit traditional classroom activities.

Strengths

The individualized method is built on the interests and needs of children, and consequently the motivation of children is high. Children are exposed to a variety of meaningful literature. The method allows children who are fast learners to progress quickly and to gain information as rapidly as they can.

Figure 2–6 presents a summary of the major characteristics of the individualized methodology.

The Basal Reader Methodology

The term *basal reader* is somewhat ambiguous and is often used to refer to two different kinds of material:

1. A set of texts and supplementary materials used to teach reading. Such a package can reflect most methodologies discussed in this chapter.

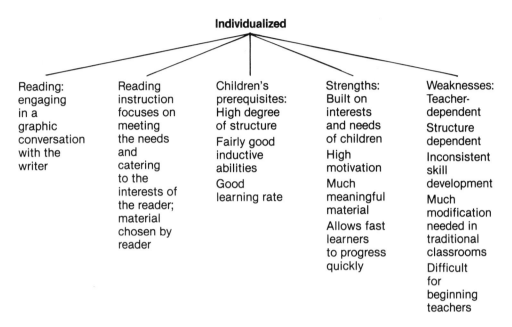

Individualized

| Reading: engaging in a graphic conversation with the writer | Reading instruction focuses on meeting the needs and catering to the interests of the reader; material chosen by reader | Children's prerequisites: High degree of structure Fairly good inductive abilities Good learning rate | Strengths: Built on interests and needs of children High motivation Much meaningful material Allows fast learners to progress quickly | Weaknesses: Teacher-dependent Structure dependent Inconsistent skill development Much modification needed in traditional classrooms Difficult for beginning teachers |

FIGURE 2–6
Major characteristics of the individualized methodology

2. A set of texts and supplementary materials specifically constructed around a developmental approach to teaching reading. Such a package is referred to as a *developmental basal reader*.

   Whereas the first type is basically a format of instructional materials, the second is not only a format but also a specific method with a clearly defined developmental approach to the teaching of reading.

The Basal Format

The basal format is an entire package of materials used to teach reading. The core consists of four major elements: readers, workbooks, teacher's manuals, and assessment instruments.

The readers or texts usually range from kindergarten through the six-grade level; some formats include seventh through ninth grades. Traditionally, the texts consist of the following:

Readiness text: kindergarten
Three pre-primers: kindergarten or first grade
Primer: first grade

First-grade reader: usually children's first hardcover text
Second-grade readers: usually two texts, 2^1 and 2^2
Third-grade readers: usually two texts, 3^1 and 3^2
Fourth-grade readers: often two texts, 4^1 and 4^2
Fifth-grade reader
Sixth-grade reader

In the basal format, each text is accompanied by a workbook for reinforcement of skills and for children's practice. Skills are taught initially in small groups and then reinforced individually in the workbooks. Exercises for each skill are repeated three to five times in the workbook and are placed at intervals throughout the book for frequent reinforcement and review.

A teacher's manual accompanies each text and workbook. The manual forms the center of the basal format because it contains not only a reproduction of each page of the text and workbook but also the detailed scope and sequence of reading skills to be taught daily, vocabulary to be introduced, directions related to the introduction of each reading selection, questions to be asked, and enrichment activities to extend each selection. In essence, the teacher's manual contains complete daily lesson plans for teaching reading.

The assessment instruments include placement tests, skill mastery tests, end-of-unit tests, and backup tests for reassessment.

Most basal formats also include optional materials such as word cards, word games, enrichment books, tape recordings or records, and additional phonic practice material.

The basal format can reflect many of the methodologies discussed in this chapter. The linguistic methodology is reflected in the *Merrill Linguistic Reader* basal series; the language immersion methodology is reflected in the Scott, Foresman *Reading Unlimited* series; and a combination of the phonic and linguistic methodologies is reflected in the *Lippincott Basic Reading* basal series.

The Developmental Basal

The developmental basal reader, often referred to simply as "the basal," is a package of reading materials arranged in a basal format and organized around a developmental approach to the teaching of reading. The developmental approach identifies important reading skills and allocates them in a logical sequence and to specific grade levels. Vocabulary counts are used to select appropriate vocabulary for each grade level. Appropriate literature is chosen and assigned to each grade level. An appropriate instructional design is created and the material is organized around this design. The developmental basal is the most widely used method for teaching reading in the United States today.

Basic Features

Philosophy   The developmental basal method views print as a language code. Reading is the breaking of this code to gain meaning from the print. Breaking this code leads to early independence in reading, and understanding meaning leads to an interest in and enjoyment of print. Since both code breaking and meaning are valued in reading, the developmental basal begins with a strong emphasis on phonic instruction. Children are expected to master word analysis early. In keeping with the emphasis on meaning, skills are taught within the context of sentences rather than in isolation. In addition, children are taught a strong sight vocabulary that is then used in reading material that reflects somewhat natural language patterns. Comprehension is important from the beginning of instruction, and teachers and texts ask questions of children from the earliest levels of instruction.

Origin   The developmental basal reader has its roots in the 1840s, when William H. McGuffey created the popular *McGuffey's Eclectic Readers*. McGuffey published a set of texts along with a brief preface to each book giving teachers explanations of procedures and instructional suggestions. These early texts were more interested in proper pronunciation and fluency than in development of comprehension skills.

In the late 1800s several other reading series appeared, stressing pronunciation and articulation. Their content heavily reflected the morals and attitudes of the middle-class family of that time.

By the early 1900s, the basal reader was a fixed part of the educational system. Most series included strong phonic strands and paid more attention to comprehension. One of the most popular series of the 1940s was the *Elson Readers* published by Scott, Foresman, which provided models for basal series for more than two decades and whose characters Dick and Jane became famous nationwide.

By the 1950s, basal series adopted the standard basal format. Teacher's manuals began to be highly detailed. Questions were included to give greater emphasis to comprehension. The content of texts often revolved around a white, middle-class nuclear family, with pets, all living in a predictable middle-class suburban home and engaging in traditional middle-class family activities. As society changed in terms of sexual equality and racial diversity during the 1960s and 1970s, so too did the tone and content of the basal series change.

Content   The developmental basal reader consists of two strands: a skills strand and a literature strand. The skills strand provides a system in which skills are introduced by the teacher, practiced in a workbook, and reinforced periodically throughout the text and workbooks. Each skill is tested, and if children have not mastered a particular skill, the skill is retaught and retested.

The literature strand consists of literature created or selected for specific grade levels. Each selection introduces new vocabulary and content, and assigned questions are asked during and after reading.

Prior to the 1970s, the literature strand consisted primarily of fiction set in suburban contexts and revolving around white, middle-class individuals and values. The 1970s and 1980s have seen a significant effort to include more expository materials, a wider selection of literary genres, better racial and sexual balance, a wider range of geographical areas, less sexual bias, and greater exposure to minorities of all kinds including handicapped individuals and senior citizens.

Prerequisites for Children   The developmental basal is arranged around a definite developmental approach. Certain sets of skills are allocated to specific grade levels, and appropriate progression through the grades demands that children learn the skills and content in definite periods of time. The skill demands are high, and adequate progress requires the ability to learn many skills in a relatively short period of time.

The developmental basal requires a child to learn many skills, words, and concepts. Because of the heavy emphasis on decoding, children must learn and hold in memory much relatively meaningless phonic information until they are exposed to meaningful print. A good memory is therefore essential.

The developmental basal is very structured. Material is introduced, presented, taught, and reinforced in the same way throughout each text. If a skill is not learned, it is often retaught in the same way that it was taught initially. Children must be able to tolerate the usual routine of instruction and also must be able to learn material in one way.

Because of the strong phonic element, auditory discrimination is also important.

Prerequisites for Teachers   The developmental basal is created for widespread adoption; therefore, it is written with the average child in mind. Teachers must be able to modify the basal to meet the needs of both slow and gifted readers. When a child fails to learn in a developmental basal format, success for that child depends on the teacher's knowledge of different ways to teach skills and content. Teachers must be able to teach *reading* rather than only teaching a series.

Teachers should be willing and able to vary the structure to affect the pervasive sameness of basal programs and to keep children interested and involved.

The developmental basal has a complex, well-defined structure. It is very easy for teachers to depend too much on the manual, to do exactly as the manual dictates, and to fall into a professional rut in which little growth, innovation, or life occurs. Teachers using developmental basals must be committed to flexibility and professional growth.

Criticisms and Weaknesses The formats of basals are often so structured that little room is left for teachers' creativity and innovation. Skills are often taught and retaught using one strategy, offering no alternative strategy for children who cannot learn from the basal structure. The structure does not adequately provide for children on either side of the norm — gifted or learning disabled.

Though major efforts during the past decade have been made to include literature that is representative of the broad racial, ethnic, environmental, and social differences in society, much more attention needs to be given to those areas.

The series are written around a developmental theme, and, particularly at the initial stages, literature is written using a controlled vocabulary. This often results in very contrived beginning reading material.

The basic format of the developmental basal is often the same throughout the grades, making a series seem monotonous.

Strengths Developmental basal series provide a systematic presentation of phonic skills and a variety of literary genres.

Emphasis is on the development of comprehension skills from the initial stages of reading, and a range of supportive material is available for practice and enrichment.

Basal series provide a relatively complete structure for teaching reading. This structure may be very helpful to beginning teachers. The assessment strand provides teachers with a way of keeping pace with children's strengths and deficits.

Vocabulary and skills are introduced at a well-defined pace, and continuity of skill development is achieved throughout a series.

Figure 2–7 summarizes the major characteristics of a developmental basal series.

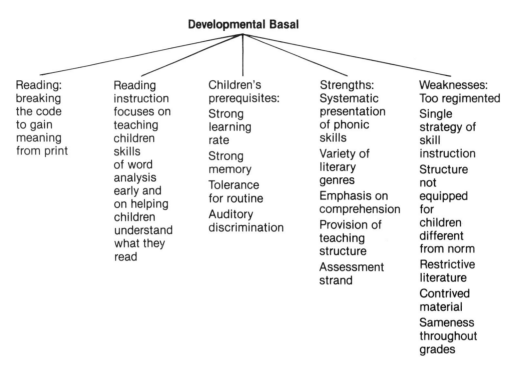

Developmental Basal

Reading: breaking the code to gain meaning from print

Reading instruction focuses on teaching children skills of word analysis early and on helping children understand what they read

Children's prerequisites:
Strong learning rate
Strong memory
Tolerance for routine
Auditory discrimination

Strengths:
Systematic presentation of phonic skills
Variety of literary genres
Emphasis on comprehension
Provision of teaching structure
Assessment strand

Weaknesses:
Too regimented
Single strategy of skill instruction
Structure not equipped for children different from norm
Restrictive literature
Contrived material
Sameness throughout grades

FIGURE 2–7
Major characteristics of a developmental basal series

Developmental Basal Materials

Addison-Wesley Reading Program
Addison-Wesley

American Readers
D. C. Heath

Ginn Reading Series
Ginn

HBJ Bookmark Reading Program
Harcourt Brace Jovanovich

Headway Program
Open Court

Holt Basic Reading
Holt, Rinehart and Winston

Houghton Mifflin Reading Program
Houghton Mifflin

Lippincott Basic Reading
Harper & Row

Macmillan Reading: Series R
Macmillan

Scott, Foresman Reading Program
Scott, Foresman

Relevant Methodological Research

In the 1960s research studies that attempted to compare the effectiveness of various reading methodologies were quite popular. Perhaps the most widely known and most comprehensive comparative study was undertaken in 1967, titled the "First Grade Studies" (Bond and Dyxtra, 1967). The studies were done in twenty-seven first-grade classrooms throughout the United States. Researchers compared five reading methods with the developmental basal. The methods studied were (1) basal plus phonics, (2) linguistics, (3) phonics plus linguistics, (4) i/t/a, and (5) language experience. Children in experimental groups were taught for one year with one of the five methods, while children in control groups were taught for one year with the developmental basal. Predictably, at the end of the year the children displayed the strengths and weaknesses of the method in which they were taught. In general, no one methodology was proved to be most effective.

The studies were continued for two additional years. After the three-year experiment, some important general conclusions were made.

1. More mature children were able to cope with the demands of less structured programs that emphasized meaning.
2. Less mature children and children of low readiness needed the structure of programs emphasizing code breaking. This does not imply that such children should be restricted to code instruction only.
3. Children with good auditory and visual discrimination have an edge in any program.
4. Familiarity with print prior to first grade benefits the development of reading skills.
5. Word-attack skills need to be emphasized early and taught systematically.
6. Combinations of teaching strategies are more beneficial than single strategies.
7. One reading program is not equally effective in all situations.

The overriding conclusion of the studies seemed to be that the most effective programs do not restrict themselves to any one instructional method. The teacher is therefore the single most important variable in success in reading. The teacher must know the prerequisites of each method and must build on the strengths and compensate for the weaknesses of each set of instructional materials. The remaining chapters of this book are designed to help teachers develop this vital "variable" that makes reading a reality for children.

Summary

There are six major current approaches to the teaching of reading. Each approach is based on a particular definition of reading. The definition determines the instructional directions that the approach takes. Each approach has clear strengths and will succeed with groups of children who possess the required skills. The effective teacher recognizes the strengths of particular approaches and constantly builds on them. Each approach has clear weaknesses and will fail with some students. The effective teacher knows those weaknesses and constantly compensates for them.

No one approach is perfect. No one approach is equally effective for all children. The success in teaching reading lies in the ability of the teacher to modify any approach to meet the needs of children. This success requires thorough knowledge, keen analysis, and commitment to ongoing change.

References

Addison-Wesley Reading Program. Reading, Mass.: Addison-Wesley, 1979.

Allen, E., and L. Laminack. "Language Experience Reading — It's Natural." *Reading Teacher,* no. 34 (March 1982).

American Readers. Lexington, Mass.: D. C. Heath, 1983.

Ashton-Warner, S. *Teacher.* New York: Simon & Schuster, 1963.

Bloomfield, Leonard. "Linguistics and Reading." *Elementary English Review,* no. 19 (April–May 1942).

Bond, Guy, and R. Dyxtra. "The Cooperative Research Program in First-Grade Reading Instruction." *Reading Research Quarterly,* no. 2 (Summer 1967).

Easy-to-Read i/t/a Program. Belmont, Calif.: Fearon Pitman, 1966.

Fries, C. C. *Linguistics and Reading.* New York: Holt, Rinehart and Winston, 1962.

Ginn Reading Series. Lexington, Mass.: Ginn, 1982.

Gray, William S. "Current Reading Problem: A World View." *Education Digest,* no. 21 (1955).

———. *The Teaching of Reading and Writing.* Paris: UNESCO, 1956.

Hall, M. A. *The Language Experience Approach for Teaching Reading: A Research Perspective.* Newark, Del.: International Reading Association, 1978.

———. *Teaching Reading as a Language Experience.* Columbus, Ohio: Charles Merrill, 1976.

HBJ Bookmark Reading Program. New York: Harcourt Brace Jovanovich, 1979.

Headway Program. La Salle, Ill.: Open Court, 1979.

Holt Basic Reading. New York: Holt, Rinehart and Winston, 1980.

Houghton Mifflin Reading Program. Boston: Houghton Mifflin, 1983.

i/t/a Edition. New York: Scholastic Book Services, 1964.

Keys to Reading Series. Oklahoma City, Okla.: Economy Company, 1975.

Lefevre, C. A. *Linguistics and the Teaching of Reading*. New York: McGraw-Hill, 1964.

Lippincott Basic Reading. New York: Harper & Row, 1981.

Macmillan Reading: Series R. New York: Macmillan, 1983.

Martin, Bill, and Peggy Brogan. *Instant Readers*. New York: Holt, Rinehart and Winston, 1974.

———. *Sounds of Language Series*. New York: Holt, Rinehart and Winston, 1974.

Merrill Linguistic Reading Program. Columbus, Ohio: Charles Merrill, 1980.

Merrill Phonics Skill Texts. Columbus, Ohio: Charles E. Merrill Publishers, 1979.

Miami Linguistic Readers. Lexington, Mass.: D. C. Heath, 1966.

Moe, A., and D. Johnson. In *Teaching Reading: Foundations and Strategies*, edited by P. Lamb and R. Arnold. Belmont, Calif.: Wadsworth, 1980.

Phonics Is Fun Series. Cleveland, Ohio.: Modern Curriculum Press, 1971.

Phonics Plus. Englewood Cliffs, N.J.: Prentice-Hall, 1973.

Phonics We Use Series. Chicago: Rand McNally, 1978.

Programmed Reading: Buchanan-Sullivan. New York: McGraw-Hill, 1963.

Scott, Foresman Reading Unlimited. Glenview, Ill.: Scott, Foresman, 1976.

Scott, Foresman Reading Systems. Glenview, Ill.: Scott, Foresman, 1981.

Stauffer, R. *The Language Experience Approach to the Teaching of Reading*, 2nd ed. New York: Harper & Row, 1980.

———. *Language Experience Activities*. Boston: Houghton Mifflin, 1976.

3

The Basal Reader: Insights

In Chapter 2, six major methods of teaching reading were analyzed. Each methodology emphasized either code or meaning. This chapter focuses on the difference in emphasis and uses the difference to reconsider the developmental basal, the most widely adopted reading method in use today. This chapter will clarify what a basal is and will suggest more appropriate use of a valuable set of instructional materials.

FOCUS QUESTIONS

☐   What is the underlying philosophy of developmental basal readers?

☐   What are the basic characteristics of code and meaning programs?

☐   What is the relationship between learning styles and learning to read?

☐   What is the major rationale behind modifying the developmental basal approach?

☐   What are the major areas in which developmental basal series need instructional modification?

The Reading Methodology Continuum

We can hypothesize that all reading methodologies or programs fall some place on a continuum that ranges from those emphasizing code to those emphasizing meaning.

Code emphasis programs are based on the philosophy that reading is primarily a code-breaking activity. Reading is breaking the code locked within the graphic content. The initial instruction must be on helping students break the code. Once they have broken the code, children are free to use and develop their comprehension abilities.

Meaning emphasis programs, in contrast, are based on the philosophy that reading is first and foremost an activity aimed at understanding meaning. The initial instruction must be on helping students bring their basic understanding of spoken language to the act of reading. Just as children use grammatical structure, meaning, and sound to understand spoken language, they must use the same three elements to understand printed language.

Figure 3–1 shows the six methodologies discussed in Chapter 2 as they would appear on the continuum between code emphasis and meaning emphasis.

Scope and Sequence

We can see the basic philosophical and instructional differences between approaches emphasizing code and meaning if we analyze the scope and sequence of specific programs within each methodology. Scope and sequence refer to the specific skills that have been identified as important to teach (scope) and the order in which each skill should be taught (sequence). The scope and sequence of a program, then, let the teacher know the priorities of a program. We will consider sections of the first-grade scope and sequence of a code emphasis program (*Distar*) and a meaning emphasis program (*Sounds of Language*) and we will see the philosophical differences between the two types of programs.

Distar Reading System: Code Emphasis

Distar is a reading program published in the early 1970s and still used widely today (Englemann and Becker, 1971). It is a very structured approach emphasizing code breaking exclusively at the first-grade level. Following is the scope and sequence of teaching several code skills at the first-grade level.

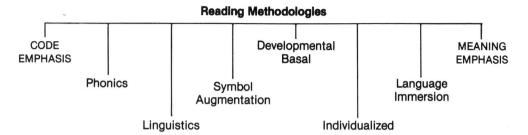

FIGURE 3–1
Reading methodologies

1. Teaching /mmm/ as in *him*.
2. Teaching /aaa/ as in *at* and teaching going with the arrow.
3. Consolidating /mmm/ and /aaa/.
4. Teaching /sss/ as in *kiss*.
5. Consolidating /sss/, /mmm/, and /aaa/.
6. Teaching /ēēē/ as in *me*.
7. Testing /mmm/, /aaa/, /sss/, and /ēēē/.
8. Reviewing /mmm/, /aaa/, /sss/, and /ēēē/.
9. Teaching /fff/ as in *if*.
10. Consolidating /ēēē/ and /fff/.
11. Teaching /d/ as in *did*.
12. Testing /d/.
13. Teaching /rrr/ as in *ran*.
14. Sound gliding /ēs/.
15. Testing /rrr/ as in *ran*.
16. Teaching /iii/ as in *it*.
17. Sound gliding /af/, /mēs/, and /raf/.
18. Sound gliding /sim/, /rē/, /fims/, and /saf/.
19. Teaching /th/ as in *this*.
20. Teaching sound gliding /if/, /sēē/, /am/, /af/, /ad/, /an/, /rēad/, and /thē/.

Initially in this program children are expected to learn the relationships between the letters and their sounds and to get some experience with blending. The priority of knowledge of the codes is very clear, given the initial emphases of instruction. This emphasis on code does not mean that meaning is ignored in the first grade. The immediate instructional focus is on breaking the code, but as children become more familiar with code breaking and can decode words in context, comprehension becomes more of a priority.

Sounds of Language Series: Meaning Emphasis

In contrast to the *Distar* program, the *Sounds of Language* series places heavy initial emphasis on whole-language comprehension and the relationship between oral language and reading (Martin and Brogan, 1974). The priority in this program is meaning. Children initially are given experiences that help them use language clues in reading such as repeated fragments, language patterns, familiar phrases, stories, and so on. The code, however, is not totally neglected. Attention is paid to letter-sound relationships and decoding, but the context for all reading is meaningful whole language.

The following is the sequence of teaching several skills at the first-grade level in the *Sounds of Language* series.

1. Recognizing that language works in chunks of meaning as in:

    Good Night Mr. Beetle,
    Good Night Mr. Fly,
    Good Night _____.

2. Reading aloud (to and with children) to deposit literary and linguistic structures in children's storehouses.
3. Innovating on literary structure to claim basic patterns such as:

    Merry Christmas
    Happy Birthday

4. Figuring out how stories and poems work as in:

    repetitive sequence patterns
    similes
    cumulative sequence

5. Helping children verbalize their intuitive literary insights through (creative) questioning.
6. Figuring out how sentences work.
7. Innovating on sentence patterns such as:

    transforming sentences
    expanding sentences
    reducing sentences

8. Figuring out how words work as in:

    rhyme

9. Figuring out how print works as in:

    highly predictable books

10. Developing skill in comprehension.
11. Linking writing and reading.
12. Cultivating literary and aesthetic appreciation.
13. Developing sensitivity to three levels of language:

     home-rooted
     public
     life lifting

14. Develop sensitivity to humanness.

Developmental Basal Series: Between Code and Meaning

A major difference between code and meaning programs is one of timing. Whereas code programs begin with the code and move to meaning, the meaning programs begin with meaning and move to code.

The developmental basal methodology occupies the middle position on the code-to-meaning continuum. The philosophy of the developmental basal attempts to take advantage of the strengths and to avoid the weaknesses of both the code and the meaning philosophies. Those who support the basal philosophy criticize code methods for their unrealistic content of initial reading material, restricted language, uninteresting content, de-emphasis on initial sight vocabulary, and lack of initial emphasis on comprehension skills. Supporters of developmental basals accept that children need instructional structure and consistent patterns. They also agree that children need to be taught to break the code quickly; therefore, immediate instruction in phonics is considered important. They differ from the code philosophy in their emphasis on a larger sight vocabulary, which results in a less restricted text and a greater emphasis on comprehension beginning in the initial stages of reading.

Supporters of the basal philosophy also criticize meaning methods for their de-emphasis of initial phonic instruction, the haphazard introduction of skills, and the overemphasis on prediction or "guessing." Basal supporters feel that these strategies teach children to rely more on their prior knowledge of language and less on their analysis of letters and letter combinations. They accept the inital attention to comprehension, the richer language, and the realistic and varied content of the material.

Analysis of the aspects of the code and the meaning methods that are accepted and rejected shows that the developmental basal attempts to accept the strengths and reject the weaknesses of both ends of the continuum. We analyze this merging of code and meaning

In the skill development section of the basal lesson plan, the teacher introduces or reviews skills that students then practice in their practice books or workbooks.

by considering segments of the first-grade scope and sequence of a developmental basal, the *Houghton Mifflin Reading Series* (1973). (See pages 54–55.) Notice that this scope and sequence gives more attention to meaning than code programs do and more attention to phonic skills than meaning programs do. It is significantly more elaborate than both the meaning and the code scope and sequence charts.

Because they are elaborate, the entire scope and sequence are not presented. Examples of skills identified in each objective are given.

Analysis of this scope and sequence demonstrates that the developmental basal draws from both the code and meaning ends of the continuum. Both word analysis and comprehension skills are given initial attention. Children are taught from the start to use phonic, context, and picture clues to decode print.

The basal lesson plan format also demonstrates a merging of both ends of the instructional continuum. This plan places more emphasis on comprehension than code programs do and more emphasis on skills than meaning programs do. The basal lesson plan closely resembles what is usually called a directed reading activity (DRA) (Burmeister, 1983). Each lesson has four major parts: (1) preparation for reading, (2) guided reading, (3) skill development and practice, and (4) extension activities.

Part 1, preparation for reading, indicates new vocabulary items (though they are not always pretaught); gives an overview of the reading selection; and discusses the selection type (tall tale, fable, myth) when appropriate. Children are often posed a question and asked to read to find the answer. In part 2, guided reading, children usually are asked to read the selection or segments of the selection silently, followed by questioning and oral rereading of sections of the story. Part 3, skill development, presents word analysis, comprehension, and/or study skills. The teacher usually introduces or reviews skills, and students practice them in their practice books or workbooks. In part 4, extension activities, suggestions for enrichment are given, including activities such as creative writing, research, additional literature, vocabulary development, or art activities.

The DRA lesson format is often modified by the use of the directed reading-thinking activity (DRTA) proposed by Russell Stauffer (1969). The DRTA begins by having children listen to the title of a story and, after looking at pictures, identify what the title and pictures make them think of and predict what might happen in the story. This brainstorming is intended to activate children's prediction and interaction abilities. Once children have made predictions, they are directed to read sections of the selection to check their predictions. At appropriate points, children are asked to predict what will happen next and to read to confirm or reject their predictions. They are also asked to indicate what material in the selection leads them to make their predictions. Teachers use four basic questions to involve children: (1) "What do you think this story might be about?" (2) "What do you think now?" (3) "What makes you think that?" and (4) "What do you think will happen next?"

HOUGHTON MIFFLIN READING PROGRAM

OBJECTIVE 1: DECODING SKILLS

In order to demonstrate ability, when reading silently, to convert printed language into the oral language it represents, the pupil reads aloud material of an appropriate difficulty level with acceptable pronunciation, taking into account regional variations; with appropriate expression; and with reasonable fluency.

COMPONENT OBJECTIVE 1: WORD ATTACK SKILLS

Given a sentence, either spoken or printed, in which a word is omitted or unknown and also given the consonants in that word (and eventually all the letters in left-to-right order), the pupil correctly identifies the word.

Skill Number	*Specific Skills and Subskills*
111	Using the meaning of spoken context as a clue to a missing word.
112	Mastering grapheme-phoneme correspondences for consonants.
113	Mastering grapheme-phoneme correspondences for vowels.
114	Mastering grapheme-phoneme correspondences for affixes.

COMPONENT OBJECTIVE 2: EXPRESSIONAL SKILLS

The pupil reads aloud material of an appropriate difficulty level with the pauses, end phases, and tonal variations indicated by the punctuation marks and/or special printing devices and by the sense of what has been said and is being said.

121	Noting correct pitch, stress, and juncture in reading.

COMPONENT OBJECTIVE 3: PRONUNCIATION SKILLS

The pupil correctly pronounces a word he/she has never heard before after looking it up in a dictionary.

131	Using a dictionary to get pronunciation of words.
132	Using context and/or a dictionary to get pronunciations of homographs and/or words with multiple pronunciations.

OBJECTIVE 2: COMPREHENSION SKILLS

The pupil correctly answers questions concerning material that has been read at an appropriate difficulty level — questions that test not only literal comprehension but also the ability to go beyond what has actually been stated in the text.

COMPONENT OBJECTIVE 1: LITERAL COMPREHENSION SKILLS

The pupil correctly answers questions that test the ability to get the explicit, or directly stated, meanings in material that has been read at an appropriate difficulty level.

211	Interpreting pictures.
212	Using spoken context and letter-sound associations.
213	Following directions.
214	Noting important details.
215	Noting correct sequence.
216	Using punctuation marks as aids in getting meaning.
217	Using special type — italics, boldface, all capital letters.
218	Recognizing word referents.

COMPONENT OBJECTIVE 2: INTERPRETIVE THINKING SKILLS

The pupil correctly answers questions that test the ability to derive implicit, or not directly stated, meanings in material read at an appropriate difficulty level.

221	Drawing conclusions and inferences and making generalizations.
222	Using direct and/or indirect experiences to get implied meanings.
223	Getting the main idea.

COMPONENT OBJECTIVE 3: MEANING ACQUISITION SKILLS

The pupil gives the meaning that a word or phrase has in material read at an appropriate difficulty level.

231	Using context to get word meanings.
232	Identifying synonyms and antonyms.
233	Using a dictionary to get word meanings.
234	Getting the meanings of compound words.
235	Using context to get meanings of figures of speech.
236	Getting the meanings of proverbs.

Use of Developmental Basal Series

Because the developmental basal takes a middle position, it is typically viewed as being appropriate for a wide range of children and abilities. It combines its elaborate scope and sequence with a very detailed, specific, and comprehensive set of directions to teachers. These often include the exact words to be used to introduce and teach skills, specific examples to present, introductory statements for each reading selection, exact questions to be asked, and specific follow-up activities for each selection. Because of the seemingly complete nature of the text, the developmental basal has often been expected to do an impossible task: take the place of teachers' knowledgeable and sensible decision making. Teachers have begun to view the basal teacher's manual less as a "guide" to teaching and more as a "manual" of teaching. This view has often been either directly or indirectly encouraged by book salespeople who tout a series as failure-proof if it is taught in the suggested ways or by district supervisors who have insisted that teachers follow the manual as closely as possible.

The fact is that the developmental basal series is indeed one of the most valuable instructional aids that teachers have, and teachers in this country are fortunate to possess such a tool. The internal structure is particularly vital and helpful to the beginning teacher who is unfamiliar with reading programs and the process of teaching reading to children. But the basal can provide us only with *guides*, *suggestions*, *alternatives*, and *models*, which can be used to expose many children to a variety of appropriate and useful strategies in reading. However, it cannot provide a complete set of suggestions, alternatives, and models to be used with *all* children. The knowledgeable teacher must be able to begin with the developmental basal and proceed outward to develop additional strategies, ideas, and methods that can meet the needs of children who do not succeed with the basal.

Effects of Children's Learning Styles on Reading

Children's learning styles in reading play a large part in the success or failure of a reading program. We can place children's learning styles on a continuum that ranges from inductive to noninductive (Enfield and Greene, 1973).

Inductive Readers

Children considered to be inductive readers usually are highly successful in reading because they possess many of the abilities that make the reading task relatively easy. Some of those abilities are among the following.

1. *A strong memory.* Inductive readers are able to remember information easily and efficiently regardless of their interest in or the meaningfulness of the content. They also are able to retain information over a period of time until they need to use it.

2. *Fast learning rate.* Inductive readers are able to learn a number of items, skills, vocabulary, or concepts in a relatively short period of time.

3. *Good vocabularies.* Inductive readers usually have large vocabularies. This is partly due to their wide range of knowledge and partly because of their use of multiple strategies of vocabulary acquisition: sight, phonics, and context.

4. *Automatic priming abilities.* Inductive readers seem to prepare themselves naturally for new information. If they realize that a new topic is, for example, "Sea Turtles," they immediately bring to the fore any information they know about turtles. This priming ability immediately provides them with a framework consisting of bits of information, questions, answers to questions, appropriate categories, and purposes for reading or listening. This active use of knowledge or mental priming is a great asset to comprehension and to the mental interaction vital to reading.

5. *Ability to see whole-to-part relationships.* A teacher can use an approach to word analysis that asks inductive readers to look at four words, say *hole*, *pole*, *file*, and *rule*, and to determine what they have in common. Inductive learners can see that (1) all the words end in *e* and (2) the first vowels all have a long sound. They can inductively understand the relationship between a final *e* and the pronunciation of preceding vowels. They can reason based on the whole and analyze and comprehend the parts.

6. *Ability to see part-to-whole relationships.* A teacher can use the opposite strategy, which might ask such students to consider the *b*, which makes a /b/ sound, then to listen to words such as *bell*, *ball*, *book*, and *box*, and to list some other words that begin with /b/. Inductive learners can respond correctly because they can abstract the concept of /b/ and are able to look to their own experience for examples.

7. *Adequately developed auditory and visual discrimination abilities.* Inductive readers usually are able to handle appropriately and efficiently both the visual and the auditory aspects of reading.

8. *Ability to deal with abstractions.* Reading involves much abstraction. We refer to "long *a*," "short *e*," "silent vowels," "main idea," and so on. Such terms require abstract thinking, which inductive readers are able to do.

Noninductive Readers

Children classified as noninductive readers do not possess many of the skills demanded in reading. They often demonstrate the following characteristics.

1. *Weak memories.* It is very difficult for noninductive readers to retain many skills, especially if those skills are based on meaningless content or are not adequately understood. Memory of isolated phonic information is often weak.

2. *Slower learning rates.* Noninductive readers take more time and practice to learn material than inductive readers take.

3. *Weak vocabulary.* Noninductive readers often demonstrate weak sight vocabulary. This is often because they depend on a single strategy of word recognition — usually phonics — and often ignore other clues.

4. *Nonautomatic priming abilities.* Noninductive readers usually do not prepare themselves automatically for information. Frequently they do not search their prior knowledge for information that will aid comprehension. They tend not to interact with print but simply to "repeat" print. This deficit is often reinforced in reading instruction by teachers who require children to begin reading with no conceptual preparation, to read long selections with no verbal interaction or thought-provoking questions, and to answer shallow, literal questions at the end of selections.

5. *Difficulty with part-to-whole learning.* Noninductive readers are unable to comprehend, retain, and use isolated rule information. Given the rule that *th* sounds like /th/ as in *them*, noninductive readers have trouble recognizing the rule because the sound /th/ has no meaning to them. They find it hard to make a bridge from a sound to their own experiences.

6. *Auditory and/or visual discrimination deficits.* Noninductive readers often have difficulty discriminating among similar auditory and/or visual stimuli.

7. *Weak powers of abstraction.* Noninductive readers often do not comprehend abstractions such as "long *a*," "short *e*," and so on.

Figure 3–2 summarizes the characteristics of inductive and noninductive readers.

Developmental Basals and Learning Styles

Noninductive children can learn to read. They simply are unable to do so using instruction that has been designed for average inductive children. The success of noninductive readers depends on the degree

Inductive Readers	Noninductive Readers
Strong memory	Weak memory, particularly for nonmeaningful content
Fast learning rate	
Good vocabulary	
Automatic priming	Slow learning rate
Whole-to-part abilities	Weak sight vocabulary
Part-to-whole abilities	Nonautomatic priming abilities
Good auditory and visual discrimination	Difficulty with part-to-whole learning
Ability to abstract	Auditory and/or visual discrimination deficits
	Weak abstraction abilities

FIGURE 3–2
Characteristics of inductive and noninductive readers

to which teachers are able to structure the reading instruction, provide adequate practice in both skills and reading, and ensure conceptual readiness for both skills and content. Does the developmental basal provide such a learning environment for noninductive learners?

Most teachers of reading would agree that the developmental basal is an excellent core program but that it fails to meet the needs of two clearly identified groups of children: poor readers and advanced readers. Figure 3–3 shows some reasons for this failure.

The developmental basal was created for widespread adoption. It was written with large groups of children — average children — in mind. Noninductive readers need instruction that focuses on the understanding and use of code, that is, phonics. They need much more practice in reading, more experience with reading for meaning, more emphasis on meaningful sight vocabulary, more interactive teaching that focuses on comprehension, and more exposure to multiple strategies of word recognition. Inductive readers require much more variety, expansion, enrichment, extension, and emphasis on critical thinking than the basal provides. Even average children may require modification emphasizing one end of the continuum a bit more than the other. Figure 3–4 shows one way that such a modification can be accomplished.

We can reasonably assert, then, that no developmental basal, indeed no reading program, can be considered adequate for all groups of children. All programs must be modified, supplemented, and expanded to meet the needs of individual children. Specific suggestions for instructional modifications of reading programs are given in Chapters 7, 8, and 9.

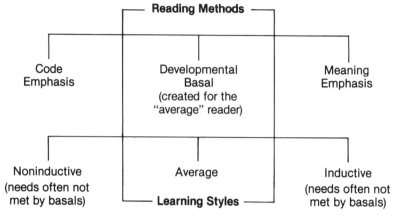

FIGURE 3–3
Intended population of the developmental basal

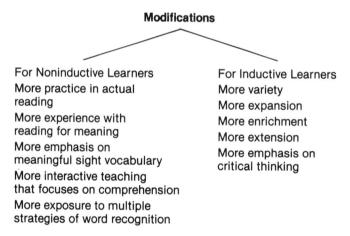

FIGURE 3–4
**Modifications of developmental basals based on children's
learning styles**

The successful teacher of reading is one who teaches *reading*, not a *program*. Teaching reading refers to the ability to analyze programs, evaluate children, and adequately modify programs to meet the needs of individual children. The ultimate responsibility of the teacher is to teach reading with the aid of the program, not to teach a program at the expense of reading.

Summary

All methods of teaching reading can be conceptualized as falling some place on a continuum that ranges from code emphasis to meaning emphasis. Code emphasis methods place heavy initial emphasis on phonics and word analysis. Meaning emphasis methods place heavy initial emphasis on comprehension. In the middle of this continuum is the developmental basal method, which initially emphasizes both phonic analysis and comprehension. Programs within this method are often viewed as balanced and total programs and often no efforts are made to modify them to suit students' needs. But no program can be considered adequate for all children. Each program has a set of prerequisites and is created for a specific type of child, but all programs must be modified to meet the needs of individual children. Success in teaching reading rests in ability of the teacher to modify programs to meet the needs of children, not in the ability of the teacher to teach programs regardless of the needs of children. The following chapters explore strategies that teachers can use to modify programs and to make reading an effective and successful experience for children.

References

Burmeister, L. *Foundations and Strategies for Teaching Children to Read*. Reading, Mass.: Addison-Wesley, 1983.

Enfield, M., and Victoria Greene. *Project Read: Reading Guide*. Bloomington, Minn.: Bloomington Public Schools, 1973.

Englemann, S., and E. Becker. *Distar Reading: An Instructional System*. Chicago: Science Research Associates, 1971.

Houghton Mifflin Reading Series, Honeycomb Teacher's Manual. Boston: Houghton Mifflin, 1973.

Martin, Bill, and Peggy Brogan. *Sounds of Language Series*. New York: Holt, Rinehart and Winston, 1974.

Stauffer, R. *Directing Reading Maturity as a Cognitive Process*. New York: Harper & Row, 1969.

4

Understanding Comprehension as a Process

The process of comprehension is one of the most complex aspects of human learning, mainly because it is an internal process and our conclusions about it must of necessity be somewhat speculative. The product of comprehension, however, is relatively simple to observe. We as teachers observe it daily when we ask children to tell us about information they have read. In essence, theorists use the products of comprehension to hypothesize about the processes individuals use to comprehend. This chapter analyzes two specific views of the comprehension process, discusses the instructional implications of each view, and presents several strategies to affect positively the products of comprehension. Besides the traditional view, this chapter presents the psycholinguistic perspective as it relates to comprehension development. The overriding theme of the psycholinguistic perspective is that a basic sensitivity to the way in which children comprehend is central to reading instruction and, in fact, to all instruction.

☐   What is your own definition of comprehension?

☐   As you read through Chapter 4, does your definition change in any way?

☐   What are the major differences between the traditional view and the psycholinguistic view of comprehension?

☐   What is the function of conceptual preparation in comprehension-centered instruction?

Traditional View of Comprehension

Traditionally, comprehension has been viewed as a major skill made up of a number of individual subskills. For several years theorists have attempted to delineate the subskills in the hope that instructional attention to subskills would result in comprehension. Four broad categories of comprehension skills are referred to in the literature: literal comprehension skills, inferential comprehension skills, evaluative comprehension skills, and critical comprehension skills.

1. Literal comprehension refers to the accessing of information explicitly stated in the text. Among these skills are recall of facts and details, recall of sequence, and knowledge of word meanings.

2. Inferential comprehension refers to the use of the literal knowledge in the text in combination with prior knowledge to make inferences that go beyond the information explicitly stated in the text. These skills include inferring the main idea, inferring comparisons and contrasts, inferring cause and effect, and predicting.

3. Evaluative comprehension refers to the forming of personal opinions based on the information in the text. Among these skills are making judgments of worth, making a choice and justifying that choice, supporting or rejecting an issue by judging acceptability or appropriateness, and justifying or rejecting an action.

4. Critical comprehension refers to the ability to analyze written material in terms of style, content, and form. These skills include distinguishing between fact and opinion, recognizing the logic of arguments, recognizing consistency of thought, distinguishing among literary forms, and recognizing the author's mood, intention, or point of view.

The traditional view of comprehension argues that the skills identified as necessary for comprehension can and should be taught to children and that instruction in the skills of comprehension will result in understanding of material. Basal reading texts almost uniformly adopt this position. Skills of comprehension are identified, allocated to specific grade levels, and presented to children. Skills are often taught in isolation during individual skill sessions and practiced and reinforced in workbooks. The questions following the reading passages in basal readers indicate that skills of comprehension are taught, checked, and monitored throughout the grades.

A premise of this approach is that once children learn the skills of comprehension, they will transfer them to actual reading situations. When they master these comprehension skills, children can bring understanding to print and, in turn, the print can expand their concepts and knowledge beyond the background they bring to the task of reading.

Children who demonstrate inadequate comprehension in reading often are identified and referred to remedial reading programs, many of which follow this model of comprehension. In a remedial program, a diagnostic comprehension test is administered, and children's specific comprehension skill deficits are identified. Usually the next step is to place each child in a comprehensive skill program, which consists of graded books that deal specifically with each comprehension skill — drawing conclusions, understanding the main idea, understanding sequence, recalling literal information and so on. After a few weeks of working through the appropriate skill books, the children are expected to have gained competence in the isolated skills and remediated their previous comprehension problems.

This traditional view of comprehension often results in the acquisition of appropriate comprehension skills in many children. Many children are able to transfer the learning of isolated skills to the reading of textual material. Many are able to understand the skills presented in skill lessons, to practice the skills in their workbooks, and to apply them in reading connected discourse. Some children, however, are unable to do this and therefore experience failure in reading. In addition, some children can comprehend some textual material but not other material, some subjects but not others, or one teacher's instruction but not another's. One reason may be that they are unable to transfer their knowledge of isolated skills to actual reading tasks. Another reason is that, although the children have learned skills of comprehension, the skills do not necessarily add up to comprehension itself.

That comprehension is much larger than the sum of its parts is the fundamental position of the psycholinguistic school of thought.

Psycholinguistic View of Comprehension

The premises of the psycholinguistic view are totally different from those of the traditional view of comprehension. The psycholinguistic view, proposed by such theorists as Smith (1982) and Pearson and Spiro (1981), says that comprehension builds a bridge between the known and the unknown, as shown in Figure 4–1. Comprehension is something humans do; we are born doing it. While there are certain limitations — native intelligence, experiences, interests, and the like — on how much and how well we comprehend, we can be successful in comprehending information if we are informed or taught appropriately.

The psycholinguistic view asserts that we comprehend incoming information by relating it to information already in our knowledge

FIGURE 4–1
Comprehension as a bridge between the known and the unknown

bank. To comprehend incoming information, we must have already established in our cognitive structure or knowledge bank basic concepts about the incoming information. In other words, we must already know something that we can relate to any new information before we can comprehend that information.

We can see how this idea operates if we consider the fact that a lawyer can read complicated legal briefs with adequate comprehension but that an equally intelligent doctor can read the same material with only minimal comprehension. Similarly, the doctor can read and comprehend medical reports that an equally intelligent teacher cannot understand. This demonstrates the nature of comprehension: the more we know about a given subject, the more we *can know* about it. Doctors can comprehend more about medicine than other people can because doctors know more about medicine. Teachers can comprehend more from pedagogical texts because they know more about teaching. Comprehension is largely dependent on prior knowledge.

The psycholinguistic approach delineates two major functions of the comprehension system: the formation of concepts and the interrelations among the concepts.

The Formation of Concepts

The first task or function of comprehension is the formation of concepts. To comprehend, we must already have a concept of the incoming information. If we are learning about an island, we must already have some concept of island — land, water, land surrounded by water, and so on. Without this concept of "islandness," we cannot comprehend island. Similarly, for children to learn syllabication, they must first have the concept of the rhythm of verbal language. Without the basic concept, they can comprehend nothing about syllables. The comprehension system abstracts concepts through meaningful experiences, either personal or vicarious. Once we have the concepts, they can be developed, expanded, and enriched through speech or print.

Frank Smith (1982) suggests that if we do not have the concepts (the basic knowledge of "thingness") for incoming information, we have three options. The first option is to investigate the information and build the necessary concepts. This is the option taken by highly interested and motivated individuals. They go to another person, the media, or books to find out about the unknown. As they learn, they constantly tie the incoming information to the information already understood and stored in their cognitive framework. Unfortunately, this is not the accepted option for most elementary students, who do not yet have the necessary concepts to comprehend a wide range of material, and who are often not motivated enough to investigate what they do not know.

The second option is to discard the information. If we cannot connect the information to what we already know, the new information is conceptually irrelevant and we throw it out. It simply does not compute. This option is widely used by learners; adults use it often. We hear topics or vocabulary items for which we have no concept and in which we have no interest, and we simply ignore them. Similarly, children may be presented with skills, vocabulary, or content for which they have no concepts or no framework, and they ignore the information. This explains why a frustrated teacher can pose the question "Don't you remember what we did yesterday?" and receive a collection of blank stares. Many children don't remember because they didn't learn in the first place. They probably did not conceptually know the information and the teacher did not make an effort to present the concept first in a comprehension-oriented way and to hook the information to the children's prior knowledge. Thus, the children did not learn the information.

The third option is to make an attempt to comprehend but, because the information is unfamiliar, to miscategorize it. In trying to conceptualize, children often place information in inappropriate concept categories. This is similar to misfiling any material: When the information needs to be retrieved, it becomes extremely difficult to find. Children often take this option. They have not been adequately prepared for incoming information, and they place fragments of the information in any available related category. When they need to retrieve the information, however, they may know it is there someplace but may not have the appropriate strategies to find it.

In the psycholinguistic view of comprehension, then, comprehension is seen as a conceptual filing system. Each concept has a file in our minds, and we add to that file by relating more and more information to it. It is the creation and the expansion of this conceptual filing system that *is* comprehension, and fostering its growth should be the major role of the teacher.

Teachers can help students form basic concepts that will prepare them for comprehension of later assignments.

Interrelations Among Concepts

The second major function of the comprehension system is the interrelationships of the concepts. It is not enough to have individual concepts. We need to know how the concepts relate to one another. When we are processing incoming information, we need to know how the incoming information relates to what is already established in our cognitive framework.

Information in our cognitive structure seems to be placed in a network of rich connections. There seems to be nothing of meaningful and lasting value that is held as an isolated entity. It is the richness of these connections that gives true meaning to our environment. The interrelationships help us to categorize and use past experiences, to understand our present experiences, and to predict the future with impressive accuracy. This ability to establish relationships allows us to use the information we have to elaborate, develop, enrich, expand, or complement incoming information, thus giving us the greatest opportunity for comprehension.

The psycholinguistic view of comprehension, diagrammed in Figure 4–2, sheds some light on what happens when children do not comprehend print. The problem often is not lack of comprehension

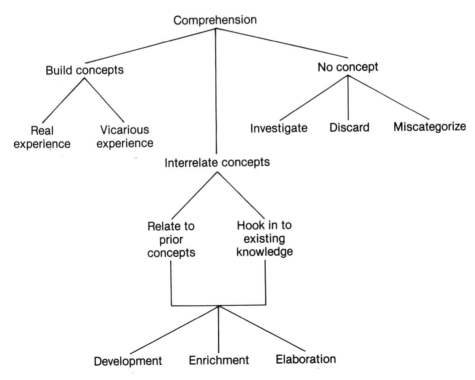

FIGURE 4–2
Psycholinguistic view of comprehension

skills but inexperience with the concepts contained in the material or inability to organize the information in the appropriate categories and in relation to relevant, meaningful, and familiar information.

Teacher as Facilitator

The role of the teacher in comprehension is twofold: (1) to provide for readers (prior to the reading task) the conceptual framework necessary to comprehend print and (2) to alert readers to the information they already have that they can use to comprehend new information, literally guiding them to the appropriate mental files to be used for learning, enrichment, and storage of new information.

The teacher is the major facilitator of comprehension. A teacher can present information in such a way that students cannot comprehend it, or a teacher can present all information in a comprehension-centered way, giving learners the best possible chance at success.

The psycholinguistic view of comprehension is relevant to all aspects of learning; it is just as applicable to learning skills as it is to learning vocabulary or content. The basis of the approach is that learning must always proceed from what is known to what is not known, and the links must be made obvious.

Teachers should be aware that traditional basal reading series usually do not begin teaching skills, vocabulary, or content at a level that is conceptually relevant and familiar to many noninductive learners. A selection from the *Houghton Mifflin Reading Series* fourth-grade book, *Passport*, provides an example of the conceptual difficulty of many basal readers. "Annie and the Old One" is a story about Annie, a young Indian girl, who is trying to cope with her grandmother's approaching death. Although the story is excellently written, it contains many conceptually difficult elements. The setting is a reservation where Annie and her family live in a hogan. Aspects of the Indian culture — environment, family relationships, food, language, and educational patterns — are subtly interwoven in the text. Many fourth-grade children are not familiar with many of the concepts necessary for comprehension of the story. The psycholinguistic approach proposes that comprehension of such a story needs to begin *before the students begin reading the story.* The teacher should discuss Indians and their culture, the relationships between the very young and the very old, the children's own older relatives whom they love and respect, death and dying, and vocabulary items of importance in the story. The teacher could even read a few short stories or show the students pictures depicting Indian lifestyles. After such preparation, or readiness, students bring to a story the vital information that makes the content more meaningful and allows them to use their comprehension skills effectively. Only then is it appropriate to expect students to consider a story in terms of sequencing, main idea, cause and effect, vocabulary, and inferences.

It is therefore important that teachers analyze basal texts and appreciate the conceptual difficulty of many selections, particularly in basal series published since 1970. Such series make an effort to be culturally, racially, geographically, and environmentally representative, and the material often assumes that readers have a great deal of background. Many children simply do not have the experiences necessary to comprehend much of the content in basal readers. The teacher's job is to provide children beforehand with the conceptual information they need to comprehend the material.

By now it should be apparent that psycholinguists view comprehension as a most active process. Comprehension demands much *doing* on the part of both student and teacher. When children passively come to the reading task, passively open their books, and passively deal with print, they have little chance of comprehension. Reading — comprehension of print — demands a high degree of involvement. Efforts to increase comprehension, therefore, must be geared toward developing interaction behaviors of teachers and children before, during, and after children's experiences with print (Jones, 1982).

Schema Theory

The psycholinguistic view, which emphasizes the importance of children's prior knowledge and their interaction with that knowledge, is supported by a more recent and conceptually parallel theory, schema theory. Schema theory is concerned with how information is stored in memory, how it is retrieved from memory, and how it is used in comprehension. The underlying assumption of schema theory is that all a person learns is organized hierarchically and stored in the brain in "files" that are open to constant growth and modification as the person learns through new experiences (Rumelhart, 1976; Adams, 1979; Adams and Collins, 1979).

The existing information in the brain about a concept is called a *schema*. A schema (plural, *schemata*) is more than a concept; a concept involves the fundamental features of information, but a schema involves concepts in addition to associations, experiences, and relationships connected to concepts. A concept for chair may include features like "seat," "legs," "back support," "hard," "off the floor," and so on. A schema for chair may include all those features in addition to associations such as "my favorite overstuffed chair," "relaxing and reading a wonderful book in a comfortable chair," "being rocked to sleep in grandmother's old rocking chair," and the like. A schema, then, is a set of associations or experiences that is brought to consciousness when we see or hear a word, phrase, sentence, or picture or experience an event.

Theorists postulate that each information file or schema is constantly open to change. In other words, each schema is incomplete. As we hear, read, see, or experience more information that is relevant to each schema, we add that information and the schema becomes more complete. Comprehension results when new information enters our cognitive field and interacts with the existing schemata, resulting in our understanding and in the expansion of our schemata.

Schema theory, therefore, acknowledges a symbiotic relationship between the reader and print. The reader brings to print the appropriate schemata. The print brings to the reader the potential of expanding and refining the existing schemata. Reading and comprehension occur when the reader *and* the print interact. This model of reading has been called an *interactive model* (Rumelhart, 1976) and can be contrasted with the "top-down" or concept-driven view, which gives supremacy to the reader's prior knowledge and sees print as secondary (Smith, 1982; Goodman, 1976; Weaver, 1980), and with the "bottom-up" or text-driven view, which gives supremacy to print and sees the reader's knowledge as important but secondary (Gough, 1972; LaBerge and Samuels, 1974).

The implications of schema theory, which are parallel to those of psycholinguistic theory discussed earlier, include the importance of building conceptual readiness for new information, of alerting children to their existing relevant and necessary schemata prior to instruction, and of mental interaction during reading through discussion and appropriate questioning.

The Memory Process

The process of comprehension and the process of memory are related and have an effect on each other. Psychologists often refer to a four-part memory process, which includes the attention stimulus, the sensory system, short-term memory, and long-term memory.

Attention   Samuels (1976) states that attention is a primary requisite for any learning and suggests that attention is a selective process. There are so many stimuli in any environment that we attend to those that are most important or that call attention to themselves. In addition, attention is an all-or-nothing function. We can attend to only one element at a time. Often it seems that we attend to more than one thing at a time, but this is really the result of switching our attention or performing subskills automatically, that is, without overt attention to them.

Attention switching is often referred to as the "cocktail party phenomenon." We walk into a party and begin to speak with one person, when we hear someone across the room mention our name. We still stare intently at the person we are speaking with, but our attention switches quickly between the first conversation and the conversation across the room. Obviously, attention switching can be successful only if we know enough about what is being said in both conversations. In that case, we end up hearing two relatively complete conversations. If we do not know enough about one of the conversations, we will miss the trend of that conversation and will find ourselves asking the other person to repeat himself or herself.

Many children try to use attention switching in class, but they fail at it because they do not know enough about the information being taught to fill in when they daydream or do not attend. Such children can miss much instruction.

We have all done two things at the same time: talked on the phone and fixed a meal, driven a car while reading directions, read notes on a page and played an instrument. Samuels states that this seemingly dual attention is possible because we have learned certain subskills or actions to an automatic level and they no longer require attention to be performed. We are then free to place our attention on something else. We listen and talk on the phone so automatically that our attention can be given to preparing a meal. We read music so automatically that our attention is free to play the music. Similarly, readers need to decode print so automatically that their attention can be free to center on comprehension. Therefore, if decoding is not fluent, comprehension is diminished to some degree.

Sensory System   Once we have placed our attention on something, that information from our environment is transmitted to the cognitive system through one or more of our physical senses. Printed information enters the cognitive system through the sensory systems of sight, hearing, or touch. When the sensory systems are functioning and capable of transmitting information, the information is passed on through the cognitive system to the next level, memory.

Short-Term Memory   Short-term memory retains meaningful information and discards the rest. The two characteristics of short-term memory most important to comprehension are its brevity and its limited capacity.

Short-term memory can be seen as the place in the cognitive system where we put a telephone number we have just looked up between the time we find it in the telephone book and the time we dial it. The usual process in such a case is to look up the number, repeat it, close the telephone book, and continue repeating the number until we dial it. If no one disturbs us, we can dial the number successfully. If someone calls our name or attempts to converse with us, we often must return to the telephone book and begin the process again.

Information in short-term memory decays very rapidly (within approximately fifteen seconds) unless we constantly rehearse it or code and pass it on to long-term memory. If the incoming material is meaningful and can be related to existing concepts, we pass it on. If not, we simply abandon and forget it.

Short-term memory has a limited capacity — according to researchers, between five and nine units of information at a time (Lindsay and Norman, 1972). Once this capacity is reached, information must be either passed to long-term memory or discarded. If the units of information are meaningful and can be associated with prior knowledge, we retain the information. If it is not meaningful, we discard it. The size of the units is not as important as their number. Consider the following sentences: "The man ran to the door and opened it quickly. He hoped it was the package he had been waiting for." A child who has no fluency in reading would decode like this: "Th - e - m - a - n - r." At this point, six units have been processed; but the units have produced six meaningless sounds — th/e/m/a/n/r — that will be rejected because the child has no conceptual files that fit the information. If the child reads the entire passage in this nonfluent way, it would not be surprising if at the end of the passage he or she cannot retell any of the information. The child remembers nothing because the units of information were meaningless and the child discarded them throughout the reading.

If, however, a child processed the units as "the - man - ran - to - the - door" or "the man - ran to - the door - and opened - it quickly. - He hoped," the meaningfulness of the material would prompt coding and passing to long-term memory, which would greatly assist comprehension. Both aspects of short-term memory — brevity and limited capacity — point to the need for fluency in decoding and word recognition as an aid to comprehension.

Long-Term Memory   Long-term memory is the place where we store our prior knowledge — our concept files and schemata. Long-term memory is the natural tie between memory and comprehension. Comprehension depends on the relating of incoming information to existing information stored in long-term memory. The more relevant information we have stored, the more we can extend, expand, interrelate, and complement incoming information, the stronger the link

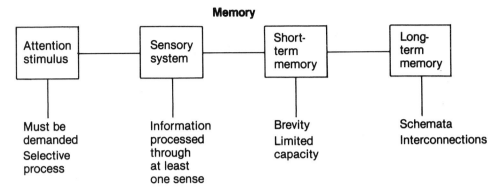

FIGURE 4–3
Elements of the memory process

to prior knowledge, the greater our comprehension, and the more stable our memory will be.

Figure 4–3 summarizes the memory process.

Comprehension from the psycholinguistic perspective can be viewed as a symbiotic relationship between the reader and the print. The reader brings to print prior knowledge, rich interconnections, relevant conceptual files, and fluency; in turn, the print brings to the reader additional material with the potential to extend the reader's concepts and understanding beyond the prior knowledge that the reader brings to the print. This symbiosis results in the strength of comprehension.

Merging the Traditional and Psycholinguistic Views

The traditional view of comprehension emphasizes the importance of learning the skills of comprehension. The psycholinguistic view emphasizes the importance of conceptual readiness and prior knowledge. Certainly both skills and conceptual readiness are essential and, indeed, vitally important to comprehension. There is a natural point at which both connect. Conceptual readiness must be attained *prior to* reading. When this is done, the reader can apply the skills of reading to the task of comprehension. The role of the teacher is to instruct children in the skills of comprehension and also to ensure that prior to reading children are given the conceptual knowledge to apply those skills successfully.

Instructional Strategies

The psycholinguistic perspective of comprehension has many implications for classroom instruction of reading. There are three major strategies that teachers can use to foster the growth of comprehension in children: conceptual awareness strategies, thinking strategies, and visual strategies.

Conceptual Awareness Strategies

Advance Organizers   One of the most useful strategies for developing readiness for comprehension is an advance organizer. By definition, an advance organizer is simply an attempt to organize students' thinking in such a way that they know what information they already have that will be important and helpful in comprehending incoming information. This conceptual organization takes place before reading. In teaching the story "Annie and the Old One," which we discussed earlier, the teacher would use a discussion of Indians, their customs, and their culture as an advance organizer.

The idea of an advance organizer is not new. It was proposed and developed by Ausubel in 1957, and, although the term *advance organizer* is somewhat outdated today, the idea is still very popular. The terms used today are *schema preparation* or *conceptual preparation* (Smith, 1982; Pearson and Spiro, 1981; Weaver, 1980).

The concept of advance organizers fits perfectly within the psycholinguistic view of comprehension. Organizers simply alert learners to the prior concepts necessary for comprehension and guide them to the appropriate files so understanding can begin. Any effort by a teacher to prepare students conceptually for incoming information by hooking the major concepts of the new information to the concepts already possessed by the learners can be interpreted as an advance organizer.

Three steps are involved in the construction of advance organizers:

1. Identify the main ideas or major concepts of the selection to be read.
2. Form parallels between the major concepts and the experiences children already have.
3. Prepare children directly for new information by a linking, or bridge, statement that shows them the relationship between what they know and what they are going to read.

The selections on pages 78–79 are taken from *The Social Sciences: Concepts and Values* (1970), published by Harcourt Brace Jovanovich. To use advance organizers to teach these selections, you would follow the three steps outlined above. An illustration of this method follows the selections.

Advance organizers should be discussed with children so that the children can verbalize the links that are necessary for comprehension. Discussion also creates interaction between the children and the information. It gives the teacher a chance to observe whether the parallels are effective.

Advance organizers need not be viewed as time-consuming additions to a teaching load. They are relatively simple to construct, but they do demand that teachers read selections beforehand to extract the important elements from the content.

Advance organizers are most beneficial in helping children create concepts. They are therefore more important for children who do not have the necessary experiences or the organizational skills to comprehend certain material.

Overviews The overview is used to give children an advance synopsis of the content to be learned. Overviews differ from advance organizers in that the latter are concept-bound (tied to children's prior concepts and experiences) while the former are content-bound (related to the content to be presented). An overview tells readers what they will read and can thus act as a comprehension check after the fact as well. Comprehension after reading should at least match the facts in the overview.

An overview for the preceding selections might consist of the following discussion:

> The selections you are about to read deal with President Lincoln's attempt to reunite the country after the Civil War. As you would expect, the people of the North and South had angry feelings toward each other. The job of reuniting the country, therefore, was a very difficult one. Unfortunately, President Lincoln was assassinated before he could reunite the country.

Overviews are appropriate when children have the necessary concepts and experiences to·deal with the material they are about to read. Overviews are not very useful if children lack conceptual experience with the content. Overviews are also appropriate for presenting names of important people and places that children will encounter during reading. The graphic code of English is quite inconsistent in its symbol/sound relationships, particularly in the pro-

BINDING THE WOUNDS

President Lincoln wanted the bitterness between North and South to end with the war. He wanted to rebuild the Union as quickly as possible. ■ If the nation was to be united again, the South had to be helped to rebuild its countryside and to take part in the national government again.

President Lincoln thought the President should decide how to *reconstruct,* or rebuild, the Union. Before the war ended, he had worked out a plan. When one-tenth of the voters in each Confederate state had declared their loyalty to the federal government, they could hold elections to form new state governments. Then they could elect representatives to Congress and join the Union again.

But many Congressmen from the North and West disagreed with the President's plan for Reconstruction. Some wanted to punish the South, and many were concerned about the black people of the South. At the end of the war, the Thirteenth Amendment to the Constitution was adopted. This amendment says that "Neither slavery nor involuntary servitude . . . shall exist within the United States. . . ." The Thirteenth Amendment freed all the slaves. What could the freedmen look forward to?

Some of the men in Congress believed that former slave owners would not respect the new freedom of black people in the South. Congressmen knew that under President Lincoln's plan for Reconstruction, many former slave owners would participate in the new state governments. Would these men protect the freedom of black people?

THE FINAL SHOT OF THE WAR

Before the President and Congress could settle their differences over a plan for Reconstruction, the nation suffered a tragic loss. While watching a play at

Ford's Theater in Washington, D.C., President Lincoln was shot and killed by an actor named John Wilkes Booth.

This happened five days after General Lee surrendered to General Grant. People throughout the North and West stopped celebrating their war victory and put on black mourning clothes. ● Thousands came to stand by the railroad tracks as the President's body was carried by train from Washington, D.C. to Illinois, to be buried.

And in the South, many people were saddened, too. President Lincoln had welcomed Southerners back into the Union and promised to treat them with "malice toward none, with charity for all." Who would take charge of Reconstruction now?

ADVANCE ORGANIZER

Step 1. Identify major concepts: Reconstruction after a disagreement may be difficult to achieve.

Step 2. Find parallels between the selections and children's experiences: Have you ever been in a situation in which two of your close friends or even your parents have been in a huge quarrel? Of course you have. Think back to that situation. Do you remember how angry each person was at the other and how it seemed as though they would never forgive, trust, or like each other again? You have at least two options at such a time. First, you can take sides: You can say one person is right and the other is wrong. You can even wish to see the "wrong" party punished. Second, you can realize that there are two sides to every argument. Realizing this, you can try to bring the two people together again. The first option, of course, is called "taking sides." The second may be called "reuniting" or "reconstruction," bringing people together again. The same thing can happen to countries or groups at war. Often, after war, presidents have the same options. They can continue to take sides or they can reconstruct.

Step 3. Make a bridge statement: The selections you are about to read are about President Lincoln trying to bring the North and South back together after the Civil War.

nunciation of place and people's names. It is very difficult to pronounce words we have not heard. (Even we teachers have trouble
pronouncing names of people and places when we are reading about
foreign countries.) If, prior to reading, teachers share with children
the important names they will encounter, children will have information and content to use to aid their phonic skills when they see
the names in print.

We do children a disservice by behaving as though somehow
what they are going to read is a secret. Children deserve to know
what they will be reading about and the purposes for which they
read.

Combination Advance Organizer and Overview   A combination of
strategies can be a very effective teaching technique. The selection
on pages 82–89, "Flight to Freedom," from *Keystone,* the fifth-grade
text in the *Houghton Mifflin Reading Series,* tells the story of Harriet
Tubman and her involvement in the underground railroad. The
combination advance organizer-overview following the selection was
prepared by John Skar, a teacher at Penrose Elementary School,
Colorado Springs, Colorado.

Notice how much conceptual and factual information these
strategies can provide to help children begin their comprehension of
print. This may seem like spoon-feeding, but remember that when a
teacher calls a group of children to the reading circle or group, the
activity that ought to be in progress is *instructional reading.* The teacher
should be teaching children how to read effectively. Instructional
reading is based on the premise that children will be successful in
reading if they are instructed by the teacher. The less prior knowledge that children bring to the print, the more they will need these
strategies.

Listing   The advance organizer and overview are very effective
when used with narrative material. A useful strategy for preparing
children prior to reading expository, nonfiction selections, particularly material in science or social studies, is listing. Instead of conceptually preparing children, as advance organizers do, listing alerts
children to the facts they know about the content to be presented,
thus providing them beforehand with useful information that can
serve as a base for comprehension. As an example, we show how the
listing procedure can be applied to the expository selection "The
Great Barrier Reef" from the *Addison-Wesley Reading Program* text
Abracadatlas (see page 90). The listing strategy, which is used before

By listing brainstorming ideas given by children, the teacher can alert children to the facts they know about the content to be presented, thus providing them with information that can be used as a base for comprehension.

children read the material, consists of eight steps. An application of these steps follows the selection.

After Step 8, on page 91, the children will be ready to read and add to their existing knowledge.

Vocabulary Preinstruction Vocabulary preinstruction means identifying and preteaching children key vocabulary items. It is counterproductive to present too many words at once. A total of five to seven items is appropriate. The words chosen for the selection "The Great Barrier Reef" may be *masses, surface, polyps, pollute,* and *damage*. All items should be explained to children and an effort should be made to relate the words to the children's experiences. Children should also be asked to predict how each word may be related to the title of the selection.

Flight to Freedom

by Frances Humphreville

One day Harriet was working near the road. She had been sent to trim some of the hedges that screened the highway from the fields.

A carriage stopped near her and a woman got out. She was dressed in the clothes of a Quaker. Pretending to fix the harness on her horse, she stood very close to Harriet.

"How did you hurt your head?" she asked. Her voice was low and kind.

Harriet knew that Quakers did not believe in slavery. She told the woman about the accident, a bad blow on her forehead, which had happened while she was trying to protect a fellow slave who was escaping.

"Have you ever heard of the Underground Railroad?" asked the woman.

"I've heard the men talk to my father about it," Harriet answered. "I know it isn't a real railroad. It's made up of people who help the slaves to freedom, isn't it?"

"Indeed it is. Over three thousand people help run our railroad. We've taken almost one hundred thousand slaves to free states."

"Why, that's wonderful!" Harriet exclaimed.

The Quaker lady glanced around her and then got into her carriage. Looking straight ahead, she said quickly, "If I were to travel north, I would follow the Choptank River. I would go up to its beginning. That is just at the border between Delaware and Maryland. Then I'd go north by northeast. It's fifteen miles from the border to John Hill's farm in Camden, Delaware."

In a few minutes she was gone. Harriet repeated the directions to herself so she would not forget them. It was good to know that somewhere there were people who believed that the slaves should be helped to freedom.

Harriet had always loved the Bible story that told of how Moses led his people, the people of Israel, out of slavery in Egypt. One of her favorite songs was "Go Down, Moses," but the slaves were not allowed to sing it now.

> *Go down, Moses,*
> *Way down in Egypt's land.*
> *Tell old Pharaoh,*
> *Let my people go.*

Then one night when Harriet was bringing in her last basket of cotton as the full moon was coming up, her spirits rose with the beauty of the evening. With her sturdy back erect and her head high, she was humming softly "Go Down, Moses" when a big black whip came down in a searing lash across her shoulders.

"How many times do you have to be told not to sing that song?" the overseer demanded. "I'm in charge here now, and you are no longer wanted. I'm going to take care of you this week once and for all when the cotton's in." The whip cracked around her bare ankles. "Think about that while you wait for the trader!"

When a slave was traded, he had to go wherever he was sent. Harriet knew the time had come. She must make a break for freedom or forever be a slave.

Later that night, Harriet crept from her bed and made ready for the journey. She had planned the route she would follow and the food she would need. Now, in a small bag, she packed some corn bread and some scraps of pork. She took the few coins that were left from her earnings. Though she felt a pang of regret, she put the family's best hunting knife into her pocket.

She walked to the nearby cabins for two of her brothers, keeping carefully to the shadows. Benjamin and William Henry did not really want to go with Harriet. They talked in hushed whispers to her now. They reminded her of the bloodhounds that could track them down so easily. They talked about the unknown route and the cold weather of the North.

"You know the rewards are getting larger," William Henry said. "The punishment gets worse for each runaway. Let's wait and see what happens here."

Harriet was furious. "Stay here, then," she said, and her voice shook with anger. "It's now or never for all of us. The trader will be here again in the next few days."

"We'll go with you," Benjamin said after a moment.

So they moved out singly and met beyond the cornfields near the woods. They hadn't walked far before a fog shut down. Harriet was used to it, for mist and fog often hung over the land along Chesapeake Bay, but it made her brothers uneasy. They couldn't see ahead of them for more than a few feet. There were no stars to help tell directions.

After a while a light rain began to fall. The men fell into holes at the swamp edge. They walked into small bushes and briers that tore at their clothes. They were terrified of the many night noises. They pleaded with Harriet to turn back. They stumbled, fell, and argued with her about the fast pace she had set and the direction she had taken.

Harriet moved as though guided by an unknown force. She seemed not to hear their pleading or their whining.

When they finally stopped for a short rest, her brothers declared they had decided to turn back.

Benjamin said, "We're going home. You'd better come, too. The dogs'll find you in an hour or so in the morning. We can't have walked very far. Come on back, Harriet. The risk is too great."

Harriet shook her head. "I want liberty," she said. "No man will ever take me alive. I don't intend to give up easily, now or later. I will fight for freedom as long as my strength lasts. What better way to go than that?"

Her brothers hugged her and turned away. William Henry's face was wet with tears. Harriet waited, hoping that her brothers might change their minds and return, but the fog swallowed them up, and she was alone.

As she started out again, the fog lifted. Soon the bright North Star was shining down to help her on her way. Harriet had a feeling of wild joy, as if this were a sign of approval for her lonely journey.

At the first sign of daylight, Harriet headed for one of the great swamps that ran behind many of the large plantations. She was almost frantic with fear as she saw two water snakes slither down into one of the swamp pools. At the next deep pool, she closed her eyes and waded in. Dogs could not track her if she walked through water.

Picking her way carefully, she kept to the sluggish pools. She walked around the hummocks, and traveled as fast as she could until the sun had risen higher. Now was the time of real danger. She found a small island in the tall swamp grass and lay down to rest. Twice during the day, she heard the distant shouts of men, but she forced herself to lie quiet and even managed to take short naps.

When it was almost dark, Harriet came out of the swamp and looked about her. Now was the time to follow the Quaker lady's advice. Harriet headed in the direction of the Choptank River.

Harriet walked at night and hid by day. She crawled into the thick underbrush and slept when she could. Once she awoke hearing voices. Three men on horseback had stopped not far from her. They were hunting for runaway slaves. She held her breath until they moved on.

Now she must try to keep her wits about her. She stopped often to check her direction by the stars. She limited herself to using only a part of her few supplies each day. She looked for and found wild grapes to eat and clean water to drink. She moved very carefully among the trees and hid whenever she heard voices or horses' hoofs. She made wide circles around farm buildings, for dogs might bark and bring out the owners to investigate.

When she reached the Choptank, she took off her shoes and waded in up to her waist. The sight of the river comforted her. The water was soothing to her tired feet. She sang softly. For the first time since she had left home, she felt a calm courage.

Harriet waded upstream until only a thin stream of water came down over the rocks. This, then, was the spot where the Choptank River began.

Now she would have to face the fifteen-mile walk to Camden. This part of the journey might prove the most dangerous of all, even at night. She would have to leave the river and the safety of the woods for the open fields and the highway.

It was almost daylight when she saw in the distance the buildings of a town. She stopped at a group of shacks that looked like the shacks slaves lived in. She dared go no farther lest she take a wrong path.

The black woman who answered Harriet's light tap on the door was already dressed in her cook's apron and cap. Before Harriet could ask a question, the woman said softly, "That's the Hill farm in the little hollow. Go to the haystack nearest the big barn. There's loose hay near the bottom. Crawl in and wait until about mid-morning. Then go to the door and give two short raps. That's the Underground's signal. Hurry!" The door closed.

Harriet followed the directions. The haystack was warm. She had a fine, safe view of the house and barns. She fell asleep.

She was awakened by the sound of horses' hoofs. Two men were riding away from the farm. Much later, a woman dressed in the Quaker garb came out to feed the chickens. Harriet waited and watched until the woman went back into the house. When she felt sure that the woman was alone, she went quickly to the door and gave it two quick knocks. The lady who had been feeding the chickens drew her into the house at once.

"Welcome," she said. "I'm Mrs. Hill. You look as though you need some food and rest right away. And a good hot bath will make you feel better, too. We can talk later."

So Harriet bathed and ate. She slept almost all day in a hidden room behind a fireplace.

In the late afternoon Mrs. Hill came into the room and sat down in a chair by the bed. "Stay right where you are," she said as Harriet sat up in bed. "Travel has to be done after dark. There's no great hurry. You just rest as long as you can."

Then, from Mrs. Hill, Harriet learned the true meaning of the Underground Railroad. She liked Mrs. Hill and enjoyed talking with her.

"I know the Railroad is a way to help my people escape to the northern states," Harriet said, "but it's not very clear to me how it works."

"The Underground is not a railroad, and of course, it doesn't run under the ground," Mrs. Hill said.

"My father used to tell me about it when I was a little girl," Harriet told her. "For some time I thought he meant that trains really ran under the ground."

Mrs. Hill smiled. "It's called the Underground Railroad because of the fast and secret way it helps Negroes to travel north. We don't talk very much about the real facts. There's danger in too many people knowing the exact details."

"I understand," Harriet said. "I'm grateful for anything you can tell me to help me along the way. And I'm interested in having my own people help, too."

Mrs. Hill nodded her head to show that she agreed. "But many of the southern slaves do help," she said. "Even when they can't escape themselves, they help runaways. They give them food and clothing. They risk their own lives to take the runaways to safe hiding places."

"That's why I think all my people will be free someday," Harriet said proudly. "If the right spirit is there, we'll be able to help each other. I feel better already," she added.

"But you aren't safe yet," Mrs. Hill warned her. "You will be in constant danger until you're out of Delaware and into Pennsylvania or New York State." She waited a moment as though not sure of how much she should tell. "Philadelphia is our eastern headquarters. The city is a natural crossroads for our work. There are a great many workers there."

"What do they all do?"

"Well, some serve as guides or conductors," Mrs. Hill said. "Others make maps showing the stations. They draw skulls to mark the places to stay away from. They write travel routes in codes. Of course, whenever possible, we send fugitives on with a guide. When that's not possible, we give them a map. And we make them learn the directions by heart, in case they lose the map."

"I'd like to be a conductor someday," Harriet said.

"All the conductors are men," Mrs. Hill answered. "Very few of them get any praise, because they aren't known by name — except for Thomas Garrett in Wilmington. His fame for his work in helping escaping slaves has spread to all the northern states. He's been a fine example to all of us."

"He's a Quaker too, isn't he?" Harriet asked. "It was a Quaker lady who told me to come here and gave me such good directions."

"Yes, Quakers believe in freedom for everyone. But we aren't the only ones who help. Other stations along the way are kept by Methodists, German farmers, and many other people who are against slavery."

That night Harriet met Mr. Hill, who was as kind to her as his wife had been. He drove her in his wagon as far as he could along a back road. "I must be back by daylight to go about my business as usual," he said. "I've already been fined for helping slaves."

Harriet thanked him for herself and for her people.

"Follow this road to my brother's farm," Mr. Hill told her. "It's at the top of a hill. The house is white with a wide stone wall around it. It has red barns exactly like mine. Meanwhile I will get word to Thomas Garrett to expect you in Wilmington."

Thomas Garrett! Harriet could hardly believe she would see the most famous conductor of them all.

James Hill was just as nice as his brother, Harriet decided.

James warned Harriet to be very careful while traveling over the twenty-three miles to Wilmington and Thomas Garrett.

"There are posters everywhere offering five hundred dollars for your capture," he said. "Also, Thomas Garrett is very closely watched."

He drove Harriet part of the way and then turned her over to another conductor—a free black. This man had a plan to outwit the patrol stationed just outside the city of Wilmington.

He dressed Harriet in ragged overalls and a big old floppy hat. He gave her a rake and hoe to carry. Then, walking together as two black workmen, they passed by the guards and into Wilmington. In the early morning they crept through the streets to the shoe store of Thomas Garrett.

Thomas Garrett was a small, gentle old man. He and his wife, Sarah, were Quakers. They had moved to Wilmington, Delaware, about the time Harriet was born. He was famous for his kindness to runaway slaves. He had been arrested a number of times for helping them to escape and fined so heavily that he had been left without a cent. At sixty he had opened a shoe store and gone on helping escaping slaves. Again he had been arrested and fined. He was criticized strongly by people who approved of slavery. Through it all, he kept his sense of humor.

Behind the shelves of shoes, Mr. Garrett had a secret room with no windows. "Rest here," he told Harriet. "Tomorrow you'll have new shoes and a ticket over the border." He smiled at her. "You are very close to being my two-hundredth passenger," he said. "Our work has spread. There's an Underground in all the northern states from Maine to Iowa."

After Harriet had rested, Mr. Garrett explained the route she must take. "Wilmington is only eight miles from the Pennsylvania border. Naturally the border is heavily guarded. Your best disguise is that of a working man. I'll take you as near to the crossing point as I can."

Very carefully he went over the directions and made Harriet repeat them until he was certain she knew them. "Head for Philadelphia as soon as you can," he advised her. "There'll be jobs there and other free Negroes to help you. You may want to visit the office of Mr. William Still. He's secretary to the committee that helps runaways. If he's very busy, you may not be able to see him, but one of his workers will help you with any problems you may have."

Harriet thanked him. She tried to put into words some of her gratitude and respect, but the words would not come.

Thomas Garrett seemed to understand. His farewell and his low bow were something Harriet would always remember.

It was only about a week after she left Maryland that Harriet crossed the border into Pennsylvania. She was tired out, the new shoes Mr. Garrett had given her hurt her feet, and she had no place to go, but she was free.

"I made it, Lord," she said aloud. "Now it's up to me to see that my family makes it, too—and all the others who want to be free."

ADVANCE ORGANIZER AND OVERVIEW

Step 1. Identify major concepts: It took great courage to oppose slavery, especially if one was a slave.

Step 2. Find parallels between the selection and children's experiences: Imagine being forced to serve someone as a slave and being totally controlled by that person for life. Imagine being totally frustrated and running away, leaving friends and family behind. Imagine knowing that capture would lead to severe punishment. Try to think about and then discuss the courage it would take to run away under those circumstances, not knowing where you are going or what awaits you. Discuss how you would feel, how you would sneak away, how you would survive, and what problems you might encounter.

Step 3. Make a bridge statement and an overview statement: The story we are going to read is about a woman named Harriet Tubman, who was a slave. The story explains how she escaped from slavery in the South and fled to the North where she helped other slaves escape.

The Great Barrier Reef

Out in the Pacific Ocean, waves curl and break, crash and foam in a long line. The waves are striking a reef lying near the surface of the water. It is the Great Barrier Reef. It is the longest coral reef in the world. If it were placed beside the United States, it would stretch from Philadelphia to Miami.

What is truly wonderful about a coral reef is the way it is made. The building begins with tiny animals called polyps. Polyps look like brightly colored flowers growing in an ocean garden. But they are a very simple form of animal life. Each little animal makes a coral cup around itself. The coral is hard, like stone. The animal unfolds from the cup to feed. It folds into the cup for safety. When the animal dies, the hard cup remains. New polyps build their cups on top of the remaining cups. As more and more cups are added, the coral takes different shapes. In time, masses of coral form a reef.

The reef is not safe from danger. Waves crash and beat at its edges. With each sweep of waves, bits of coral are carried away. Some kinds of fish feed on live polyps. When live polyps are killed, the reef breaks down. People also cause damage. They pollute the waters. They even tear off pieces of beautiful coral.

It has taken millions of years to build the Great Barrier Reef. Day by day parts of it are destroyed. Day by day the building goes on.

LISTING

Step 1.   Write the title on the chalkboard: "The Great Barrier Reef."

Step 2.   Read the title to the children. Ask if anyone has heard the phrase "coral reef" before. Ask children to tell you anything they know about coral reefs.

Step 3.   If there is no response, give a clue, such as "it has to do with something in the ocean."

Step 4.   List all responses on the board. Do not generate discussion at this point; simply look for many responses. Some possible responses include the following.

> they are hard
> different colors
> they are sharp
> break easily
> found in the ocean
> people collect them

Step 5.   Stop when you feel you have enough responses.

Step 6.   Reread the responses and ask for clarification or discussion if necessary.

Step 7.   Have children look for general categories, such as size, uses, location, color, shapes.

Step 8.   Leave the information in sight so that it can be used to give children a purpose for reading and to check and elaborate the information as they read.

Initial Prediction   Prediction is a major skill in reading. Prediction strategies should be taught to children from the beginning of reading instruction. (They can also be used even before formal instruction in reading begins, as teachers read literature to young children.) Children should be encouraged to look at the title of a selection and predict what the selection will be about; to look at the pictures and make further predictions about the characters, setting, mood, seasons, feelings, emotions, and so on; look at the boldface type, italicized words, and major and minor headlines, as aids to predicting content.

Once children make predictions, their reading has a purpose and becomes a vehicle for accepting or rejecting their predictions. This mental interaction is vital to comprehension (Burmeister, 1983; Eeds, 1981).

During reading, teachers should also stop children at appropriate spots and ask questions like "What do you think will happen next?" "What will this character do?" or "What do you think the outcome will be?" Children then read to check their predictions.

Prediction can further be trained via the cloze procedure, a method of aiding comprehension by omitting every nth (fifth, seventh, tenth) word in a passage and having children fill in the space with an appropriate word. The activity is scored by comparing the substitutions with the actual omitted words. The more identical matches children make with the text, the higher their prediction and comprehension of the passage.

This procedure can be modified and used for developing comprehension skills not directly related to specific material. Children may be encouraged to produce words that make sense in a paragraph. This helps them to use their oral language knowledge to understand print. For example, children can be given passages similar to the following.

It was Saturday morning. John _____ out of bed. It was a great day. The sun was _____ brightly. It was a good day to _____ outside. John wanted to _____ a treehouse. He had _____ wanted a treehouse.

The exercise can be done orally with children who have minimal sight vocabularies. It can be further modified by

1. including the first letters of omitted words;
2. including the first and last letters of omitted words;
3. deleting words with the same initial letters (all words with *gr* or *tr* blends) to reinforce certain skills; or
4. deleting special classes of words (contractions, compounds, nouns, verbs) to reinforce certain skills.

Thinking Strategies

The strategies presented so far are tools teachers can use to prepare children for material or to help children achieve an appropriate level of readiness for material. Thinking strategies are designed to assist children to interact adequately with material and to develop effective ways of thinking to process textual material. These strategies develop thinking skills that are of great importance in reading and understanding (Cassidy, 1981).

Bloom's Taxonomy   Perhaps the most well-known attempt to describe levels of thought is Bloom's taxonomy of educational objectives (Bloom, 1956). The taxonomy grew out of an attempt to standardize examination questions used to evaluate comprehension. Bloom and other educators tried to identify various levels of thinking used by individuals. Bloom's taxonomy was created and has since become a landmark in the field of education.

Six major levels of thought were identified by the taxonomy.

Level 1: Knowledge.   Knowledge refers to the recall of facts and details. This step does not necessarily include any understanding of information but simply the ability to state facts, recall events, list specific details, name items or conventions, and so on. The statement an individual can make at this level is "I know and I can state what I know."

Level 2: Comprehension.   Comprehension refers to the ability to go beyond knowledge and understand information. At this level we can process information and translate it into our own words. We can explain information and compare and contrast elements. Because comprehension involves relating incoming information to prior knowledge, we can also predict events. The statement a person can make at this level is "I can understand and I can explain."

Level 3: Application.   Application refers to the ability to apply information to real or hypothetical situations. Application includes the abilities to manipulate elements and to abstract and apply rules. Because we can use, apply, and manipulate, we can solve problems. This level, then, is the beginning of problem-solving ability. The statement one can make at this level is "I can use information. Therefore, I can solve problems by doing and by manipulating elements or ideas."

Level 4: Analysis.   At this level we can analyze elements, principles, and relationships. We can pull apart the whole to understand it better. We can analyze reactions, relationships, patterns, use of vocabulary, and so on. Because analysis involves the critical investigation of information, this level is the beginning of critical thinking.

The statement one can make is "I can pull selections apart and can analyze the parts to gain a greater understanding of the whole."

Level 5: Synthesis.   Synthesis refers to the ability to put the parts back together in a new whole with a unique and creative perspective. This level is the beginning of creative thought. The statement one can make at this level is "I can put the parts back together and add my own unique and creative perspective to the whole."

Level 6: Evaluation.   Evaluation is the ability to place value on an idea and judge it with some internal logic or external set of principles. The statement one can make at this level is "I can give and support my own opinions and can share my values with others."

At each level of thought the individual can engage in very specific behaviors, as listed in Table 4–1.

One of the goals of education is to help children operate effectively on all levels of thought. In fact, I believe that attention to all levels of thinking may form a central theme in the development and teaching of comprehension skills to children.

Using Questions   One important way that teachers can help children operate on all levels of thought is by exposing them to questions designed to tap each level of thought. Teachers need to be aware of the power of questions to stimulate children's thinking, to increase their interaction with the material, and to extend comprehension.

Although a variety of questions are always included with basal reading selections, teachers should independently construct questions to develop children's comprehension. Questions asked in basal series primarily tap the knowledge and comprehension levels of thought. In addition, the development of thinking skills through the use of questions is not limited to the reading program. Teachers must emphasize appropriate questions in all areas of the curriculum.

Gallagher (1965) offers a useful questioning scheme, with two categories of questions: narrow and broad. Narrow questions are text-bound; their answers are always in the text. They have one right answer and require little or no mental interaction. They depend heavily on memory. Broad questions are reader-bound; the answers begin in the text but end in the mind of the reader. These questions have many responses and demand a high level of mental interaction.

Gallagher identifies two types of narrow questions: cognitive-memory and convergent. Cognitive-memory questions require students to recall, identify, answer yes or no, define, name, and designate information. These questions tap the knowledge level of thought only. They often begin with the words "Who," "What," "Where," and "When." They are the most often asked questions in school.

TABLE 4–1
Possible operations at each level of Bloom's taxonomy

TAXONOMY LEVEL	OPERATIONS
1. Knowledge	tell, cite, show, list, locate, state, recite, repeat
2. Comprehension	describe, explain, review, infer, translate, paraphrase, predict, summarize, discuss
3. Application	use, model, try, operate, manipulate, diagram, apply, demonstrate, utilize
4. Analysis	organize, categorize, analyze, scrutinize, dissect, take apart, break down, prove, inspect
5. Synthesis	create, imagine, suppose, compose, hypothesize, improve, reorder, originate, formulate, elaborate, design
6. Evaluation	justify, appraise, recommend, criticize, support, reject, judge, award, censure

Convergent questions are text-bound but their answers require students to use information from different parts of the text and to explain, state relationships, compare, and contrast. They tap the comprehension level of thought. They often begin with the words "Why," "How," "Explain," "Compare," and "Contrast." The vast majority of questions asked of children during a school day fall in the cognitive-memory and convergent categories. It is very important for teachers to realize that these questions tap only the first two levels of thought.

Gallagher also identifies two types of broad questions: divergent and evaluative. Divergent questions require students to predict, hypothesize, infer, reconstruct, solve problems, and trace alternatives. Divergent questions tap the levels of application, analysis, and synthesis. Because these questions utilize so many levels of thinking, they are very important to the development of comprehension. They often begin with phrases and words like "What if," "Suppose," "How do you know that," "What will happen next," "What leads you to believe that," "How many ways can you think of to," "How could the outcome have been different if," and "Predict."

Evaluative questions require students to give and support an opinion, justify a choice, defend a position, place a value, and make a choice. These questions tap the level of evaluation. They often begin with phrases such as "What do you think," "Do you agree — why or why not," "Can you support," "How do you feel about,"

TABLE 4–2
Gallagher's (1965) questioning scheme

QUESTION TYPE	LEVEL OF THINKING	PURPOSE	FIRST WORDS
Narrow			
Cognitive-memory	Knowledge	Recall Identify Observe Answer yes/no Define Name	Who What When Where
Convergent	Comprehension	Explain State relationships Compare Contrast	How Why Explain Compare Contrast
Broad			
Divergent	Application Analysis Synthesis	Predict Hypothesize Infer Reconstruct Trace alternatives Guess	What if Suppose How do you know How many ways Predict
Evaluative	Evaluation	Judge Give an opinion Justify Choose Support Value	What do you think Do you agree Can you support How do you feel about

"Would you," and "Would you suggest." Gallagher's scheme can be represented graphically as in Table 4.2.

It is very important that teachers read textual material prior to instruction and that they construct questions to stimulate children's thinking on all levels of thought. There is nothing wrong with any question type, but none should be overused or underused. Questioning strategies are independent of grade level and content, and teachers should make an effort to stretch children's thinking at any age through listening or reading in all areas of the curriculum.

On pages 97–101 is a selection from *Windchimes*, a third-grade reading text (Durr et al., 1978). Sample questions of all four types—cognitive-memory, convergent, divergent, evaluative—based on "The Burning of the Rice Fields" follow the selection.

THE BURNING OF THE RICE FIELDS

by Lafcadio Hearn

Far away in Japan, many years ago, lived good old Hamaguchi (hah-mah-**goo**-chee). He was the wisest man of his village. and the people loved and honored him.

Hamaguchi was a rich farmer. His farmhouse stood on a hillside acre above the seashore. Down by the shore, and scattered up the hill, were the houses of his neighbors. Around his own house the ground was flat, like the top of a huge step in the hillside, and all about him stretched his rice fields.

It was the time of harvest. Hundreds of rice stacks dotted Hamaguchi's fields. There had been a fine crop, and tonight down in the village everyone was having a good time.

Hamaguchi sat outside his house and looked down into the village. He would have liked to join the merrymakers, but he was too tired — the day had been very hot. So he stayed at home with his little grandson, Tada (**tah**-dah). They could see the flags and the paper lanterns that hung, fluttering, across the streets of the village, and see the people gathering for the dance. The low sun lighted up all the moving bits of color.

It was still very hot, though a strong breeze had begun to blow in from the sea. Suddenly the hillside shook — just a little, as if a wave were rolling slowly under it. The house crackled and rocked gently a moment. Then all became still again.

"An earthquake," thought Hamaguchi, "but not very near. The worst of it is probably far away."

Hamaguchi was not frightened, for he had felt the earth quake many a time before. Yet he looked anxiously toward the village. Then, suddenly, he rose to his feet and looked out at the sea. The sea was very dark, and, strange to say, it seemed to be running away from the land.

Soon all the village had noticed how the water was rolling out, and the people hurried down to the beach. Not one of them had ever seen such a thing before.

For a moment, on the hillside. Hamaguchi stood and looked. Then he called, "Tada! Quick — very quick! Light me a torch!"

Tada ran into the house, picked up one of the pine torches that stood ready for use on stormy nights, lighted it, and ran back to his grandfather. The old man grabbed the torch and hurried to the rice fields. Tada ran with him, wondering what he was going to do.

When they reached the first row of rice stacks, Hamaguchi ran along the row, touching the torch to each as he passed. The rice was dry, and the fire caught quickly, and the seabreeze, blowing stronger. drove the flames ahead. Row after row. the stacks caught fire. and soon flames and smoke towered up against the sky.

Tada ran after his grandfather, crying, "Grandfather, why? Why?"

Had his grandfather gone mad, that he was burning the rice that was their food and all their wealth? But Hamaguchi went on from stack to stack, till he reached the end of the field. Then he threw down his torch and waited.

The bell-ringer in the temple on the hill saw the flames and set the big bell booming. And, down on the beach, the people turned and began to climb the hill. If Hamaguchi's rice fields were afire, not the strangest sights of the shore should keep them from helping him.

First up the hill came some of the young men, who wanted to fight the fire at once. But Hamaguchi stood in front of the fields and held out his hands to stop them.

"Let it burn, lads," he commanded. "Let it burn."

The whole village was coming. Men and boys, women and girls, mothers with babies on their backs, and even little children came. Children could help pass buckets of water. Even the old men and women came very slowly, as best they could.

Still Hamaguchi stood in front of his burning fields and waited. Meanwhile the sun went down.

The people began to question Tada. What had happened? Why wouldn't his grandfather let them fight the fire? Was he mad?

"I don't know," sobbed Tada, for he was really frightened. "Grandfather set fire to the rice on purpose. I saw him do it!"

"Yes," cried Hamaguchi. "I set fire to the rice. Are all the people here?"

The men of the village looked about them and answered, "All are here, but we cannot under-stand —"

"Look!" shouted Hamaguchi. as loud as he could, pointing to the sea. "Look! Now do you think I've gone mad?"

All turned and looked through the dim light, over the sea. Far, far out, where sea and sky seemed to meet, stretched a cloudy line that came nearer and nearer, and broadened out larger and larger. It was the sea coming back to the shore. It towered like a great wall of rock. It rolled more swiftly than a kite could fly.

"The sea!" shrieked the people. Hardly had they spoken, when the great waters struck the shore. The noise was louder than any thunder. The hillside shook. A sheet of foam was dashed up to where the people stood. When the sea went back, not a house was left below them on the hillside or along the shore. The village had been swept away.

The people stood silent, too frightened to speak, until they heard Hamaguchi saying gently, "That was why I set fire to the rice. . . . My house still stands, and there is room for many. The temple on the hill still stands. There is shelter there for the rest."

Then the people woke, as if from a dream, and understood. Hamaguchi had made himself poor to save them, and they bowed their foreheads to the ground before him.

POSSIBLE QUESTIONS

Cognitive-Memory

Identify: What occupation did Hamaguchi have?
Designate: Who was with Hamaguchi on the night of the fire?
Identify: Where did the story take place?
Name: What was Hamaguchi's grandson's name?

Convergent

Explain: Why did Hamaguchi tell Tada to get the torch?
Explain: How did Tada feel about his grandfather's actions?
Compare: How was Tada's reaction to his grandfather different from that of the villagers?

Divergent

Infer: How did the people really feel about Hamaguchi? How do you know?
Predict: What might have happened if Hamaguchi had been at the party?
Reconstruct: How might the story have been different if Hamaguchi had *not* been liked by the townspeople?
Alternative
  finding: How many other ways can you think of to have Hamaguchi save the village?
Infer: Why did the author say that the people woke "as if from a dream"?
Infer: Why did the people bow their heads to the ground at the end of the story?
Reconstruct: Create a different ending to the story.

Evaluative

Opinion: Do you think that Hamaguchi was wise in his actions? Why or why not?
Value: Would you have burned your fields to save the village? Why or why not?
Value: What five things do you think the townspeople will do *immediately* after the tidal wave?
Defend: Would you have reacted like Tada did if your grandfather had acted like Hamaguchi? Would your reactions have been different if you were younger (five years old) or older (fifteen years old)?

The Herber Three-Level Guide   Hal Herber (1978) views comprehension as a three-level process. Level 1 is the literal level, in which readers determine what the author *says*. Level 2 is the interpretive level, in which readers use prior knowledge and literal information to infer what the author *means*. Level 3 is the applied level. Here readers search for broad principles or generalizations that are illustrated both by the content and through ideas they have previously encountered.

To help children develop comprehension skills, Herber uses statements rather than questions because he feels that questions give the impression that there is one exact answer, which greatly limits critical and creative thought. In Herber's method, students are asked to support or reject declarative statements based on the text. All responses that can be supported by the text are viewed as correct.

A Herber three-level guide based on "The Burning of the Rice Fields" might look like the model below. Children should be guided to find information in the text to support or dispute each statement.

The Herber guide can be used as an instrument for discussion

HERBER GUIDE

Literal: What did the author say?

_____ Hamaguchi was a farmer.
_____ Hamaguchi had a granddaughter.
_____ The story took place in Japan.
_____ Before the tidal wave there was an earthquake.

Interpretive: What did the author mean?

_____ Hamaguchi was sitting outside because it was too hot in the hut.
_____ Hamaguchi was a quick thinker.
_____ The people were celebrating because they had a good crop.
_____ Rice was the most important crop to the villagers.

Applied: What do you agree with, based on the story and on what you know about life?

_____ If people love and respect you, they will help you in time of trouble.
_____ Sometimes if you help others you also help yourself.
_____ Actions often seem ridiculous to others when in fact they are very sensible.
_____ Always follow a crowd.

with children until they become familiar with the process and adept at the critical reading skill demanded by the guide. Once children are familiar with this tool, modifications can be made. For example, children can be assigned selections as independent reading material and can respond to the literal statements before coming to the reading group. During the group reading period, time can be spent discussing the interpretive and applied statements. Or children can read a selection in the group, discuss all the statements, and then respond to literal and/or interpretive statements in writing. Children can work independently, in pairs, or in small groups.

Visual Follow-up Strategies

We have so far considered conceptual awareness strategies, which aid comprehension before reading and questioning strategies, which are designed primarily to aid comprehension during reading (although questions are also important before and after reading). Visual follow-up strategies are designed to foster further comprehension and promote divergent thought primarily after reading.

Once children have read and comprehended narrative selections, teachers can help them extend their understanding of the material and of general story structures by focusing on three areas: character analysis, plot and major theme, and setting.

Children can be helped to analyze characters through discussion. Individual characters can be identified. Children can be asked to find words that best describe each character and support their choices with information from the text. Children can find words or phrases from the text that give an insight into characters' personalities. In addition, they can be assisted in comparing and contrasting characters.

Children should be taught how to identify the major theme or themes in a narrative. Main idea as a skill is often taught to children, but rarely do children apply these skills to reading selections. Remember that there may be more than one main idea in a selection. Recalling sequentially the key elements in the plot is an important skill. Children can also be taught to identify major problems presented in the story along with their solutions or resolutions.

Some stories describe setting very graphically. They lend themselves to children's creativity in appreciating setting. Children can be asked to read particularly descriptive passages and to represent them in pictures, sketches, papier-mâché, charts, maps, and so on. They can also focus on key words that visually describe the setting. Children can be helped to identify the different settings described in the story and to understand the significance of each setting to the story.

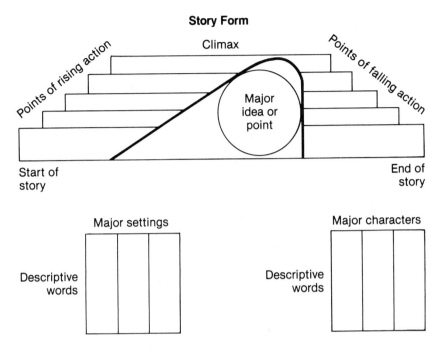

FIGURE 4–4
Story form

The Story Form   Enfield and Greene (1973) have created a very useful graphic scheme, called a *story form*, to accentuate characterization, plot, and setting for children. An adaptation of that scheme for elementary students is shown in Figure 4–4.

In addition to reinforcing elements of setting, plot, and character, the story form gives children a basic underlying structure for a story and helps them internalize that structure for all narrative material. This graphic representation should be discussed in detail several times with children. When they understand the idea of the structure, they can complete it independently after reading a story. The strategy reinforces comprehension skills of identifying sequence, climax, main idea, and characterization, and of appreciation of setting and plot.

Once children have become familiar with this scheme, it can be used as a skeleton structure to assist creative writing. Segments of the form can be filled in by the teacher, and children can fill in the remaining details. As children gain confidence in writing, the teacher can provide fewer segments. An example of such modification is shown in Figure 4–5.

The importance of children's internalizing the structure of a story cannot be minimized. During the past decade, psychologists

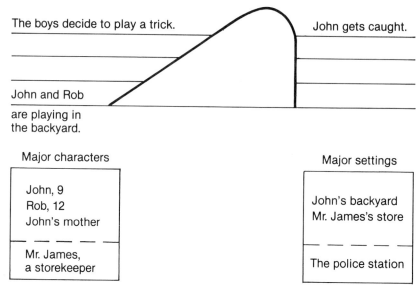

The boys decide to play a trick.   John gets caught.

John and Rob
are playing in
the backyard.

Major characters

John, 9
Rob, 12
John's mother

Mr. James,
a storekeeper

Major settings

John's backyard
Mr. James's store

The police station

FIGURE 4–5
Story form skeleton for creative writing

have investigated the way in which humans process whole language units such as stories and have found that stories have identifiable, internal structures that consist of syntactic or structural elements — setting, plot, episodes — and semantic elements — time frame, location, specific events. The semantic elements vary from story to story, but the syntactic elements remain relatively stable. These internal structures are called *story grammars* (Whaley, 1981; Sadow, 1982). Research suggests that many children are successful in processing narrative material because they have abstracted the concept or schema for story structure that helps them to understand, store, and retrieve information in a story (Bruce, 1978; Nezworski, Stein, and Trabasso, 1979; Stein and Glenn, 1979).

Stein and Glenn (1979) have proposed that a simple story usually contains two main components: setting, which includes place, character, and general background information; and episode, which includes an initiating event that sets the stage for a problem or an event, a response that sets up a goal, an attempt that makes an effort to accomplish the goal, a consequence that gives the result of the attempt, and a reaction that is the concluding response to the situation.

The following example is the application of Stein and Glenn's story grammar to a simple story, "The Belling of the Cat."

Setting

Once there was a family of mice who lived in the attic of a *big old house*. In the house lived a big, fat, mean, hungry cat.

Initiating event

One day the two young mice were sent out to find food. They sneaked quietly downstairs, picked up a pinch of cheese and a crumb of bread. As they were going back home, they *almost got captured by the silent cat*.

Response

When they got back home, they told their family of the near escape. The family decided that someone had to *bell the silent cat* so that they could be warned of his approach.

Attempt

They bought a bell and placed it on a collar. The father mouse waited until the cat was deep in sleep *and gently slipped the collar round the cat's neck*.

Consequence

From then on, the mice *could easily hear the approaching cat* and were able to seek their food without fear.

Reaction

The mice *were pleased* at their newly found freedom and *honored the father mouse* for his bravery.

Not only does a story grammar explain a story, but it also serves as a tool to analyze the story. The story form can be an initial method of helping children begin to internalize story structure by focusing on elements of sequence, problems and their resolution, characters, and setting. Once children conceptually understand the structure of a story, they can be introduced to the more complex elements of events, responses, attempts, consequences, and reactions.

The Report Form   Children in the elementary grades have a great deal of exposure to narrative material and relatively little exposure to expository material. In the secondary grades, the tables are turned, and expository material abounds. Many children find it quite difficult to make the transition because the strategies used to deal with each type of textual material are quite different. In narrative material, the whole is vitally important — the plot, the characterization, the abstraction of main idea, and so on. In expository material each sentence may be important because each may state an important fact.

Enfield and Greene (1973) have devised a visual representation of expository writing, called a *report form*, that is very helpful to

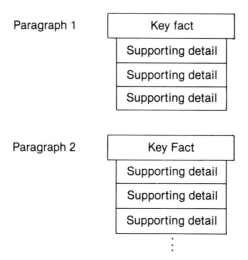

Paragraph 1

Key fact
Supporting detail
Supporting detail
Supporting detail

Paragraph 2

Key Fact
Supporting detail
Supporting detail
Supporting detail

FIGURE 4–6
Report form

children. They suggest that each paragraph in expository selections is often composed of a major key fact and supporting details. The report form is shown in Figure 4–6.

The report form is very useful in helping children abstract major facts and relevant details from expository material. It also gives children an internal structure that is helpful in reading texts. This should be used as a teaching strategy, that is, discussed with children, before they are expected to do it on their own. Figure 4–7 provides an example of a third grader's application of the report form to the first three paragraphs of "The Great Barrier Reef" (page 90).

The report form aids analysis of structure, of major facts, and of supporting details. It also forms the foundation for outlining and provides a good structure for test review.

Semantic Webbing   In 1980, Freedman and Reynolds introduced a visual strategy designed to assist children in organizing and integrating written information and in developing divergent thinking abilities. Their strategy is called *semantic webbing*. A semantic web is constructed using four basic elements: a core question, the web strands, the strand supports, and the strand ties.

At the center of the semantic web is a core question, a question related to any of several areas and with several possible answers. The question can relate to conclusions, generalizations, predictions, characters, evaluations, and so on. The only restriction is that the question must have many possible answers. All the information generated by

The Great Barrier Reef is in
the Pacific Ocean.

Waves break and
curl on it.

It is close to the
surface of the water.

It is the longest reef
in the world.

It is wonderful how
the reef is made.

It starts with tiny
animals called polyps.

They look like bright flowers.

They are really animals.

Each polyp makes a coral cup
around itself.

The coral is hard.

The polyp comes out to eat.

It goes in its shell for safety.

When polyps die, the
shell remains.

New polyps build their
cups on the dead shells.

Many shells make
the coral reef.

The reef is not safe from danger.

Waves destroy parts.

Fish feed on polyps.

People cause damage.

FIGURE 4–7
**Report form for "The Great
Barrier Reef"**

FIGURE 4–8
Core question for "The Burning of the Rice Fields"

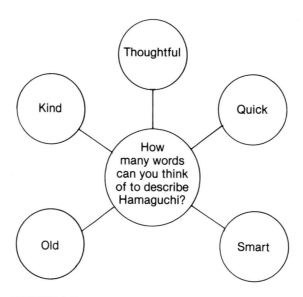

FIGURE 4–9
Core question and web strands for "The Burning of the Rice Fields"

the semantic web relates in some way to this core question. The question is placed in a circle. A sample core question based on "The Burning of the Rice Fields" (pages 97–101) is shown in Figure 4–8.

The responses to the core question are called *web strands*. They are placed in small circles extending from the core question, as shown in Figure 4–9.

Strand supports are the facts or inferences in the reading selection that support each strand. These supports extend from each strand, as shown in Figure 4–10.

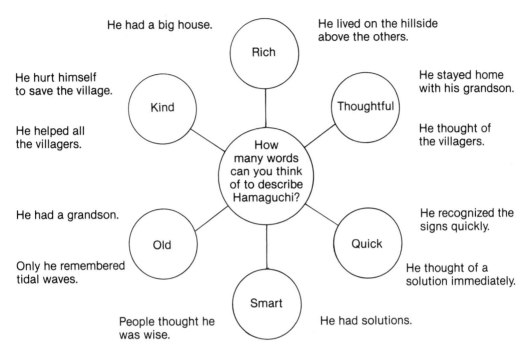

He had a big house.

Rich

He lived on the hillside above the others.

He hurt himself to save the village.

Kind

He stayed home with his grandson.

Thoughtful

He helped all the villagers.

How many words can you think of to describe Hamaguchi?

He thought of the villagers.

He had a grandson.

Old

He recognized the signs quickly.

Quick

Only he remembered tidal waves.

Smart

He thought of a solution immediately.

People thought he was wise.

He had solutions.

FIGURE 4–10
Core question, web strands, and strand supports for "The Burning of the Rice Fields"

Strand ties are simply possible relationships that exist among the strands. *Smart* and *quick*, for example, may be related and *kind* and *thoughtful* may also be related.

Semantic webbing is an effective strategy that can be used to develop awareness and critical reading at many levels. In "The Burning of the Rice Fields," there are many possible good core questions, among them the following.

Characterization

How many words can be used to describe Tada?

Prediction

What do you think the villagers will do *immediately* after the tidal wave recedes?

Problem solving

How many other ways can you think of to have Hamaguchi save the village?

Analysis

What emotions were experienced in the story?

Comparison and contrast

How were the reactions of Tada and of the villagers the same *and* different? (In this case, two webs would be created and comparisons made between each.)

Vocabulary

What words does the author use throughout the story to show excitement?

Because webs can be created from a wide variety of questions, this strategy is a very versatile and powerful one.

Expository Fact Analyzer   Besides the report form, a strategy that can be used for comprehension of expository material is the expository fact analyzer. The purpose of this strategy is twofold: (1) to help children recall important facts in expository material and (2) to help children relate content-area material to their own experiences and environments. One problem in content-area instruction, particularly in science and social studies, is that, although teachers are adept at teaching the facts, seldom do they help children personally interact with the material and recognize the subject matter in their own lives. The fact analyzer, which combines elements of the story form and of semantic webbing, ensures children's interaction with the material. The basic structure of the expository fact analyzer is shown in Figure 4–11.

At the top of the fact analyzer, students must recall and list the major facts presented in a selection. Then they must respond to two semantic web core questions. One question is called a textual extension question, which aims to extend students' understanding of the text. The other core question is an experiential expansion question, which aims to show students how the material in the text can be related to their own experiences.

Figure 4–12 presents a fourth-grader's fact analyzer for "The Great Barrier Reef" selection on page 90.

The fact analyzer is an excellent structure for review, and it also extends analysis of the text and shows students how elements of the text are related to their own lives.

Using Instructional Strategies

Many strategies for developing and extending comprehension have been presented in this chapter. The strategies are in no way meant

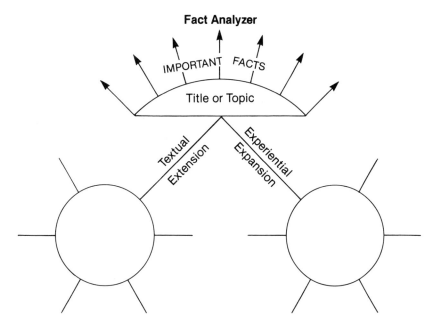

FIGURE 4–11
Expository fact analyzer

to be applied to all reading selections. The strategy or combination of strategies a teacher uses should depend on two important factors: the group of children to be taught and the complexity and familiarity of the material to be taught.

Students who have a slow learning rate, who have difficulty decoding, who are unfamiliar with many key vocabulary items, and who lack basic concepts and experiences may need a different combination of strategies than a group of children who have a fast learning rate, have mastered decoding, and have adequate vocabulary and concepts for the material.

Material that contains few unfamiliar or difficult vocabulary items and that is written about a familiar topic may require fewer and different strategies than material that is written in a complex style, contains difficult and unfamiliar vocabulary, and is written about abstract, unfamiliar, or complicated content. It is very important, therefore, that teachers read material prior to instruction, analyze the difficulty of the vocabulary and concepts in relation to the group of children to be instructed, and decide which strategies would best develop and extend the comprehension of the children.

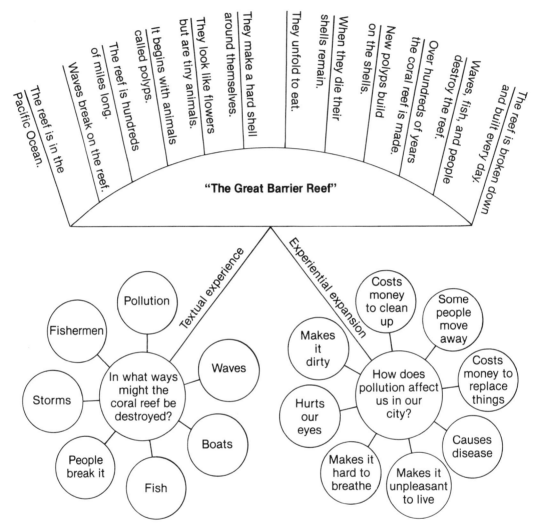

FIGURE 4–12
Expository fact analyzer for "The Great Barrier Reef"

Summary

Comprehension should be the major focus in reading instruction, and development of comprehension should involve the following factors:

1. preparing children for material by providing necessary concepts, alerting them to already known concepts, providing clarification for unfamiliar vocabulary, building an interest in material to be read, and generating predictions of the content;
2. generating interaction with and comprehension of the text by continuing prediction throughout reading, having children retrieve facts about content, and helping children develop thinking and comprehension skills through higher-level questions that focus on critical thinking, creative thinking, and problem solving; and
3. extending children's understanding of, interaction with, and motivation toward material by elaborating on the material they read and by helping them use the information in a variety of situations.

Research in reading instruction indicates that we need to review our instructional priorities. The National Assessment of Educational Progress in Reading (1981) reports that, while our educational system does an admirable job teaching decoding and literal recall of information, it falls short in the instruction of inferential thinking, a cornerstone of comprehension. In addition, research by Durkin (1978–1979) shows that in twenty-four classrooms for more than four thousand minutes of reading instruction over an eight-month period, very little instruction in comprehension took place. Durkin reports that while 0.63 percent of the time was spent in teaching comprehension and 0.25 percent of the time in prediction, 2.13 percent of the time was spent making assignments, 5.46 percent of the time clarifying and helping with assignments, 5.53 percent of the time in preparation, and 17.65 percent of the time in assessment of comprehension. Durkin reports that the majority of questions asked were designed to test children's knowledge of facts, that vocabulary instruction was usually very brief and shallow, and that little transfer of comprehension skills was expected or made in content areas. Based on her observations, Durkin characterized teachers as predominantly interrogators, assignment givers, and assignment checkers.

Priorities in instruction need to shift from merely having children regurgitate information to helping them develop, recognize, use, and extend their thinking abilities as they practice reading tasks. The strategies presented in this chapter are designed to help teachers build and enhance children's comprehension during all phases of reading instruction.

References

Adams, M. J. "Models of Word Recognition." *Cognitive Psychology*, no. 11 (1979).

Adams, M. J. and A. Collins. "A Schema-Theoretic View of Reading." In *New Directions in Discourse Processing*, edited by R. O. Freedle. Vol. 2. Norwood, N.J.: Ablex, 1979.

Addison-Wesley Reading Program. Abracadatlas. Palo Alto, Calif.: Addison-Wesley, 1979.

Ausubel, D. P. "The Use of Advance Organizers in Learning and Retention of Meaningful Verbal Material." *Journal of Educational Psychology*, no. 51 (1960).

Bloom, B. S. *Taxonomy of Educational Objectives: Handbook 1, Cognitive Domain*. New York: David McKay, 1956.

Bruce, B. "What Makes a Good Story?" *Language Arts*, no. 55 (1978).

Burmeister, L. *Foundations and Strategies for Teaching Children to Read*. Reading, Mass.: Addison-Wesley, 1983.

Cassidy, J. "Grey Power in the Reading Program: A Direction for the Eighties." *The Reading Teacher*, no. 35 (December 1981).

Durkin, D. "What Classroom Observations Reveal About Reading Comprehension Instruction." *Reading Research Quarterly*, no. 14 (1978–1979).

Durr, William K., et al. *Windchimes*, third-grade text. Boston: Houghton Mifflin, 1978.

Eeds, M. "What to Do When They Don't Understand What They Read: Research Based Strategies for Teaching Reading Comprehension." *The Reading Teacher*, no. 34 (February 1981).

Enfield, Mary L., and Victoria Greene. *Project Read: Reading Guide*. Bloomington, Minn.: Bloomington Public Schools, 1973.

Freedman, G., and Elizabeth Reynolds. "Enriching Basal Reader Lessons with Semantic Webbing." *The Reading Teacher*, vol. 33 (March 1980).

Gallagher, John. *Productive Thinking with Gifted Children*. Urbana, Ill.: Cooperative Research on Exceptional Children, University of Illinois, 1965.

Goodman, K. "What We Know About Reading." In *Findings of Research in Miscue Analysis: Classroom Applications*, edited by P. D. Allen and D. J. Watson. Urbana, Ill.: N.C.F.E., 1976.

Gough, P. G. "One Second of Reading." In *Language by Ear and by Eye*, edited by J. F. Kavanagh and I. G. Mattingly. Cambridge, Mass.: M.I.T. Press, 1972.

The Social Sciences: Concepts and Values. New York: Harcourt Brace Jovanovich, 1970.

Herber, H. *Teaching Reading in the Content Areas*. Englewood Cliffs, N.J.: Prentice-Hall.

Houghton Mifflin Reading Series. Keystone, fifth-grade text. *Passport*, fourth-grade text. Boston: Houghton Mifflin, 1976.

Jones, L. "An Interactive View of Reading: Implications for the Classroom." *The Reading Teacher*, no. 35 (April 1982).

LaBerge, D., and S. J. Samuels. "Toward a Theory of Automatic Information Processing in Reading." *Cognitive Psychology*, no. 6 (1974).

Lindsay, P., and D. Norman. *Human Information Processing*. New York, N.Y.: Academic Press, 1972.

National Assessment of Education Progress. *Reading in America: A Perspective on Two Assessments*. Denver, Col.: N.A.E.P., 1981.

Nezworski, T., N. L. Stein, and T. Trabasso. *Story Structure Versus Control Effects on Children's Recall and Evaluative Inferences*. Tech. Rep. no. 31. Urbana, Ill.: Center for the Study of Reading, University of Illinois, June 1979.

Pearson, P. D., and R. J. Spiro. "Toward a

Theory of Reading Comprehension Instruction." *Topics in Language Disorders*, no. 1 (1981).

Rumelhart, D. E. *Toward an Interactive Model of Reading*. CHIP Rep. no. 56. San Diego, Calif.: Center for Human Information Processing, March 1976.

Sadow, M. "The Use of Story Grammar in the Design of Questions." *The Reading Teacher*, no. 35 (February 1982).

Samuels, S. J. "Automatic Decoding and Reading Comprehension." *Language Arts*, no. 53, 1976.

Smith, Frank. *Understanding Reading: A Psycholinguistic Analysis of Reading and Learning to Read*. New York: Holt, Rinehart and Winston, 1982.

———. "Making Sense of Reading — and of Reading Instruction." *Harvard Educational Review*, no. 47 (1977).

Stein, N. L., and C. G. Glenn. "An Analysis of Story Comprehension in Elementary School Children." In *New Directions in Discourse Processing*, vol. 2, edited by R. R. Freedle. Hillside, N.J.: Erlbaum, 1979.

Taylor, W. L. "Cloze Procedure: A New Tool for Measuring Readability." *Journalism Quarterly*, no. 30 (1953).

Weaver, C. *Psycholinguistics and Reading: From Process to Practice*. Cambridge, Mass.: Winthrop, 1980.

Whaley, J. "Story Grammars and Reading Instruction." *The Reading Teacher*, no. 34, (April 1981).

5

Reading Readiness

Reading readiness is often viewed as a specific set of subskills that must be acquired before reading instruction begins. If any of these prerequisite skills are lacking, they must be identified and taught prior to reading. It is often assumed that when children learn the skills, they have achieved readiness for reading. This view places the major responsibility for learning on the child. We will approach readiness from a much broader perspective, using the definition proposed by Ausubel (1959) as our focus. Ausubel states that readiness is "the adequacy of existing capacity in relation to the demands of a given learning task" (p. 248). This definition describes readiness in its broadest sense. It has major implications for the instruction of any content to any child at any level of development.

☐ How has the concept of readiness changed over the past eighty to one hundred years?

☐ What factors affect children's readiness for reading?

☐ What is the role of the teacher in making children ready to read?

☐ How is readiness to read related to readiness to learn any subject?

☐ How does readiness relate to students at all grade levels learning any content?

Historical Perspective

The concept of reading readiness has undergone several changes both in definition and in emphasis since the turn of the century, many of them due to larger philosophical shifts in education and psychology. Before 1900, the issue of readiness was of little concern. But by the 1920s, readiness was a major topic. The reasons for this relatively sudden change will become apparent as we analyze the historical aspects of readiness.

1900 to Mid-1930s

The first major catalyst for the readiness movement came in 1904 in the writing and philosophy of the psychologist G. Stanley Hall (1904). Hall was a major proponent of the theory of recapitulation, which stated that individual human beings pass through predetermined stages similar to those through which the race passes. As such, physiological and mental maturation determines the individual's progression through each stage. The 1920s saw major acceptance of this "stage theory." By 1925, Hall's views were supported by many influential leaders in the country, among them Arnold Gessel (1925, 1946), a physician whose natural interest in physical maturation made him a close ally of Hall's views. By the end of the 1920s, it was generally accepted that individuals passed through automatic, fixed stages of physical, mental, and behavioral development.

A parallel emphasis on scientific testing and measurement of behavior grew in the 1920s, contributing to the rather rapid development of achievement and intelligence tests and their wide use in the schools. As a result of this emphasis, it was determined that many first-grade children were unprepared for second-grade material and that the major cause for this failure was their inability to read appropriately.

Given the overpowering emphasis on developmental stages, the young children's failure to read was interpreted as a result of failure to achieve appropriate levels of readiness prior to reading instruction. This conclusion may seem somewhat rash and unfounded today, but the reasoning as based on the philosophy of the 1920s is quite understandable: (1) all development occurs in fixed stages; (2) passage through the stages is due to maturation; (3) since all behaviors occur in stages, reading behavior must be no exception; (4) reading success is thus dependent on instruction in reading only when one has matured to the appropriate stage; (5) teaching reading prior to the stage of readiness will result in failure. The natural outgrowth of this line of reasoning was a major effort to find the stage at which readiness for reading occurs.

Starting in 1925 and continuing to the early 1930s, theorists tried to determine that stage. By the end of the 1920s, it was generally accepted that a mental age of between 6.0 and 6.5 was necessary for reading success in first grade. The term *mental age* describes the level of mental functioning of an individual. The two major factors that contribute to this measure are intelligence quotient and chronological age. The accepted formula for computing mental age is $IQ/100 \times$ chronological age (Wilson, 1977).

The search for a specific stage came to an end in 1931 when Morphett and Washburne, two educators in Winnetka, Illinois, published research demonstrating that a mental age of 6.5 was necessary for reading success in the first grade. In actuality, the study was a very crude one in which one method of instruction was used in one school system. It seems irrational that such a small study was given such major importance; but because of the preeminence of the stage theory and the emphasis on scientific testing and measurement, the educational community was well prepared to accept this conclusion without close scrutiny.

By the mid-1930s, the Winnetka results were so entrenched that in that city teachers kept charts showing approximately when each child would reach mental age 6.5, and no formal reading instruction was begun until that time. Indeed, this mental age concept was to be accepted in varying degrees in the educational community across the country for the next twenty years (Durkin, 1983).

This initial view of readiness accepted from 1900 to approximately the mid-1930s focused on physical and mental maturation. The total responsibility for readiness was placed on the child. If the child matured appropriately, readiness would occur at about the start of first grade. If not, reading instruction would be postponed until the child matured. No responsibility for readiness was placed on any external factors, such as parents, teachers, or instructional methods. It was precisely this point of view that pushed the readiness issue into its next phase.

Mid-1930s to Late 1950s

By the late 1930s, educators began to question the mental age concept. Perhaps its most vehement opponent was Arthur Gates. Acting on the conviction that readiness for reading was affected somewhat by factors outside the child, Gates (1936, 1937) identified ten low achievers in four first grades. All those children were not ready for reading instruction because of their mental age. Gates assigned the children to tutors and modified their instruction, and within three months all were successfully reading. On the basis of these results, Gates made the following conclusions:

1. Readiness is not totally dependent on the child.
2. The appropriate time for beginning reading is also determined by the method of reading instruction used.
3. Success in reading is to some extent due to the teaching environment.
4. Readiness for reading is something that can be developed rather than waited for.
5. Different methods of teaching reading may require different levels of readiness.

Although the evidence from Gates's study was quite strong, his message did not gain wide acceptance in the 1930s. The mental age concept was so deeply entrenched and its underlying assumptions so widely accepted that they were not easily dispelled. Even though Gates's conclusions did not replace the prevailing ones, they did have an effect on some of the practices of the day. Educators began to identify individual skills that contributed to a readiness for reading and also accepted that the skills necessary for reading readiness could be developed in children through training. This was a significant departure from the maturational philosophy that dominated the 1920s.

The 1940s and 1950s saw a rapid increase in the use of reading-readiness tests and programs. The content of these programs varied considerably. Some were very structured, consisting of training in visual discrimination, auditory discrimination, left-to-right orientation, vocabulary, letter names, top-bottom orientation, and so on. Other programs were experience-based, providing children with wide experiences, exposure to much literature, language development, and social interacton.

Until the late 1950s conditions remained relatively stable. Many people still accepted the notion of mental age; others were swayed by Gates's ideas. Some programs were very structured, while others were quite flexible. No drastic change in attitudes toward readiness was evident. This tranquillity was to end in 1957.

The Turning Point: 1957

On October 4, 1957, the Soviet Union launched Sputnik I. That a foreign country was so advanced and had accomplished such a significant feat ahead of the United States caused immediate and drastic changes in the way education was viewed in this country. The educational system in the United States was seen as too lax, too undemanding, and too nonstructured. There was an immediate mandate to correct these inadequacies by teaching more information in a more structured way to more children at an earlier age. The attitude was that if children weren't ready for instruction, they should be made ready. This was a total reversal of the earlier concept of readiness; Now readiness was something to be created, to be made to happen.

The early 1960s saw an emphasis on structured preschools, academic kindergartens, preschool programs for disadvantaged children, and accelerated academic programs for high achievers.

Predictably, this new view of readiness was endorsed and supported by noted psychologists of the day. Jerome Bruner (1960) stated that any subject can be taught to any child at any age provided that the topic is explained in understandable language and that the child has or is given the necessary preliminary experiences. This validation from the field of psychology added momentum and credibility to prevailing beliefs of the post-Sputnik era.

Ausubel's View

In the wake of the educational upheaval begun in 1957, the Aristotelian principle of the golden mean was operationalized in the definition of readiness proposed by Ausubel in 1959. His definition — that readiness is "the adequacy of existing capacity in relation to the demands of a given learning task" (p. 248) — implies that readiness is not totally dependent on the child, the teacher, or the method of instruction. Readiness is the result of interaction between the learner and the task to be learned. Every task demands from a learner certain prerequisites — cognitive, experiential, conceptual, intellectual, or a combination. Readiness occurs when the learner possesses these prerequisites either through natural acquisition or through instruction.

Some very important implications can be drawn from Ausubel's definition:

1. All learning tasks demand some level of readiness.
2. Readiness factors cannot be limited to the discussion of reading instruction: they are relevant to the learning of all subjects.
3. Readiness factors cannot be limited to the discussion of instruction of young children; they are relevant to learning at all age levels.
4. Different methods of instruction impose different readiness demands on learners.
5. Readiness must be linked to some degree to prior knowledge and experience.

6. Certain aspects of readiness can be taught.
7. Because one's "existing capacity" is limited to some degree, one's readiness for a topic or ability to learn a given task by one method or another may also be limited.
8. The closer one's "existing capacity" matches the demands of the task, the higher one's level of readiness.
9. Since "existing capacity" is related to experience, the more experience one has with the task to be learned, the higher one's level of readiness.
10. A high level of readiness should ensure high levels of understanding and learning.

These implications are reminiscent of the discussion of comprehension in Chapter 4. Indeed, a comparison of the two definitions will demonstrate how close these concepts really are.

> Comprehension is building a bridge between the known and the unknown.
> Readiness is the adequacy of "existing capacity" in relation to the demands of a given learning task.
> Readiness=Existing Capacity *in relation to* demands of task
> Comprehension=What is known *in relation to* what is unknown.

Both readiness and comprehension are affected by prior knowledge and experience. If one is ready to learn a task, comprehension occurs. The higher the level of readiness, the greater the comprehension. If one is not ready for learning, comprehension will not occur.

The definition of readiness formulated by Ausubel is the accepted definition in this text. It places readiness, like comprehension, at the base of all learning. It also makes readiness a central concern not only in initial reading instruction but in all instruction. All teachers must take the responsibility for making their students ready for instruction. The strategies of vocabulary preinstruction, overviews, advance organizers, concept preparation, and listing discussed in Chapter 4 are all pertinent to readiness. Readiness can appropriately be viewed as the preparation of the cognitive field for any information to be learned.

Readiness and Child-Centered Factors

To a significant degree reading readiness can be fostered and developed in children, but some individual factors in each child also contribute to reading readiness. Teachers should be aware of these factors and use them to observe and check children and to provide experiences in the skills they lack.

Visual Factors

1. **Visual Acuity** Visual acuity refers to the clearness or sharpness of vision. Reading is a visual activity, and to engage in it appropriately children must be able to see the stimuli clearly. Impaired vision interferes with easy acquisition of reading. It is advisable that children have a vision check prior to entering school.

2. **Visual Discrimination** Visual discrimination is the ability to distinguish similarities and differences beteen graphic symbols. In reading, the graphic symbols are letters and words. Though most children come to school well practiced in general visual discrimination, many are not adept in the discrimination necessary in reading, particularly letter and word discrimination.

   Visual discrimination exercises are prevalent in readiness programs, but such exercises often train children to discriminate between pictures, geometric forms, objects, and the like that bear little resemblance to the forms of print. Research by Weintraub (1968), Robinson (1972), and others has shown that such exercises do not influence readiness for reading. Exercises that help children discriminate between letters and words do affect readiness. Further research by Samuels (1973) shows that visual discrimination and learning are more positively affected if children are required to discriminate between letters that are similar (*p / b t g p*) rather than between letters that are quite dissimilar (*p / o r s p*).

   This discrimination ability is developed through activities such as matching games with letters and words and "same-different" games with letters and words along with analyzing responses with children.

3. **Visual Memory** Visual memory as it relates to reading readiness refers to the ability not only to recognize letters or words but also to remember and reproduce them. This ability is related to the frequency with which children are exposed to and have first-hand experience with letters and words. It can be developed through frequent practice with letters and words each day; multimodal practice with elements (seeing, saying, writing, tracing, spelling, and so on); practice viewing letters or a word, discussing them, and recalling them from memory by identifying, spelling, or writing them; and practice in writing and spelling names and common sight words.

Auditory Factors

Auditory Acuity   Auditory acuity refers to the clearness or sharpness of hearing. It can be tested by instruments such as the Beltone Audiometer. This ability is important in readiness, particularly in learning the isolated sounds of the language. Losses in acuity at the upper pitch range affect an individual's ability to hear some single consonants, such as /s/, /l/, and /t/, and their blends. Losses in acuity at the lower pitch range affect an individual's ability to hear isolated vowel sounds as well as some consonant sounds, such as /m/, /g/, /b/, and /h/. Such losses negatively affect reading behavior as well as performance in all school subjects. Children's hearing should be tested before they enter first grade.

Auditory Discrimination   Auditory discrimination is the ability to hear differences between sounds in the language. It has been shown to be one of the best predictors of reading success at the end of first grade (McNinch, 1970). Many children entering first grade are weak in this ability.

Some researchers view auditory discrimination as a metalinguistic ability, which is the ability to reflect on language, analyze it, and make decisions regarding acceptability, ambiguity, humor, and so forth. Some researchers have found that many children do not fully develop their metalinguistic abilities until they are five, six, or even seven years old (Knafle, 1974).

Research results in auditory discrimination skills are quite mixed. Some research suggests that auditory discrimination skills should be trained in children who are weak in the ability (Lyon, 1977). Other research suggests that teaching auditory discrimination may be a useless activity (Moskowitz, 1970, 1982; Rozin and Gleitman, 1977). Common sense suggests that the truth lies somewhere in the middle. Some children do come to school with poor auditory discrimination skills. Particularly in phonic-based programs, auditory discrimination is an important skill that is demanded of children. If children are expected to perform this skill, they should be provided with formal opportunities to learn and practice it.

An ability related to auditory discrimination is auditory segmentation, the ability to divide words into syllables or individual letter sounds (*bat* = /b/ + /a/ + /t/; *stop* = /st/ + /o/ /p/. This is an important reading skill in the instructional sequences of many published reading programs. Good readers often learn this skill inductively, while poor readers find it very difficult. Training in auditory segmentation does improve children's ability to segment words (Rosner, 1982).

Some activities that train auditory abilities are as follows:

☐ Children listen to pairs of words and decide if they are the same or different: *bat–fat, pet–Pete, hall–ball, flip–flop.*

☐ Children produce words that begin or end like a key word or have the same middle sound as a key word.

☐ Children find words that rhyme with key words.

☐ Children listen to words that have symbol-sound consistency (hat, bed, stop) and identify the sounds they hear.

☐ Children play "Guess a Word." "I am thinking of a three-letter word." First letter *h*. (Children guess.) Second letter *a*. (Children guess.) Third letter *t*. What is the word? (Children respond.) Cover the stimuli and have children spell from memory.

☐ Children clap the syllables in words.

Oral Language Factors

As part of the language system, reading is closely related to oral language. Like oral language, it is affected by syntax or word order. Words are strung together in predictable strings. The order of words makes it easy to predict what class of word will follow a given word. In the sentence "the boy ran _____," the verb *ran* will most likely be followed by a noun, an adverb, or a preposition. It will not likely be followed by a verb or adjective.

Like oral language, reading is affected by meaning or semantics. Readers expect certain types of words to occur in certain contexts. In the previous example, "The boy ran _____," we would fill in the slot with a word or phrase like *home, down the street, quickly,* or *slowly,* but never with a word like *chair, bed,* or *sick.* Like oral language, reading is also affected by sound. Knowing that the open slot in the previous example begins with the sound /h/ leads us to guess a word like *home.*

Use of the three language cues is an important readiness skill. Children who can use context to predict deleted or unknown words are at a significant advantage in reading; their knowledge of language will assist them in learning reading.

In addition to use of language clues, facility in oral language is an important readiness skill. Children who have many experiences with discussion, who are involved in and talk about experiences valued by schools and texts, who can engage in various language tasks such as acting out stories, who actively expand their oral vocabulary, who ask and answer questions, and who are able to use language to solve problems are at an advantage in learning to read. Facility with language is particularly important in the comprehension of print.

Environmental Factors

The following are some experiences children have in their home environment that predispose them to develop reading readiness.

- ☐ Having many experiences with books
- ☐ Being read to often
- ☐ Knowing what letters or words are and finding them in print
- ☐ Looking at books and enjoying being read to
- ☐ Following along with the print when a book is being read
- ☐ Learning some letters and words from their parents
- ☐ Retelling stories based on pictures
- ☐ Having parents who value reading, who read for pleasure, and who enjoy reading to and with their children
- ☐ Having basic left-right and top-bottom orientation when dealing with books
- ☐ Being encouraged to predict word endings, words, phrases, events, episodes, and so on as they are read to
- ☐ Watching TV programs like "Sesame Street" and "Electric Company" regularly and beginning to learn a basic sight vocabulary and letter-sound relationships
- ☐ Having enough experience with print to realize that reading should make sense
- ☐ Having a basic knowledge of signs they see often in the environment ("McDonald's," "Burger King," "School," "Stop")
- ☐ Having a repertoire of stories, poems, nursery rhymes, TV commercials, and so on that they know and can repeat from memory

These factors point to the importance of parents in the preparation of children for school. They also suggest possible readiness activities for preschool and kindergarten classrooms. Durkin (1978) and Clay (1980) have identified the following activities as essential to reading readiness instruction of kindergarten children. Notice how closely they relate to the environmental factors we identified.

- ☐ Interest children in learning to read.
- ☐ Help children acquire some understanding of what reading and learning to read are all about.
- ☐ Teach about left-to-right and top-to-bottom orientation of written English.
- ☐ Teach the meaning of *word* and the function of space in establishing word boundaries.
- ☐ Teach children the meaning of terms that are involved in reading instruction.

Parents can help prepare children for reading readiness by reading to them often.

☐ Teach children to discriminate conceptually and visually among letters and words.
☐ Teach children the names of letters.
☐ Teach children strategies for using their knowledge of oral language for prediction and self-correction in reading.

One of the essential tasks of teachers is to observe children at the beginning of the school year, identify those who already have or who need certain readiness skills, provide the skills the children need, and extend the children's abilities continuously throughout the year. Teachers should also discuss readiness factors with parents and suggest strategies that parents can use at home. Many activities identified as "environmental factors" earlier in this section would be very appropriate to suggest to parents. Readiness for reading is a responsibility that should be shared by the home and the school.

Readiness Skills and Methodology

In Chapter 2 we noted that each method of teaching reading demanded certain prerequisites from children. It should be apparent now that those prerequisites are actually factors that determine children's level of readiness for instruction in a given method. We will now review some of the prerequisites for the programs presented in Chapter 2 to see how they relate to children's reading readiness.

The Phonic Program

If children are to be taught in a phonic program, they need the following skills to be ready for that method of instruction.

1. *Strong auditory discrimination.* Phonics demands that a student be able to hear and respond to isolated sounds that are very similar, such as /b/, /d/, and /p/.
2. *Good visual discrimination.* Phonics isolates letters in instruction. To read letters like *b* and *d*, *o* and *e*, or *p* and *q*, a child must discriminate between very similar stimuli.
3. *Good auditory segmentation abilities.* Phonics requires that children hear and produce isolated sounds in words. As we saw earlier in this chapter, this might be a metalinguistic ability that is related to maturation.
4. *Good auditory memory.* Auditory memory is the ability to hold sounds or combinations of sounds in memory and retrieve them at the appropriate time. This skill is vital for sounding out letters and blending letters into words. If children do not know the word *stop*, they must sound out /st/ and hold it in memory; sound out /o/ and hold it in memory; and sound out /p/ and hold it in memory. Then they must retrieve the entire sequence from memory in correct order.

The preceding list is certainly not complete, but it covers some of the most important readiness skills related to phonic instruction. Children who do not possess prerequisite skills can be trained in these abilities; but they also must be given alternative strategies for learning. Such children may need a strong sight-word strand as a supplement to the phonic program. They may also need many opportunities for incidental learning. This can be done through frequent use of language experience, writing and then reading texts they create for wordless storybooks, and much experience with reading predictable print books. Chapter 11 contains bibliographies of wordless storybooks and predictable print books along with instructional strategies. Exposure to word families or patterns can also be helpful.

The Linguistic Program

Some of the more important readiness skills for a linguistic program are the following.

1. *Good visual discrimination.* Linguistics requires that children discriminate visually among very similar stimuli, such as *cat, mat, rat, sat.*
2. *Good visual memory.* Children must remember a variety of phonograms (*at, in, et, up, ot*), retrieve them from memory quickly, and use them to decode words.
3. *Knowledge of consonant sounds.*
4. *Flexibility in grammatical and semantic expectation.* Linguistic programs contain very restrictive sentences, such as "Nat is a cat. Nat is fat. Nat is a fat cat." Children who have strong language expectations may be very confused or bored.

Teachers whose students lack these prerequisite skills should modify their linguistic program by providing much exposure to meaningful print such as language experience and predictable print books, by helping students build a strong sight vocabulary, and possibly by giving students experience with phonic analysis.

The Basal Format

As we have seen, a basal format can emphasize any methodology. If the emphasis is either phonic or linguistic, the readiness skills and modifications mentioned in the two preceding sections apply. The readiness skills for developmental basal programs include the following.

1. *Good auditory discrimination, auditory memory, and auditory segmentation abilities.* These are needed because developmental basals often have strong phonic strands.

2. *Tolerance for routine.* Most developmental basals use one basic instructional plan throughout a text. Each lesson is presented in the same format, and skills are instructed in the same way. Children must be able to withstand routinized learning conditions.

3. *Ability to learn skills in the way they are presented.* If children do not learn a skill, the skill usually is retaught in the same way as it was initially taught. Children must be able to learn in that one way.

4. *Average to better than average learning rate.* Developmental basals contain a certain amount of material that must be completed in a specified time frame. Each skill is practiced a definite number of times. Children must be able to learn at the required rate.

5. *Wide range of experience.* Children are expected to know much background material about a variety of countries, people, values, regions, races, activities, and ideas.

Teachers whose students do not possess these readiness skills must modify programs by providing more or fewer skill practices for slow or gifted learners, respectively; reteaching skills using techniques different from those used in initial instruction; varying the instructional format; providing a strong sight vocabulary; or providing the concepts and experiences children need prior to instruction. The importance of analyzing learning tasks, identifying necessary prerequisites, providing practice in certain skills for children if needed, and modifying instruction cannot be overemphasized.

Developing Readiness for Reading

Readiness for Initial Reading

Many strategies can be used to develop readiness for beginning reading, among them the following.

Read to children often and vary the reading experience using some of the following suggestions.

☐ While reading to children, show them the pictures and discuss the story.

☐ Before or after reading, choose interesting vocabulary and discuss the words.

☐ Read to children and discuss issues only when children raise them.

☐ Have children participate in your oral reading by joining in on repeated fragments, finishing predictable sentences, predicting outcomes, and generating solutions to problems.

☐ Let children follow along with the print as you read. Point out familiar words and phrases and have children read them. Encourage them to read sections with you.

☐ Have children lie down in a relaxed position, close their eyes, and conjure up visual images as you read to them. After reading, let them share what they "saw."

☐ After you have read a relatively easy or predictable book, encourage children to read it to you, to a friend, or to the group.

Give children experience in following oral directons. Start with one-step directions and slowly increase the complexity. Directions can involve both physical activity ("Go to the bookcase; bring me a green book; put it on the chair") or paper-and-pencil tasks ("Make a yellow circle at the top of your paper and a green square at the bottom of your paper").

Provide many experiences in rhyming. Start with brainstorming words that rhyme with key words and extend that to finishing short verses: "The little mouse / Lived in a _____. Finally, practice adjective-noun rhyming; "a fat cat," "a sad dad," "a funny bunny."

Provide much experience in learning the forms and names of the alphabet. Make an attempt to incorporate the alphabet into as many activities as possible, such as matching, verbalizing similarities and differences, and clapping the alphabet song.

Give children experiences with solving and creating riddles. Start with the "I am thinking of a word" game. Let children guess the word after each clue. Keep adding clues until they guess correctly. Move to the riddle format: "What is round, red, grows on a tree and is good to eat?" (Apple, cherry, and the like.) Accept any logical answer.

Provide many opportunities for children to understand the use of prepositions. Provide experiences both with bodily movement ("Stand *on, beside, in* the circle") and with paper-and-pencil tasks ("Put a line *under* the picture of the dog," "Draw a circle *around* the word *boy*"). An ideal stimulus to use for these activities is the traditional reading or language arts workbook that contains many pictures or words.

Give many experiences with oral cloze exercises. Give children a sentence, delete a word, and have them fill in the space with a word that makes sense. You can begin with simple exercises and increase the complexity as the children's responses become more refined: "I have a pet _____," "I like to _____ chocolate," "_____ I went to school."

Showing pictures to children while you are reading them a story is one of the strategies a teacher can use to develop readiness for beginning reading.

Develop a working sight vocabulary. For young children this might begin with labeling key items around the room, naming and discussing the words often, and gradually removing the labels and having children replace them. You can also create a "word of the week" bulletin board and have children choose special words they want to learn each week. Once they learn a word, children can be encourged to make collages of the word from old newspapers, magazines, and so on.

Give students many opportunities to memorize short, interesting poems, songs, sayings, and the like. Once children memorize

them, write them on a chalkboard or large sheet of paper and plac̲
them where they can be seen easily, and periodically have children
repeat the segments as you point out the words. Eventually, individual
children may point to words as others respond.

Give many experiences in identifying similarities and differences among objects. Begin with the obvious (a red car and a red
truck) and move to the more complex (the letters *L* and *M*). Remember that you are attempting to make children ready to read, so move
closer and closer to graphic clues.

Give students opportunities to clap, tap, or march to the rhythm
of words, sentences, poems or songs. Help them respond to each
syllable within languge units. If children find this difficult, teachers
can hold their hands and clap them as the syllables are repeated.

Ensure children's understanding of necessary concepts such as
"word," "letter," "sound," "sentence," "page," "line," and so on.

Provide opportunities for children to train their ears to hear
separate sounds within words. Many children (even many linguistically developed children) are unable to perceive separate sounds
within words when they enter school (Durrell, 1971; Elkonin, 1973).
Such children need what Elkonin calls "phonematic hearing," which
trains them to hear the separate sounds in words. Activities to develop
this skill include games that segment words and require children to
produce the whole word (/c/ + /a/ + /t/ = *cat*) and activities that
provide children with a complete word and help them to segment
the word into individual sounds (*cat* = /c/ + /a/ + /t/). Frequent
exposure to such activities is vital to the development of auditory
segmentation abilities, a prerequisite to the use of phonics for word
analysis.

Readiness for All Stages of Reading

To develop readiness for reading at stages beyond beginning reading,
the following activities can be used.

Provide many language experiences. Children should be given
many opportunities to develop their oral language abilities. Provide
chances for discussion of stories, pictures, experiences, trips, presentations, and so on. In the discussions vary question types and emphasize divergent questions.

Provide direct or vicarious experiences with places, people,
events, and activities that children will encounter in their reading.
Use discussion before, during, and after the experiences.

Teach children to retell stories. One marked difference between
good and poor readers is that good readers approach a retelling with
a sense of sequence, logic, and order while most poor readers often

have no obvious plan of action. Teachers can discuss story segments, characters, and sequence with children and help them recall stories in sequential order, with attention to detail. If necessary, short stories can be used at first, and the length of stories can be increased gradually.

Provide many opportunities to finish stories with one or several different endings. This can be done by reading most of a story and letting the children brainstorm possible endings.

Give children practice in sequencing by providing them with pictures that tell a story, discussing the plot, mixing up the pictures, and having them rearrange the pictures in correct sequence.

Provide students with a problem, ask them to generate as many possible solutions as they can, and evaluate the result or feasibility of each.

Provide students with illustrations of completed events (a man sitting in the snow, a girl with an irate look on her face, an explosion). Have children brainstorm possible causes or results of each event.

Give students groups of objects that have one or more characteristics in common. Have them group similar objects together. Then start over and regroup according to a different characteristic. It is important to have children explain their decisions. Vary the patterns as much as possible. For example, items can be chosen based on the following characteristics.

> description: same color
> function: used for cooking
> quality: made of cloth
> action: can fly
> class: fruits
> size: tiny
> possession: have wheels
> location: found at beach

Remember, for young children it is necessary that the basic characteristics be observable. With older children, more abstract qualities can be used.

Provide many experiences with role playing. Start with single objects, people, or emotions (act out the role of a hammer, a doctor, someone showing anger), and then move to scenes or episodes.

Provide experiences with picture language and sign language. Discuss environmental signs such as the symbol for poison; red, amber, and green traffic lights; handicapped signs, and so on. Discuss how communication can occur without words. Read comic strips to children and discuss the clues the pictures give about the words. Provide comic strips without words and fill in possible dialogue based on the pictures, then compare with the original dialogue. Have children create their own picture and sign languages. Finally, consider sign language in reading, that is, punctuation: the period, question mark, exclamation point, comma, and quotation marks. Discuss their meanings and demonstrate their use by reading passages with appropriate expression.

Provide constant vocabulary development activities. Make collections of words with multiple meanings, synonyms, antonyms, descriptive words, and so on, and give students much practice in word use.

Provide many opportunities for sentence manipulation.

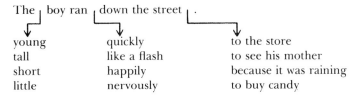

Expansion

The | boy ran | down the street | .

young	quickly	to the store
tall	like a flash	to see his mother
short	happily	because it was raining
little	nervously	to buy candy

Transformation

The boy ran down the street.

girl	walked	road
horse	rushed	corridor
fire fighter	hopped	stairs
dog	dashed	path

Reduction

The *furry gray* cat with *deep* blue eyes climbed *slowly* up the *creaky* stairs to eat its *long-awaited* meal. (The italicized words would be deleted to reduce the sentence.)

Constantly involve children in prediction activities. Have children look at titles and pictures and predict content. As you read to them, stop at appropriate times and ask, "What do you think happens next?"

Provide many opportunities for students to develop imaginative thinking and problem-solving abilities. Ask questions beginning "What would happen if," "What would you do if," "How do you know that," "What in the story makes you feel that," "Explain to me why," and "How many ways can you think of to."

Read a section of a story to children and have them draw or act out what they think will happen next.

Prior to content-area teaching, use pictures, filmstrips, models, experiments, and the like to provide conceptual readiness for material.

Summary

Readiness is one of the most important concepts in the field of teaching. Indeed, understanding and acting on the basic principles of readiness are the keys to effective instruction. Readiness has often been viewed as the responsibility of the preschool, kindergarten, and possibly the first-grade teacher. The definition of readiness given by Ausubel (1959) clearly endorses concern for readiness at all grade levels and in all subject areas. All learning tasks require a certain level of readiness. It is the responsibility of each teacher to analyze each task; identify what students need to know before the task is begun; decide what information students have and what they need; provide the information they need, that is, make the students ready for instruction; and instruct students in the task.

Readiness must be viewed as a mandatory program that parallels all instructional activities. A teacher who accepts this challenge to ensure readiness in students embarks on a very time-consuming and demanding journey. This is particularly true for teachers who are new to readiness strategies. Practice in this philosophy of instruction, however, results in greater facility in its use and, consequently, less time required to prepare for instructon.

The results totally justify the effort. Teaching means imparting knowledge. If the student does not learn, teaching has failed. Teachers' attention to readiness factors helps ensure students' learning, motivation, and retention of material.

References

Ausubel, David P. "Viewpoints from Related Disciplines: Human Growth and Development." *Teachers College Record*, vol. 60 (February 1959).

Bruner, Jerome. *The Process of Education*. Cambridge: Harvard University Press, 1960.

Clay, M. M. *The Early Detection of Reading Difficulties: A Diagnostic Survey*. 2nd ed. New York: Heinemann. 1980.

Durkin, Dolores. *Teaching Them to Read*. Boston: Allyn and Bacon, 1978.

———. *Teaching Them to Read*. 4th ed. Newton, Mass.: Allyn and Bacon, 1983.

Durrell, D. Address given at the International Reading Association Conference, Billings, Mont., Spring 1971.

Elkonin, D. "U.S.S.R." In *Comparative Reading: Cross National Studies of Behavior and Processes in Reading and Writing*, edited by J. Downing. New York: Macmillan, 1973.

Gates, Arthur I. "Reading Readiness." *Teachers College Record*, vol. 37 (May 1936).

———. "The Necessary Mental Age for Beginning Reading." *Elementry School Journal*, vol. 37 (March 1937).

Gesell, Arnold L. *The Mental Growth of the Preschool Child*. New York: Macmillan, 1925.

———. *The Child from Five to Ten*. New York: Harper, 1946.

Hall, G. Stanley. *The Psychology of Adolescence*. New York: Appleton, 1904.

Knafle, J. D. "Auditory Perception of Rhyming in Kindergarten Children." *Journal of Speech and Hearing Research*, no. 17 (1974).

Lyon, Reid. "Auditory-Perceptual Training: The State of the Art." *Journal of Learning Disabilities*, no. 10 (November 1977).

McNinch, G. "Auditory Perceptual Factors and Measured First-Grade Reading Achievemment." *Reading Research Quarterly* (Summer 1970).

Morphett, M. V., and C. Washburne. "When Should Children Begin to Read?" *Elementary School Journal*, vol. 31 (March 1931).

Moskowitz, A. I. "The Two-Year-Old Stage in Acquisition of English Phonology." *Language* (1970).

———. "The Acquisition of Phonology." In *Developing Readers in Today's Elementary School*, edited by M. Aulls. Boston: Allyn and Bacon, 1982.

Oliver, M. "Initial Perception of Word Forms." *Elementary English*, no. 44 (1967). (1967).

Robinson, H. M. "Perceptual Training: Does It Result in Reading Improvement?" In *Some Persistent Questions on Beginning Reading*, edited by R. C. Aukerman. Newark, Del.: International Reading Association, 1972.

Rosner, J. "Phonic Analysis Training and Beginning Reading Skills." In *Developing Readers in Today's Elementary School*, edited by M. Aulls. Boston: Allyn and Bacon, 1982.

Rozin, P., and L. R. Gleitman. "The Structure and Acquisition of Reading 2: The Reading Process and the Acquisition of the Alphabetic Principle." In *Toward a Psychology of Reading*, edited by A. S. Reber and D. L. Scarborough. Hillsdale, N.J.: Erlbaum, 1977.

Samuels, S. J. "Effects of Distinctive Feature Training on Paired Associative Learning." *Journal of Education Psychology* 64, no. 2 (1973).

Weintraub, Samuel. "Research: Oral Language and Reading." *Reading Teacher*, no. 21 (1968).

Wilson, Robert M. *Diagnostic and Remedial Reading for Classroom and Clinic*. 3rd ed. Columbus, Ohio: Merrill, 1977.

6

Word Recognition and Word Analysis Skill Instruction

This chapter applies the principles of psycholinguistic theory to skill instruction. It discusses the various available clues that aid word recognition and recommends ways to expose children to the use of multiple clues in reading. It also analyzes the skill instruction format (teach/practice/reteach/repractice/reteach) used in many developmental basal series and points to an inherent fallacy within this model. For many children who fail in the basal format, the problem rests with the way in which the skill is taught initially. Simply reteaching the skill in the same way as it was taught initially usually leads to miscomprehension of and failure in the skill. This text opts for a conceptual instructional framework and presents a skill instruction model that adheres to psycholinguistic theory. This chapter suggests effective strategies for using workbooks based on the demands and format of each task.

FOCUS QUESTIONS

☐ What are the available clues to word recognition found in written language?

☐ What are the basic limitations of the traditional skill instruction format used in most reading series?

☐ How does the skill instruction model presented in this chapter facilitate understanding of a skill?

☐ What are some strategies that teachers can use to modify workbook instruction and increase children's comprehension and memory of workbook skills?

Skill Instruction

Basic Problems

Instructing children in the skills of reading is undoubtedly one of the most frustrating tasks in the teaching of reading. This frustration is felt by children and teachers alike. Some of the factors that contribute to this frustration are the following.

☐ In many traditional reading series, skills are presented a specific number of times with no adjustments made for children who need less or more exposure to them.

☐ Many traditional reading series use one instructional strategy to introduce, practice, and review skills making no adjustments for children who cannot learn with that strategy.

☐ Many teachers of reading focus on teaching a series or a program rather than on teachng reading. Consequently, little effort is spent on modifying programs or series to meet the needs of children.

☐ Instruction in skills is often not sufficiently thorough, and many children quickly forget information that teachers were certain they learned.

☐ Often skills are introduced and practiced in isolation. Many children can "do" skills but are unable to apply them in real reading situations.

☐ Most reading programs overemphasize some decoding strategies and underemphasize or ignore others, thus minimizing children's options for word recognition and analysis.

☐ Skill instruction often is given in contexts that have little or no meaning for some children; consequently, they learn little and forget quickly.

☐ Instructional energy often is directed toward changing children to fit the program rather than modifying the program to meet the needs of the children.

In the skills component of the reading program, perhaps more than in any other component, success in teaching relies on the willingness and ability of the teacher to be sensitive to the needs of children and to modify instruction to meet their needs.

Principles of Skill Instruction

Certain pedagogical principles are fundamental to the successful teaching of any skill. They help ensure maximum learning, comprehension, retention, and use of skills.

1. Skills should be presented in the most meaningful contexts. Skills often are introduced and demonstrated in single-sentence contexts, however, which are not adequate for providing the concepts necessary for learning. DeCecco and Crawford (1974) support the principle of meaningful contexts: "Not only is meaningful material more rapidly learned than meaningless material, but it is also remembered for longer periods of time."

2. Skills must be taught thoroughly, particularly to children who have difficulty learning or who have slow learning rates. Children often fail to learn skills because too many skills are taught too superficially and too rapidly. Cronbach (1977) states that the key to reducing failure in learning is solid, thorough, meaningful initial learning.

3. Children's attention must be ensured prior to skill instruction. Very simple strategies can be used to get their attention, including the following.

☐ Start instruction only when you have all children's attention. Use statements like "I will know you are ready when your eyes are on me" or "John isn't quite ready. Let's wait until he is."

☐ Group the children around an uncluttered table, making sure that they have nothing in their hands. Keep all pencils, texts, paper, and workbooks and distribute those supplies only when needed.

☐ Seat children who tend to be disruptive apart from each other and close to you.

☐ If you need to write examples on the chalkboard, do so before children are called to the reading group. If you spend time writing on the chalkboard after the children have been grouped for reading, the tone of the session will invariably be set by the most disruptive child.

☐ As much as possible, involve children kinesthetically in learning.

4. Teachers must make an intentional effort to give children experience in applying their newly gained skills immediately in real reading situations. Often children are taught a skill, are directed to practice it in the sparse context of a workbook, and days later are exposed to the skill in actual reading. Unfortunately, by that time they have probably forgotten the skill or have no idea of the relationship between the isolated skill and the reading situation. Not only do they need to practice skills immediately, but the teacher must draw their attention to the application of the new skill.

5. The abilities and knowledge of each group of children must be taken into account during skill instruction. Fast learners need less exposure to skills; slow learners require more exposure.

6.   There are three basic phases of skill development: the cognitive awareness phase, in which children become conceptually aware of the task; the accuracy phase, in which children master the task through practice and significantly minimize error; and the automatic phase, in which the skill has been overlearned to such a degree that its performance no longer requires conscious effort or overt attention. Researchers have often argued for the importance of retaining the automatic phase in learning. In fact, many have shown that fluent reading depends on readers' learning the skills of decoding to an automatic level (Oliver, 1976; Samuels, 1976; Chapman and Hoffman, 1977). It is important that teachers move children through each phase of skill development and provide enough meaningful practice for students to achieve automatic performance of skills in reading.

Clues to Recognizing Words

The clues that can help children recognize words during reading are as follows.

1.   Sight vocabulary clues— *instant recognition*
     a.   Structure words - *hold the lang. together [in, an, the]*
     b.   Context words - *strong in meaning +*
2.   Meaning clues
     a.   Anticipatory clues
     b.   Context clues
     c.   Picture clues
3.   Visual clues
     a.   Configuration clues
     b.   Salient feature clues
4.   Structural clues
     a.   Affixes
     b.   Compounds
5.   Phonic clues
     a.   Initial single consonants
     b.   Final consonants
     c.   Short vowels
     d.   Long vowels and vowel teams
     e.   Consonant combinations
     f.   Blending
6.   Dictionary clues
     a.   Pronunciation clues
     b.   Meaning clues

Sight Vocabulary

Sight vocabulary consists of the words a student recognizes instantly by sight. There are two basic types of sight vocabulary: structure words and content words.

Structure Words Structure words are those small words or high-frequency words that hold the language together: *in, an, the, through, them,* and *although,* for example. They are usually low in imagery. Structure words are the most difficult words for children to learn because they lack concrete meaning.

Content Words Content words are strong in meaning and usually high in imagery: *table, mother, car, run, elephant, book,* and so on. These words are significantly easier to learn than structure words.

One unfortunate instructional practice is to overemphasize structure words as early as kindergarten and to underemphasize content words, thus forcing children to process the most difficult words first.

It is very important that teachers help children develop a strong sight vocabulary. Basal series provide many opportunities for learning sight words, although they often select too many words, present too many difficult words at once, and give children insufficient practice.

Principles of Instruction Six principles should guide sight-word instruction.

1. Sight-word instruction should not violate children's learning rates. Children with average-to-slow learning rates should not be expected to learn more than five to seven new vocabulary items in each instructional period. If the maximum is approached or exceeded, there must be a balance between words that are easy to learn and those that are difficult to learn. Many factors make words difficult or easy to learn. Generally, structure words are more difficult to learn than content words. Generally, low-imagery words are more difficult to learn than those that have a strong image. Generally, words whose sounds are inconsistent with their letters (*lean, the, though, are, this*) are more difficult to learn than words whose sounds are consistent with their letters (*hat, stop, plan, and, pin*). Generally, words that have a low emotional content (*moth, wire, shown, made*) are more difficult to learn than those that have a high emotional content (*mother, mad, love, friend*). These factors can operate together to affect the difficulty or ease of learning words.

Sight-word instruction should be compatible with children's learning rates.

2.   There should be an inverse relationship between the thoroughness of sight-word instruction and the performance and learning rate of the children. The slower the learning rate, the more thorough the instruction must be. Manning (1980) presents a "Three by Three by I" design for sight-word instruction that is a most thorough and intensive strategy. Manning's design consists of three methods of introducing each word and three levels of skill development, balanced by the individual differences within each group of children. Following is a description of this procedure.

SET 1 — THREE METHODS OF INTRODUCING WORDS

Method 1: External Learning

The sight words to be learned are placed on individual flash cards: *stand*, *pony*, *enough*, *bring*, and *umbrella*, for example. The first method of presentation is to show each word and say the word for children: "This word is *stand*." "This word is *pony*." The teacher may wish to block certain parts of the word with a hand to direct children's attention to other parts, for example showing only *st* and then *and*.

Method 2: Internal Learning

This method is designed to elicit an internal response in all children. The teacher shows each word, waits briefly, and then asks: "Did you say 'stand'? You were right. The word is *stand*. Did you say 'pony'? Good. This word is *pony*." It must be remembered that some groups of children may need three to five presentations of method 1 before they are ready for method 2.

Method 3: Visual Memory and Review

The third method is simply a review and a building of visual memory abilities. Each word is shown. After approximately one second, the flash card is removed and children are asked to repeat the word. For example, the teacher shows the word *enough*. After one second, the teacher removes the flash card and asks, "What was that word?" When a child responds correctly, the teacher shows the word again and possibly spells it. The teacher might say, "Right; *e-n-o-u-g-h* spells *enough*."

SET 2 — THREE LEVELS OF SKILL DEVELOPMENT

Skill 1: Word Meaning

The teacher may show the word *pony* and ask, "Is this word animal?" thus drawing attention to the meaning of the word. If children say yes, the teacher may say, "What is this word? Right. The word is *pony* and a pony is an animal."

Skill 2: Word Analysis

The teacher draws attention to the phonic elements within a word. For example, the word *stand* is shown. The teacher may ask, "Does this word begin like *stop*?" or "Does this word end like *bend*?" or "Does this word rhyme with *hand*?" As children answer, the phonic elements can be more closely analyzed. The teacher may ask, "What letters represent the sound you hear at the beginning of the word *stand*?" or "Can you think of another word that begins like *stand*?" or "If we take away the *st* from *stand*, what little word do we have left?" Thus the teacher is forcing children to attend to and process phonic information.

Skill 3: Word Recognition

Some words, primarily structure words, defy both meaning and phonic explanation. For such words, teachers can develop automatic recognition by simply showing the words and asking for a very quick response. For example, the word *enough* is shown for one second. The teacher may ask, "What is this word?" Once a correct response is given, the teacher may have children spell the word quickly and may use it in a sentence.

SET 3 — *I* — INDIVIDUAL DIFFERENCES

The *I* in the design refers to the individual differences that exist within the group. Even though an effort is made to group children homogeneously, teachers must remember that there is always a range of abilities within any group and should instruct with this in mind. Consider a group with six children, where child 1 is the weakest and child 6 is the strongest. To accommodate individual differences, a teacher who wanted all children to respond to newly learned words could ask children 1 and 2 to respond, then children 1 and 3, then children 1 and 4, and so on, rather than asking each child to respond once. In this way the weakest child would receive the most practice. Instead of simply putting the cards away at the end of the lesson, the teacher could call on individual children to hand in the cards while reading the words, thus giving the weakest children additional practice.

3.   Sight words instructed in isolation should be placed back in a whole language context. It is very important that children learn sight words; but words seldom occur in isolation. Children need to learn the word *enough*, for example, but if a sentence in the reading selection reads "They had enough to eat," children also need to see the phrase "enough to eat" or the sentence "They had enough to eat" during some level of sight word instruction, before or after

reading. This helps them develop contextual expectations of words and gives them incidental exposure to other words.

It is often helpful, particularly for weak readers, to see and read words, phrases, and sentences from the text. Children often have difficulty moving from the large print used on flash cards to the small print used in texts. Providing exposure to text print aids transfer and gives students additional practice.

4. Sight vocabulary must be learned to an automatic level. Children can be timed on lists of sight vocabulary and encouraged to pratice until they can better their previous times.

5. Sight vocabulary instruction must focus on the most useful and vital words. It is unrealistic that all groups of children can be taught all the sight vocabulary they need prior to each reading selection. This may be feasible for groups of high achievers who know most of the necessary vocabulary and who can learn the rest quickly. For groups of average or below-average readers, however, the teacher must make an effort to choose from among several words only those that warrant direct instruction, using the following guidelines.

□ Teach words most essential to the meaning of the selection. If the selection is about a glacier, the word *glacier* is essential.
□ Teach words that occur most frequently in print.
□ Teach words that have highly generalizable segments. The word *slide* is very useful not only because it is often used but also because it includes the *sl* blend, which occurs frequently in print, and the final *e* construction, which is a very useful structure to learn.
□ Do not teach words that are unique to the selection and that children rarely meet in print. Such words can be presented to children prior to reading the selection or can be explained during reading. Instructional time is better spent on more useful items.
□ Do not teach person and place names. These can be presented during the content and conceptual preparation prior to reading.

6. Intensive practice must be provided in sight vocabulary that is frequently confused or quickly forgotten. Manning (1980) presents an intensive structure-word practice that is very effective in helping children to learn structure words automatically and to eliminate confusion among similar word forms. The procedure is as follows.

a. Choose between four and six key structure words that children need to practice (say *even*, *enough*, *through*, and *then*).
b. For each key word, choose distractors, three or four words

that children often confuse with the key word or that are structurally similar (*even/ever/every/envy*; *then/thin/than/when*).

c.   Divide a sheet of paper into four parts. Label the sections A, B, C, and D.

d.   In each section, place the key words and their distractors. Vary the positions of the words horizontally and vertically. Make copies of this sheet for the students.

A	B
1. even, every, ever, envy 2. ever, enough, though, away 3. when, than, thin, then 4. though, thing, through, throw	1. through, though, throw, thing 2. ever, even, envy, every 3. away, though, enough, ever 4. then, when, than, thin
C	D
1. then, than, when, thin 2. though, through, thing, throw 3. envy, every, even, ever 4. though, away, ever, enough	1. enough, away, ever, though 2. ever, every, envy, even 3. when, then, thin, than 4. though, throw, through, thing

e.   Place each key word on a flash card. Use the flash cards to present the words to the group. Point out distinctive features of each word, use each in a sentence, and spell each word.

f.   Fold the papers so that only block A can be seen. Give each child paper. Begin with block A. Show the flash card with the first word, *even*. Say to the children, "Look in line 1. Find the word *even*. Put a box around the word *even*. Show the word *enough*. Say, "Look in line 2. Find the word *enough*." Underline the word *enough*. Continue through all the words in block A.

g.   Refold the papers to expose block B. Give fewer oral directions and move through the words at a faster pace. Show the card that says *through*. Say, "Line 1. Circle the word *through*. Line 2. Cross out the word *even*. Line 3. Put a 3 beside the word *enough*." Continue in this way through all the words in block B.

h.   Expose block C. Now give still fewer clues and go faster. This time provide the directions before the children begin the task. You might say, "I am going to show you a word quickly and tell you what to do with the word. Listen carefully and do just what I say. We are going to go a little faster." Show the first word for approximately one second and then remove the flash card. Say, "Circle." Show the second word, remove the card, and say, "Underline." Continue in this way through all the words in block C.

i. Expose block D. Now you might say each word and have the children mark it. You might say, "In line 1, circle *even*. Line 2, underline *enough*." You might also ask children to circle in each line the key word they have been working with.

This is an excellent strategy to provide children with intensive practice and to help them to discriminate quickly among words that are easily confused. The strategy can be modified to the instruction of any type or class of word. It need not be limited to structure words. Teachers can also use the structure-word practice to force children to focus on particlar parts of words. To draw attention to the beginning of words, a teacher might use distractors that vary the initial letter(s) only (*pay/play*; *day/say/may*). To draw attention to the middle of words, a teacher can use distractors that vary the middle letter(s) only (*ride/rude/rode*). To draw attention to the end of words, a teacher can use distractors that vary the final letter(s) only (*them/then/this/these/there*).

Meaning Clues

Meaning clues are clues within the semantic component of language that help readers anticipate and expect words they will meet in reading. These clues are vital to efficient reading. Failure to use meaning clues in reading invariably leads to an overdependence on sight-word and phonic clues; the result is slow, fragmented, nonfluent word calling and faulty comprehension. Use of meaning clues should be taught and emphasized in all phases of reading instruction beginning with the readiness phase.

Three important types of meaning clues are anticipatory clues, context clues, and picture clues. They help children use what they know about their own language to assist them in reading.

Anticipatory Clues Every topic, heading, or title should generate within children a set of words, ideas, or experiences that are closely related to the concept presented in the selection. This process of expecting certain words or ideas given a specific topic is called *anticipation*. Anticipatory clues are topics, headings, titles, events, and even pictures that cause readers to expect certain meaning from print. If children are about to read a story entitled "A Trip to the Zoo," they should anticipate words like *animals, cage, lion, tiger, monkey, zookeeper*.

This strategy of anticipation can be clearly observed in the reactions good readers have to print. As a teacher instructs good readers, he or she may direct their attention to the title and the pictures. Children's hands will begin to go up and invariably they will want to share their experiences related to the topic. This demonstrates that the title and pictures have triggered their anticipation and prediction, and they have summoned prior experiences relevant to the anticipated information. This prior information is extremely important to comprehension, as we have seen. Poor readers, on the other hand, most often react quite differently. Given the title and pictures of a selection, they have little reaction. They have not learned to anticipate meaning or to predict content. The information does not trigger their prior knowledge to the extent that it will be useful to them as they read. This lack of anticipation is detrimental to comprehension.

Recently, I was demonstrating the importance of anticipatory clues to a teacher in a classroom. I asked for two groups of children, one group of good readers and one group of poor readers. I wanted readers at approximately the same grade level, so I chose a high third-grade reading group and a low fifth-grade reading group. The story I chose to use was "Annie and the Old One" from the *Passport* text of the *Houghton Mifflin Reading Series*. I instructed the good readers first. I said to this group, "Boys and girls, today we are going to read a beautiful story. The title of the story is 'Annie and the Old One.' Before we go any further, however, I want you to look at the title, the pictures, and the major headings, and then we are going to discuss what the story might be about." The children performed this task quickly, and immediately the hands went up. These were their comments, unedited.

Child 1: I think the story is going to be about Navajo Indians because last year when my parents took me to New Mexico I got a Navajo blanket and it is the same pattern of the blanket in the picture.

Child 2: I think it will be about a girl named Annie and maybe her grandmother, who is the old one. Indians don't treat their old people like we do. Even if you are an adult, you have to respect older people. They would not talk back to them or put them in old people's homes or anything like that.

Child 3: These Indians are living in hogans so it must be spring or summer or something. I think they live in different homes during the winter.

Child 4: I recently watched a documentary on the Indian culture. There are many Indian tribes who do not have their languages written down and people called transformational linguists are spending time with them and listening to them and making a writing system for them.

Child 5: I think the story is going to be mainly sad. The expressions are so sad. Maybe the old one is dying or something or maybe it's even the girl.

If I hadn't stopped this discussion, it would have continued. The information given by the children may not be entirely accurate, but they made excellent use of anticipation and prediction, and their prior knowledge was appropriately triggered. These children were ready for instruction, so I continued the lesson.

I gave the identical instructions to the poor readers. They performed the task a bit slower and looked up at me, pleasantly waiting for me to continue. I said to them, "Do the title, pictures, or headings remind you of anything or make you want to ask any questions?" They repeated the task slowly and looked up at me once more. No comment. I asked, "Do you have any questions you want to ask?" Still no response. Finally, one hand went up. The question was, "What is an old one?" Obviously, these children were not ready for reading. They had not anticipated meaning, predicted content, or triggered their prior knowledge. We closed the book, discussed Indians and the children's experiences with the Indian culture. We looked at pictures of reservations, Indians, and Indian ceremonies, and slowly the concepts and anticipation started to build. These children were not often exposed to the use of anticipation in reading, and their comprehension — or lack of it — demonstrated this failure to use anticipation.

Anticipatory clues are available throughout reading selections. If during a story it is stated that the children were visiting the zoo right before feeding time, that fact should lead children to anticipate or predict certain events: The animals are hungry. The animals are eager to eat. Someone will feed the animals. Each group of animals will require a different type of food.

Teachers should not assume that children will use anticipatory clues on their own. Generally, good readers are quite adept at using anticipatory clues, but many average and below-average readers use them insufficiently and inadequately. Use of these clues must be taught directly. Prior to teaching a selection, teachers should read the title, the major headings, and words in boldface type to the children and ask them to identify what they expect to find in the selection. Teachers can write down their predictions and check them as they read the selection. They can also look at pictures and use them to expand their expectation further. In addition, as they read, children should constantly be asked questions like "What do you think will happen next?" or "What could possibly happen next?"

Context Clues   Context clues are clues found in surrounding words that allow a reader or speaker to predict the pronunciation or meaning of an unfamiliar or unknown word. Though the efficient use of context is necessary for fluent reading, certain factors limit the potential information gained from context clues. Two of the most important factors are that context clues are useful only if the reader or speaker has prior experience with and knowledge of the topic and that context reveals only one of a word's meanings. Before children are expected to use context clues efficiently, they must be conceptually and experientially familiar with the topic.

Very early in their experiences with language, both oral and written, children need to be taught that they can decipher an unknown word more easily if they use its context. By using context, they can greatly limit the number of alternative word choices that can fit into a slot in a word or sentence.

Even before children are taught to read, they should become familiar with context. They can be exposed to exercises that teach them the value of context. Teachers can read sentences containing deleted words and can assist children in using the context to supply possible words to complete the sentences appropriately.

> The little boy ran through the _____.
> The little _____ ran through the room.
> The little boy _____ through the room.
> The little boy ran _____ the room.

Note that the deleted words can occupy different positions in the sentence. This provides practice in predicting word classes. As children fill in the deleted words, teachers should analyze their responses with them. The most important question that constantly needs to be asked and answered is "Does it make sense?"

Once children begin to learn letter-sound relationships and sight vocabulary, the same exercises can be used with print. The task can be varied in many ways, among them the following.

1. Only context clues are used. No other information is provided about the deleted word.

    The bird flew into the _____.

2. The beginning letter of the deleted word is provided.

    The boy hit the b _____ over the tree.

3. The length of the deleted word is indicated.

    In the summer the weather is _ _ _ _ .

4. The first and last letters of the deleted word are provided.

    It is time to eat s __ __ __ __ r.

5. Children are provided with a number of words from which to choose an appropriate word. (The word choices must be in the child's meaning vocabulary.)

    It was so hot that I turned on the _____. (stove, fan, bed, light)

6. The consonants in the deleted word are provided.

    I wanted to jump over the f __ nc __ .

7. The initial consonant combination is provided.

    I have thr_____ sisters.

It is most important that such exercises be done with the children so that their responses, both correct and incorrect, can be analyzed, evaluated, and discussed.

Use of context clues should also be practiced during reading. As children meet an unknown or forgotten word, they should be encouraged to skip over the word, finish the sentence, and use the context and initial letter to guess at the word. When a child substitutes a word that makes no sense in a sentence ("Joan *want* to school"), the teacher should repeat the entire sentence and ask, "Does that makes sense?" The child should then be assisted to use the sentence context along with the letter sounds to determine the correct word. For example, the teacher may say, "Listen to what you just read. 'Joan want to school.' Does that make sense?" When the child says no, the teacher should say, "That's right; it does not make sense. Look at the sentence. It says, 'Joan _____ to school.' The word you need begins with *w*. It is spelled *w-e-n-t*. Joan _____ to school. What could that word be?" The child should respond "went." "Right. Joan *went* to school. Does that make sense?" The child should respond yes.

If the child demonstrates an inability to judge semantic or grammatical acceptability, the teacher must provide much oral experience in language context.

Picture Clues Pictures can be very useful in reading. They can describe objects, clarify concepts, and generate predictions about the text. Pictures can also be helpful in expanding concepts by presenting objects in more detail. Pictures provide the vicarious experience necessary for concept building when direct experience is not an option. Although pictures provide useful clues, children should not be allowed to overrely on them and minimize the more important clues of word recognition, context, and phonic analysis.

Visual Clues

Reading is partially a visual act, and there are important clues to word recognition embedded in the graphic system of print. Two of the most important visual clues available to readers are configuration clues and salient-feature clues.

Configuration Clues   Configuration clues are provided by the general shape of words. Mature readers often use word shape to validate their expectations of words and to eliminate alternative choices. It is well known, for example, that readers can recognize whole words from distances too far to identify any individual letters. Say that you are traveling on a highway and know that you need to exit at a particular street, Parker Lake Ave. Before you are close enough to recognize any individual letters, you can recognize the configuration ⌐Parker⌐ ⌐Lake⌐ ⌐Ave.⌐ and are able to distinguish it from other signs such as ⌐Main⌐ ⌐Street⌐ or ⌐Academy⌐ ⌐Blvd.⌐

Although configuration is a clue that is available to readers, it may not be a particularly helpful one in initial reading instruction because so many words have the same general shape: ⌐cap,⌐ ⌐map,⌐ ⌐rag,⌐ ⌐cup.⌐ Children should be given practice in visual awareness to lead them to appropriate use of visual clues. Exercises like the following will help children develop necessary attention to word shape.

1. Find the word that is the same as the key word.

    cap/   rat   cat   pan   cap

2. Which word will fit in each shape?

	/ wall	still	were	ring
	/ seen	cart	stop	call
	/ car	mate	girl	mug

Salient-Feature Clues   A more useful strategy to help children attend to visual features is the intentional discussion of the salient features of words and the analysis of the similarities and differences among words. In teaching words to children, teachers should point out their visual features. If the words *stand* and *stare* are being introduced, the teacher can help children recognize the following facts about the words.

☐   The words are somewhat similar.
☐   They begin the same: *st.*

☐   They have different endings: *and* and *are*.

☐   They have different shapes: stand and stare.

☐   The word *stand* has two tall letters, s*t*and, while s*t*are has only one.

☐   The word *stand* has the letters *s-t-a-n-d*, while *stare* has the letters *s-t-a-r-e*.

☐   The word *stand* contains the little word *and* within it.

In this way, children will become more aware of the visual features of words and will begin to develop their own strategies of visual analysis.

Structural Clues

There are two basic strategies used by readers to break down an unknown word to better analyze and decode·it: phonic analysis, which involves analyzing the individual sounds (phonemes) within the word, and structural analysis, which involves analyzing the meaning-bearing units (morphemes) in a word. Graphic language contains many structural clues that, if used appropriately, are of invaluable assistance in both decoding and comprehension. Two major structural clues are affixes and compounds.

Affixes   Affixes consist of one or more letters or sounds that are attached to the beginnings (prefixes) or the ends (suffixes) of words and that serve to give added meaning to words. Affixes cannot stand by themselves. They must be attached to base words to have meaning. Affixes, therefore, can provide readers with at least two important clues: decoding clues and meaning clues.

It is very important that children learn to recognize and understand common prefixes and suffixes. Of course, children also must thoroughly understand the base words before using affixes with them.

The following list contains common affixes.

SUFFIXES

Suffix	Meaning	Examples
-ess	female	princess giantess
-eer	a calling or profession	auctioneer buccaneer
-ful	full of	helpful playful

-ing	related to	banking fishing
-ist	practicer, doer	pianist violinist
-less	without, lacking	careless painless
-ling	young, small	duckling sapling
-ly	in a certain way	softly quietly
-ly	having characteristics of	queenly neighborly
-ward	in a specific direction	westward backward
-y	full of, like	rosy glassy

PREFIXES

Prefix	*Meaning*	*Examples*
auto-	self-propelling, self	automobile autobiography
bi-	two	bicycle bilingual bicentennial
dis-	opposite	disagree disable
ex-	out	exhale exhaust
hyper-	over, excessive	hypersensitive hyperactive
mis-	wrong	misplace misfit
over-	too much	overactive overheated
re-	again	redo recall
sub-	under	submerge submarine
tele-	afar, of or by	television telescope

tri-	three	triangle
		tricycle
un-	not	unfair
		unnecessary
under-	below	underpaid
		underground

It is not enough to give children a list of affixes. They must be thoroughly taught and frequently practiced. Teachers must focus on one or two per week, instruct children in their use, taking care to introduce them in highly meaningful contexts, and provide practice with them throughout the week. It is imperative that base words be totally familiar to children before they add affixes. If the word *unnecessary* is being used, for example, the base *necessary* must be familiar to children.

To make use of affixes, children also must be able to recognize and identify a root word within a longer word. Early in their reading experiences children should be presented orally with familiar, meaningful words and asked to detect smaller words (base words) within the words. Some common examples are *unhappy*, *helpful*, *kingdom*, *jewelry*, *giantess*, *hopeful*, *violinist*, *useful*, *poisonous*, and *disagree*. Once children are able to perform the strategy orally, they can be introduced to the visual forms and they can receive instruction in affixes.

Other meaningful word parts are inflectional endings, which include -*s* (*beds*), -*es* (*horses*), -*ed* (*wanted*), -*ing* (*talking*), -*er* (*bigger*), and -*est* (*slowest*). Inflectional endings differ from suffixes in that the addition of a suffix usually results in a change in the word's class or part of speech while the addition of an inflection does not change the word's part of speech.

One very valuable strategy that helps children develop their skills in using affixes is word expansion. Start with a common root word and have children build as many words as they can from the root, as shown in Figure 6–1. For each new word, children should be encouraged to construct sentences.

Another strategy involves starting with a complex word and having children identify as many smaller words as they can. A teacher can begin with a word like *unfaithfulness* and help children identify *unfaithful*, *faithfulness*, *faith*, and *faithful*.

Compound Words Compound words are single word units formed from the combination of two morphemes that can each stand independently as root words: *mailbox*, *steamboat*. The recognition of compound words requires that children use both visual analysis skills to segment the compound visually into the two words (*saw/dust* rather

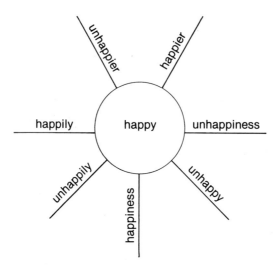

FIGURE 6–1
Adding affixes to a root word

than *sawd/ust*) and meaning skills to realize that the meaning of the compound word is similar to the combination of its parts (*moonlight* = the moon's light, *towtruck* = a truck that tows). Children should be given both oral and graphic practice in recognizing the base words within compounds and in interpreting the meaning of compounds.

Johnson and Pearson (1978) identify six specific types of compounds:

1. Root 2 is *of* root 1.

    nightfall (fall of night)
    riverbank (bank of the river)

2. Root 2 is *from* root 1.

    sawdust (dust from a saw)
    moonlight (light from the moon)

3. Root 2 is *for* root 1.

    bathroom (room for a bath)
    wallpaper (paper for a wall)

4. Root 2 is *like* root 1.

    cottontail (tail like cotton)
    frogman (man like a frog)

5. Root 2 *is* root 1.

    bluebird (bird is blue)
    pipeline (the line is a pipe)

6. Root 2 *does* root 1.

    towtruck (a truck does towing)
    scrubwoman (a woman does scrubbing)

Johnson and Pearson do not suggest that the structures of these six groups of compounds be overemphasized or formally taught. Instead, they recommend that teachers engage in the following activities.

☐   Ask children questions like "What would you call a woman who scrubs or a truck that tows?" They suggest that one category be practiced at a time.

☐   Reverse the process and ask questions like "If a scrubwoman is a woman who scrubs, how would you define a towtruck or a racecar?"

☐   Have children use compounds in sentences, select compounds to fit cloze passages, and the like.

Phonic Clues

Phonic clues are available in the graphic symbol system of textual material. Readers are able to use phonic clues when they learn symbol-sound relationships either through direct instruction or through abstracting symbol-sound relationships from their experiences with print. Like the other clues to word recognition, phonic clues provide very important and valuable information in decoding words.

Phonic instruction centers around teaching children rules governing letter-sound relationships. Major emphasis is placed on the following rules.

1. Initial single consonants and their sounds

    /h/ as in *hop*
    /b/ as in *bed*

2. Short vowel sounds

    /ă/ as in *hat*
    /ŭ/ as in *rub*

3. Final single consonants and their sounds

    /t/ as in *cat*
    /p/ as in *lip*

4. Long vowel sounds

/ī/ as in *pine*
/ō/ as in *rope*

5. Consonant combinations and their sounds
   a. *Blends*: Blends are two or three letters that represent two or three consonant sounds. Each letter in the blend represents a distinguishable consonant sound.

      /st/ as in *stop*
      /str/ as in *strong*
      /nd/ as in *bend*

   b. *Digraphs*: Digraphs are formed by combining two or three letters to represent a single consonant sound. This sound is different from the sound typically identified with any of the individual letters in the digraph.

      /ch/ as in *chain*
      /sh/ as in *shop*
      /ng/ as in *ring*

6. Vowel combinations and their sounds
   a. *Digraphs:* Digraphs are two letters that represent one vowel phoneme or sound.

      mistake — /ē/ as in *bead* — *Correction* 'ĕ
      /ō/ as in *toad*

   b. *Diphthongs:* Diphthongs are two vowels blended together to form a unique sound not associated with either of the two vowels.

      /oi/ as in *oil*
      /oy/ as in *toy*
      /au/ as in *taught*

   c. *Vowel clusters:* Vowel clusters are vowel combinations that cannot be consistently categorized as either digraphs or diphthongs.

      /ei/ as in *weight*
      /ei/ as in *either*
      /ou/ as in *tough*
      /ou/ as in *cough*

   d. Final *e* constructions: In many cases, when the letter *e* is at the end of a word, the first vowel sound in the word is the long vowel sound and the final *e* does not represent a sound.

      fīle, hōme, pāle

The purpose of phonic instruction is to teach children the rules that govern letter-sound relationships. In synthetic phonic instruction, the smallest units—letters and their sounds— are taught first.

7. *R*-controlled vowels and their sounds
   When a vowel is followed by the letter *r*, it results in a unique sound.

   /ar/ as in *car* or *mare*
   /or/ as in *for* or *worn*

Instructional Strategies   The purpose of phonic instruction is to provide readers with tools to analyze unknown words based on their letter-sound relationships. Phonic information is usually presented to children via two major strategies: synthetic instruction and analytic instruction.

Synthetic phonic instruction focuses on breaking the reading task down into individual, isolated skill segments, teaching the smallest units first, and continuously building until larger units are taught.

Children are first taught the names of the letters and then the sound or sounds each letter represents. Once these two skills have been learned to an automatic level, blending is taught. For example, children might be taught the letter names *m*, *a*, and *t*. Next they would be taught the sound each letter represents: *m* = /m/, *a* = /ă/, *t* = /t/. Finally they would be taught to blend the letters together to form a word: /m/ + /a/ + /t/ = *mat*. The word *mat* would then be used in a sentence. In this strategy, children are often explicitly taught the rules that govern various letter-sound relationships.

Analytic phonics, on the other hand, teaches children the larger units first and then helps them induce the relationships that exist among letters and their sounds. For example, if the goal is to teach children that the letter *m* represents the sound /m/, first sight words such as *man*, *mother*, and *mat* would be taught, and then used in sentences. Next the words would be taken out of sentence context, and children would be directed to listen to and look at the three words and to identify their similarities and abstract other general rules about the words:

> All the words begin with the same sound, /m/.
> All the words begin with the same letter, *m*.
> The sound /m/ is represented by the letter *m*.
> Words that begin with the sound /m/ also begin with the letter *m*.

Children would then be encouraged to generate other words that begin with *m*, and finally the rule *m* = /m/ would be presented.

There are several similarities between the analytic and synthetic approaches: Both present the rules of phonics. Both present the isolated sounds of letters and letter combinations. Both use the phonic segments in whole words. The major difference is timing. Synthetic phonic instruction begins with language parts and moves to the whole, and analytic phonic instruction begins with the language whole and moves to the parts. Analytic phonic instruction is the preferred strategy of most developmental basal series.

Pros and Cons   Much controversy surrounds the issue of phonic instruction. During the last decade, there has been a growing trend to divide the field of reading instruction into two seemingly dichotomous camps: pro–phonic instruction and anti–phonic instruction. Those in the pro-phonic camp support their position with the following arguments.

1. The meaning of print is locked in a letter and letter-combination code. To unlock meaning, children must learn to break

the code by learning symbol-sound relationships to an automatic level. In fact, the relationship between decoding and meaning has often been identified by research. Automatic decoding does facilitate comprehension (LaBerge and Samuels, 1976; Perfetti and Lesgold, 1977).

2. Analysis of English spelling patterns identifies phonic rules that account for the many ways letters and letter combinations can be pronounced. For several years researchers have succeeded in identifying the significant letters and letter combinations in English and in formulating rules that govern the relationships between letters and letter combinations and their sounds (Berdiansky, Cronnell, and Koehler, 1969; Venezky, 1970). Instruction in the rules that govern spelling patterns is expected to result in the ability to decode unknown words.

3. Since all rules have exceptions, children also need to be taught the exceptions to phonic rules.

4. Once children learn phonic rules and their exceptions, they are able to apply those rules to the decoding of unknown words and to move quickly toward independence in reading.

5. Early emphasis on phonic instruction results in early acquisition of and success in reading. There is a fair amount of research evidence to support this claim. In the classic book *Learning to Read: The Great Debate,* Chall (1967) reviewed more than sixty experimental studies tht compared many programs that emphasized meaning and code. Her conclusion was that "research from 1912 to 1965 indicates that a code emphasis method — i.e., one that views beginning reading as essentially different from mature reading and emphasizes learning of the printed code for the spoken language — produces better results, at least up to the point where sufficient evidence seems to be available, by the end of third grade" (p. 307). Chall's evidence, however, did not support any one code method over another. She also recommended code emphasis programs as beginning reading methods and stressed the importance of helping children read for meaning in any reading experience.

Those in the anti-phonic camp support their position with the following arguments.

1. A rule-based approach to English spelling is counterproductive because there are too many rules to learn. Researchers have repeatedly attempted to identify a specific number of rules for English spelling. Berdiansky, Cronnell, and Koehler (1969) analyzed more than 6,000 one- and two-syllable words in the meaning vocabularies of six-to-nine-year-old children.

The words were taken from commonly used reading books. Some of the research results were as follows:

a. There are 69 graphemic units in the 6,000 words. A graphemic unit is a group of two or more letters whose sound cannot be accounted for by single-letter rules: *ch, th, ea, oi, bb, ll,* and so on.

b. The 69 graphemic units were related to 38 different sounds.

c. There were 166 rules needed to account for the letter-sound relationships.

d. There were 45 exceptions to the rules.

e. There were 60 rules related to the pronunciation of 21 consonants and 106 rules related to the pronunciation of 7 vowels (*a, e, i, o, u, y, w*).

The findings relate to only 6,000 words and not to the many hundreds of other words children meet in the first three years of reading.

2. Few phonic rules are sufficiently consistent to warrant direct instruction. Indeed, research studies show that most phonic rules are so inconsistent and have so many exceptions that teaching them may be unjustifiable (Emans, 1967; Bailey, 1967; Burmeister, 1968; Moskowitz, 1973; Vaughn-Cook, 1977). May and Eliot (1978) suggest that only the following seven rules provide enough consistency to be taught directly.

a. When the letter *g* comes at the end of a word or comes immediately before the letter *a, o,* or *u,* it usually represents the hard sound, as in *nag, gave, go,* and *gun.* Otherwise, it usually has the soft sound. (Exceptions: *get, girl, begin, give.*)

b. When the letter *c* comes immediately before the letter *a, o,* or *u,* it usually represents the hard sound, as in *cap, code,* and *cut.* Otherwise, it usually represents the soft sound, as in *cell, city,* and *ceiling.*

c. When a single vowel is followed by a consonant or consonant combination in either a word or a syllable, the vowel represents the short sound, as in *if, on, candy,* and *dinner.*

d. When a vowel digraph is included in a word or a syllable, the first letter in the digraph usually represents the long sound and the second letter is usually silent. This rule is very consistent in the digraphs *ee,* as in *see, oa* as in *boat,* and *ay* as in *may.* It is moderately consistent in the digraphs *ea* as in *each* and *ai* as in *paid.* It is only minimally consistent in the digraphs *ei* as in *rein, ie* as in *piece,* and *oo* as in *boot* (Clymer, 1963).

e. In one-syllable words containing two vowels, one of which is a final *e*, the first vowel usually represents the long sound and the *e* is silent, as in *file*, *made*, and *cute*.

f. When the letter *r* immediately follows a vowel, it modifies the sound of the vowel resulting in a second sound that can not be classified as either long or short, as in *bar*, *her*, and *girl*.

g. When a word or syllable contains only one vowel that comes at the end of the word or syllable, the vowel usually represents the long sound, as in *go*, *me*, *hotel*, and *motor*.

3. Phonic rules alone will not help the reader decode most high-frequency words met in reading because so many of these words are exceptions to the rules.

4. Phonic rules do not need to be taught directly to children. Though phonic *knowledge* is imperative in reading, phonic rule *instruction* is not. This is supported by the following facts.

a. Many children who have learned to read at home have received no formal instruction. They simply internalized the rules through direct experiences with print.

b. Many mature readers can apply the rules in reading even though they have never been taught the rules directly and cannot adequately verbalize them.

c. Many mature readers who were once taught to verbalize the rules have forgotten those rules but retain the application of them in practical reading situations.

d. Verbalization of phonic rules in no way guarantees the ability to apply those rules in reading.

5. Emphasis on phonic instruction often results in overdependence on phonics. This overdependence leads to underutilization of other language clues and results in slow, laborious, nonfluent reading and inefficient comprehension.

6. Phonic instruction is often presented in isolation or in language contexts that contain sparse meaning, such as phrases or sentences. This often results in children's memorizing the rules of phonics but failing to understand, remember, and use them.

Certainly, both points of view present valid and justifiable arguments. The polarity, however, seems unnecessary. The real issue is not whether to give phonic instruction but *what* phonic instruction should be given *when*, *how*, and *to which* children. The remainder of this section considers these questions: *What* phonics should be taught? *When* should phonics be depended on? *How* should phonics be taught? *Which* children need *what kind of* phonic instruction?

How Words Convey Meaning   Phonics is one strategy readers can use to arrive at the appropriate pronunciation of an unknown word. To use this strategy most efficiently, readers must learn that they do not have to depend equally on all the phonic clues within a word to provide the information necessary to decode the word. In fact, only a few such clues are essential. To demonstrate the parts of words that are most important and that carry the most information in reading, we will consider segments of the story "When Christmas Comes" by Doris Whitman. The intact parts of the story are printed at the end of this exercise, on pages 169–70. Here we reproduce the entire first two paragraphs and then in subsequent paragraphs we delete certain parts of almost every word. As you read through each paragraph, decide which parts of words provide you with the most essential information.

> For three days it snowed without stopping. The Mallorys couldn't remember when it had snowed so much. All the schools were closed. Snow plows had broken down because the snow was so heavy. It was a real snowstorm.
>
> Sara and Tim Mallory talked excitedly as the flakes drifted down. But their brother Jake didn't seem to care. He didn't look up when Tim ran into his bedroom.

(Ends Deleted)

"Di__ yo__ he___ th__ ne____?" Ti__ as_____, hi__ br_____ ey___ shi_____. "We'___ no__ go_____ to b___ a Chris_____ tr____ th___ ye____. "We'___ go_____ to cu__ ou__ ow__! On__ of th_____," he sa____, poin_____ to th__ tw__ spr_____ tr_____ out_____ Ja___'__ win_____. "Ho__ do yo__ li___ th____?" Ja___ shr_____. "It'__ al__ ri_____," he sa___.

(Beginnings Deleted)

"__ou __an ___tch ___om __he ____dow," ___id __im, ___ying to __et __is ___other _____rested. "__'ll ___ll '____ber' so ___u'll ___ow ___en __t's ___ming ___wn." ___ke ___id ___thing, __nd ___nt on ____ding.

(Middles Deleted)

J___e fe__t so l___t o__t of it a__l! He fe__t n___e of t__e exc_____ent of ha_____g th___r o__n tr__e. He co_____n't h___p c__t it, a__d he ha___d t__e i___a of si_____ng at t__e wi___ow wat_____ng t__e ot___rs h___e

f＿n. He de＿＿＿ed he wo＿＿＿n't wa＿＿h
th＿m c＿t it d＿＿n, a＿d he wo＿＿＿n't h＿＿p
dec＿＿＿te it ei＿＿er. He di＿＿'t w＿＿t to
h＿＿e an＿＿＿＿ng to do w＿＿h th＿＿r
Chr＿＿＿＿as tr＿e!

(Vowels Deleted)

J＿k＿ h＿d b＿＿n v＿ry ＿ll wh＿n h＿ w＿s
s＿x y＿＿rs ＿ld. N＿w h＿ w＿s tw＿lv＿.
H＿ st＿ll w＿r＿ br＿c＿s ＿n h＿s l＿gs, ＿nd
h＿ h＿d t＿ s＿t ＿n a wh＿＿l ch＿＿r. H＿
w＿＿ld n＿v＿r b＿ ＿bl＿ t＿ r＿n ＿nd pl＿y
＿s ＿th＿r ch＿ldr＿n d＿d, b＿t th＿ d＿ct＿rs
s＿＿d h＿ m＿ght w＿lk ＿g＿＿n ＿f h＿
r＿＿lly tr＿＿d. ＿t f＿rst J＿k＿ s＿＿m＿d t＿
＿cc＿pt th＿s ＿nd l＿＿rn＿d t＿ t＿k＿ ＿
f＿w st＿ps ＿n h＿s ＿wn.

(Consonants Deleted)

＿u＿ a＿ ＿a＿a a＿＿ ＿i＿ ＿o＿ o＿＿e＿
a＿＿ ＿a＿e ＿ea＿＿ ＿＿e＿ ＿e＿＿ o＿ a＿＿
＿＿e a＿＿e＿＿u＿e ＿＿e＿ ＿a＿, ＿e
＿e＿a＿ ＿o ＿o＿e i＿＿e＿e＿＿ i＿
＿a＿＿i＿＿. ＿e ＿ee＿e＿ ＿o ＿ee＿ ＿＿a＿
i＿＿e ＿ou＿＿＿＿'＿ ＿o a＿＿ ＿＿e ＿＿i＿＿＿
＿＿e o＿＿e＿＿ ＿i, ＿＿e＿e ＿a＿ ＿o
＿oi＿＿ i＿ ＿a＿＿i＿＿ a＿ a＿＿.

Here is the complete text for the preceding five paragraphs.

"Did you hear the news?" Tim asked, his brown eyes shining. "We're
not going to buy a Christmas tree this year. We're going to cut our
own! One of those," he said, pointing to the two spruce trees outside
Jake's window. "How do you like that?" Jake shrugged. "It's all
right," he said.

"You can watch from the window," said Tim, trying to get his
brother interested. "I'll yell 'timber' so you'll know when it's coming
down." Jake said nothing, and went on reading.

Jake felt so left out of it all! He felt none of the excitement of having
their own tree. He couldn't help cut it, and he hated the idea of
sitting at the window watching the others have fun. He decided he
wouldn't watch them cut it down, and he wouldn't help decorate it
either. He didn't want to have anything to do with their Christmas
tree!

Jake had been very ill when he was six years old. Now he was twelve.
He still wore braces on his legs, and he had to sit in a wheelchair. He

would never be able to run and play as other children did, but the doctors said he might walk again if he really tried. At first Jake seemed to accept this and learned to take a few steps on his own.

But as Sara and Tim got older and Jake heard them tell of all the adventure they had, he began to lose interest in walking. He seemed to feel that if he couldn't do all the things the others did, there was no point in walking at all.

As you attempted to decode the story, you probably became aware of some important points.

□   Reading is most successful when both phonic clues and context clues are used cooperatively.

□   The more you read and comprehended the material, the easier it became to decode the later segments. This is true because the more you understood the semantic context, the easier it was to predict what information should logically follow. In short, familiarity with the content enhances the ability to use phonic clues quickly and efficiently.

□   Consonants provide the most important clues to word recognition.

□   Vowels provide relatively few clues to word recognition.

□   The beginnings of words provide the most information.

□   The middles of words are the least useful in word recognition.

□   A combination of the beginnings and ends of words (deleting the middles) provides almost all the information necessary for decoding print.

The information presented to this point can be summarized as follows.

□   Phonic instruction emphasizes the relationships that exist between letters or combinations of letters and their sounds.

□   Instruction can be given either through analytic or synthetic strategies.

□   A large number of rules account for letter-sound relationships. The rules are often difficult and inconsistent.

□   Rules about consonants are more consistent than rules about vowels.

□   There are at least seven rules that are consistent enough to warrant direct instruction to children.

□   Phonic knowledge is indispensable in efficient reading.

□   Different parts of words carry different amounts and quality of information.

□   Consonants are more useful than vowels in decoding.

□   Beginnings and ends of words are more useful than middles in decoding.

☐   The most effective reading occurs when phonic clues are used in conjunction with context clues.

☐   Direct instruction of phonic rules and verbalization of those rules may not be necessary.

☐   Verbalizing phonic rules and understanding phonic principles are not the same.

Based on these points, we can make certain suggestions about phonic instruction:

☐   Phonic instruction should be given in meaningful language contexts that allow children to conceptually understand skills and to use them efficiently.

☐   Meaning and phonic analysis are mutually dependent clues. Phonic skills help readers gain meaning from print while meaning helps them use phonic clues more efficiently. Children must be taught to use both clues cooperatively. For example, children might read the sentence "The girl ran down the *street* to the school" but be unable to read the word *street*. Instead of insisting that the child laboriously sound out each letter, the teacher might suggest (1) that the children skip the word, finish the sentence, and then use the initial sound /str/ to predict the word; (2) that the children note the initial letters and recall the sound and then guess at the correct word based on context; or (3) that the children note the beginning letters *str* and final letter *t*, reread the beginning of the sentence, and use the phonic information in addition to the context to help decode the word.

☐   Initial and final consonants and consonant combinations are very important in decoding. Children must be taught to attend to those clues and to use them efficiently.

☐   Few phonic rules are consistent enough to be taught directly. Some, however, are reliable. Children should be encouraged and guided to learn these as generalizations.

☐   There is considerable variation in the spelling of vowel sounds, particularly long vowel sounds. It is important to teach children both long and short vowel sounds. But directly teaching rules for the relationship between each sound and its letter or letter combination seems highly counterproductive. It may be more productive to teach children to be flexible in the application of vowel sounds. If they try one sound (say short) for a vowel and it does not suggest a word they know or the resulting word doesn't make sense in the sentence, they should try the second vowel sound (long). Children might see the sentence, "The road was wide" but read, "The *rod* was wide." The teacher might say, "Let's look at this word again — *road*. You know the sounds of the letter *o*. You used the short sound; you said *rod*. Why don't you try the other sound?" Children read *road*. The teacher might say, "Now read the sentence." The children read correctly and the teacher might say, "Does that make sense? Good. That makes sense. *R-o-a-d* is *road*." This suggestion in no way implies that children should not be given reliable generalizations about the ways in which vowel sounds are represented. It simply means that children must learn strategies that will allow them to make quick and appropriate decisions regarding decoding. This strategy also gives them a workable approach to use prior to learning all the complex vowel associations.

☐ Once children have been taught both short and long vowel sounds, they should be urged to use that knowledge in combination with context to decode new words.

☐ It may be unnecessary to require children to verbalize phonic rules formally. Rather than directly teaching rules, it may be more helpful to provide children with sets of words such as *ride*, *hide*, *side*, *tide* and to lead them to discover the consistent spelling of sound patterns. Another strategy is to present children with minimally contrasting pairs of words and to help them identify the differences in the patterns: *hid/hide, rid/ride, Sid/side; ad/aid, mad/maid, pad/paid, lad/laid.*

☐ It is imperative that children be allowed to practice all phonic skills in actual reading situations. Skill instruction has not been successful nor have skills been learned until children can apply those skills and use them in real reading situations. If children are taught the skill *oa* = /oa/ as in *boat*, then they ought to be allowed to also read textual material that contains a number of related words such as *road*, *boat*, *goat*, and *load*. In this way the children will learn to apply the phonic skill in actual reading material.

The six principles that were described earlier as fundamental to all skill instruction are very important in phonic skill instruction, and we repeat them here.

1. Skills should be presented in the most meaningful contexts.
2. Skills must be taught thoroughly, particularly to children who have difficulty learning or who have slow learning rates.
3. Children's attention must be ensured prior to skill instruction.
4. Teachers must make an intentional effort to give children experience in applying their newly gained skills immediately in real reading situations.
5. Fast learners need less exposure to skills; slow learners require more exposure.
6. Skills should be learned to the automatic level.

Modifying the Skill Strand   Throughout this text we have stressed the importance of modifying existing programs to meet the needs of children. Phonic skill instruction is an area of reading instruction that demands constant and thoughtful modification. The suggestions and fundamental principles presented in the previous section can be used by teachers to make modifications that may be vital to the successful learning of phonic skills for many children. Even further methodological modifications are necessary for children who still have difficulty learning skills.

Teachers spend a major part of their instructional time during reading periods teaching reading skills. Unfortunately, significantly more time is often spent teaching children skills than providing them with firsthand experiences with print. Still many children fail to learn phonic skills and are unable to use them in reading. This failure is particularly evident in noninductive children and children with slow learning rates. Failure to learn skills can often be traced to some very specific reasons, such as the following.

- □   Instructional modifications are not provided for children.
- □   In typical classroom situations, teachers follow basal directions too closely, and basals usually present too many skills, too quickly and too superficially.
- □   Often teachers do not provide enough conceptual preparation for skills; because of this, many slower learners learn skills by rote but have little real understanding of how those skills actually work.
- □   There is often too little immediate transfer of skills to actual reading. In a typical basal reading lesson, children are taught one or two phonic skills in isolation or in the context of a single sentence. Then they complete a workbook page that often does not reinforce the newly learned skill. Finally, they read a selection. But no specific effort is made to incorporate examples of the new skill in the text. This strategy works appropriately for some average or highly inductive readers who conceptually understand the skill, read enough on their own to provide themselves with immediate and relevant practice of the skills, or knew the skill prior to instruction. Many poor readers are at a clear disadvantage on all three counts.

To instruct poor readers more effectively in phonic skills, teachers must make an effort to teach skills more thoroughly and in a more meaningful manner. The following skill instruction model is very effective in helping children process, learn, use, and remember phonic skills.

SKILL INSTRUCTION MODEL

Level A: Awareness

Conceptual
    Auditory and/or visual

Level B: Instruction

Introduce language
Teach in isolation
Place back in language

Level C: Practice

Contrived
Integrated
Incidental

Level D: Evaluation

Formal
Informal

INSTRUCTION OF PHONIC SKILL *CH*

Level A: Awareness

The purpose of this level is to prepare children for instruction by bringing to the conceptual level an awareness of the skill to be taught. To do this, find a passage that is meaningful to children and that has many examples of the skill to be taught. Sources can be language series such as the *Sounds of Language Series* or *Instant Readers* (Martin and Brogan, 1974a, 1974b). The most effective awareness material, however, is written by teachers themselves. The following example, "Charlie Chan," was written by Brenda Vogt, a teacher in the Colorado Springs Public Schools, to instruct the skill *ch*:

> Charlie Chan lives in a big house. He has a secret hideout at the top of his cherry tree. Charlie has a table in his hideout. He keeps pieces of chalk to write secret messages to his friends. Charlie quickly climbs down a strong chain when he smells something good coming from his mother's kitchen. Today she has baked chocolate chip cookies.

At this level, the selection is simply read to children to create an awareness of the skill. Note the constant use of the skill element and the meaningful level of the information.

Level B: Instruction

The objective at this level is to go beyond the awareness level to the learning stage. To do this, use the following steps:

1. Step 1: Introduce the words in language. Reread the story, but this time ask questions that force children to focus on the skill element.

   What is the name of the boy in the story? (Charlie Chan)

   Extend the questions:

   Have you ever heard that name before? Where? What kind of name do you think it is?
   Where is his secret hideout? (cherry tree)

   Extend the questions:

   What is a "secret hideout"? Do you have one at home? Why would someone need a secret hideout?
   Charlie has a table in his house. What other piece of furniture does he have? (chair)

   Extend the questions:

   What other furniture would you want in a hideout?
   What does he have to write with? (chalk)

   Extend the questions:

   What material did Charlie Chan write on? How do you know? Could he have used regular school paper? Why or why not?
   How does he get down from the tree? (chain)

   Extend the questions:

   What other ways could he have used to get down from the tree?
   What kind of cookies is his mother baking? (chocolate chip)

   Extend the questions:

   What is your favorite cookie?

   The main purpose of the questioning is to elicit from the children and to focus on the words conforming to the skill element to be learned. Extension questions are included to expose children (even on a skill level) to interpretive and evaluative thought. Once all the questions have been asked and discussed, the teacher should go back to the skill questions, elicit the answers once more, and write the answers on the chalkboard so that children can attend to and focus on the skill more closely.

2. Step 2: Teach the words in isolation. List answers on the chalkboard or on paper. Draw children's attention to the phonic element by asking questions such as:

   What do you notice is the same about all these words?
   What letters make the sound you hear before all these words?

Isolate the letters *ch*. Have children generate words that begin with the letters *ch*. List the words. Encourage children to read the words. Choose a few key words and place them in sentences. Encourage children to read the sentences. Say a number of words, both *ch* words and non-*ch* words. Have children tap or clap when they recognize words that begin with *ch*.

3.   Step 3: Place the words back in the language. Go back to the story and have children read it. Encourage them to use their newly acquired skill. If the passage is too difficult for them, write another passage using the skill taught at their instructional level and have them read it.

Level C: Practice

Contrived practice.   The traditional workbook is useful for practice. Assist children in completing workbook pages or skill pages relevant to the skill being taught. Children can also be given listening exercises to hear the *ch* sound and to distinguish between *ch* and other sounds such as *sh*. It is important that children be encouraged to practice to the point of accuracy. If accuracy does not occur, the teacher needs to return to the instruction phase. There should be as little time lapse as possible between the instruction and practice phases.

Integrated practice.   As children read material throughout the day, the teacher should make an effort to have those who need additional practice in the *ch* skill read sections containing the skill. Remedial readers need all the reading practice and reinforcement they can possibly get.

Incidental practice.   During free reading or sustained silent reading periods each day, the teacher can have available materials that contain the skill in question so that the skill can be reinforced in an informal, incidental way.

Level D: Evaluation

Formal evaluation.   This is accomplished through assessment tests and standardized or nonstandardized testing instruments. Results of testing should be used to help children — to assess their strengths and needs and to identify the need for reteaching. This level of evaluation is rarely necessary during normal classroom instruction.

Informal evaluation.   As children read in the normal course of the school day, the teacher should make an effort to assess informally children's use of the *ch* skill. When children apply it, they should be verbally rewarded; when they omit it, they should be reminded. And when they consistently ignore it, the teacher should reteach it. Modifications of the initial teaching strategy should be made so as to more closely meet children's needs.

Modifying Workbook Use   In most basal readers, workbooks are used for the practice and reinforcement of phonic, structural, and contextual analysis skills and comprehension and syllabication skills. Workbooks can be invaluable instructional tools; but they are often misused or at best underutilized in most elementary classrooms.

The major cause of this misuse is that many teachers use the workbook as seatwork activity and expect children to be able to do the exercises independently. A workbook is an instructional tool written on children's instructional level, however, which means that it is expected that children receive instruction in the tasks. Research shows that workbooks are often more difficult than their corresponding texts. Fitzgerald (1979) analyzed forty-two workbooks from seven reading series at grades three, four, five, and six. Using a readability formula, Fitzgerald assessed the difficulty level of the prose sections of the workbooks. Results showed that only three of the forty-two workbooks analyzed agreed with their grade-level designations. Third- through fifth-grade workbooks were up to three grade levels more difficult than their designation. The sixth-grade workbooks were up to one and one half grade levels more difficult. These results point to the error in using workbooks as independent practice activities. It is true that many high-achieving readers can correctly respond independently to many workbook assignments mainly because the workbooks in which they are placed are closer to or are at their *independent* reading levels. For most average and below-average readers, workbooks may be closer to their *frustration* levels. Success in these cases greatly depends on the teacher's providing appropriate instruction prior to independent use. In addition to being quite difficult, workbooks are notorious for their highly confusing directions and awkward prose construction.

The use of workbooks can be made substantially more effective by some relatively general modifications, such as the following.

Teach the workbook. Do not expect children who are functioning on or below grade level to perform appropriately without adequate instruction.

Teach each workbook page to the maximum. Each page can be used to teach or reinforce many more than the intended skills. A page designated for teaching suffixes can also be used to reinforce skills such as sight vocabulary, fluency in reading, vowels, initial and final consonants, vocabulary development, following directions, drawing inferences, and so on. Use each page to its fullest. This is particularly important in teaching slow readers.

Especially for young readers (grades K–3), use each workbook page as a kinesthetic response page. Have children circle words, underline word parts, point to words or phrases, mark an *x* through words, and so on. These activities not only force each child to become involved with learning but also allow the teacher to observe which children are fluent in skills and which children require further practice or reteaching.

Remember that workbooks do not usually provide enough meaningful context to allow children to transfer their skills into actual reading. Workbooks provide only partial context. Further opportunities must be provided for children to practice skills in whole-language contexts.

In addition to these general modifications, more specific strategies should be used to modify workbook instruction. Following are five specific strategies, based on the clarity of the directions, the format of the presentation, and the nature of the task.

Strategy 1: Teach the workbook page as the directions suggest. Some activities are totally appropriate. The directions are extremely clear, the task is straightforward, and the vocabulary is familiar. Such pages can be instructed as they are presented.

Using Context Clues

Draw a circle around the word below each sentence that makes sense in the blank space.

1. John was feeling very tired. He wanted to _____.
   run sleep see play

Strategy 2: Read directions with the children. Some activities are relatively simple. The directions are not ambiguous or awkward, although they may be somewhat long or they may include multiple steps. Children have already been taught the skill and have had several occasions to practice it. The vocabulary is familiar and the task is clear. In these cases, you might wish to read the directions with children to make sure that they understand them. You might also wish to do half the exercises in the reading group. If there is no sign of difficulty, children may be directed to finish the page independently, in pairs or in small groups.

Compound Words

Compound words are so called because they are made of two smaller words. If you watch for the smaller words in a compound word, you will be better able to figure out what the word means.

Some of the words below are compound words and others are not. If you think a word is a compound word, write the two small words in the blank spaces beside it. If the word is just one long word, put an *x* in the blank space beside it.

1. elephant   _____   _____
2. finger   _____   _____

3. birthday   _____   _____
4. bookmark   _____   _____
5. mailman   _____   _____
6. basket   _____   _____

Strategy 3: Forget about reading the directions and tell children what they should do. Some directions are hopelessly awkward. Often teachers themselves have difficulty deciphering their meaning. In these cases, simply forget the directions and verbally tell children what they need to do. Depending on how familiar the children are with the task, you might wish to do half the exercises in the group and have children finish them independently.

Using Syllables

You have learned that when you meet a new word in which a single consonant sound comes between two vowels, you should divide it before the consonant and use the long sound for the first vowel. If that does not sound like a word you know, try dividing the word after the consonant and using the short sound for the vowel. Use what you know about dividing syllables to divide the following words.

1. liver
2. polite
3. ravish
4. legal

Strategy 4: Use the workbook for vocabulary development before using it for skill development. Many workbook pages use vocabulary that does not appear in children's listening vocabularies. Although they may be able to decode the words, they don't know the meanings. In other cases, children may understand the vocabulary but need quick recognition practice. In such situations, you might (1) have a different child read each word and call on children to give definitions or use the words; (2) read each word for the children and ask them for meanings; or (3) give children definitions and have them circle, underline, or somehow mark the appropriate word. Once children have practiced the vocabulary, they can complete the page as intended.

Practice with Ending -ous

Many words end in the letters *ous*. In the following sentences, a word is missing. Find the missing word in the list on the right. Write the correct word in the space.

1. John gets _____ when he has to give a speech in class.
2. When I am sad, I look very _____.
3. Some plants are good to eat but others are _____.

jealous
serious
famous
poisonous
nervous

4. Sometimes when I get something new, my little sister is _____.
5. If many people know you, you are _____.

Strategy 5: Use the workbook for auditory skill development. Some skills cannot be appropriately completed until they have been auditorially processed. Such skills should be presented in the group orally by the teacher. Children need several oral/auditory experiences before they can easily perform some tasks visually. In addition, many skills require fine auditory discrimination abilities. Many children experience extreme difficulty doing these tasks independently because of the confusion that results from trying to pronounce and to discriminate auditorially at the same time.

Counting Syllables

Use what you know about dividing words into syllables to decide how many syllables are in each of the following words. Write the number of syllables in the space beside each word.

1. landed _____
2. figured _____
3. perfected _____
4. barked _____
5. rocked _____

Using Stress and Intonation

Sometimes in speech we make some words sound more important than others. We say that we *stress* those words. Often a sentence can have different meanings depending on which word we stress.

Each of the paragraphs below has two endings. All the words in both endings are the same, but different words are stressed so they mean different things. Underline the best ending for each paragraph.

1. Mother took Mary shopping. They looked at two dresses, one red and one blue. Mary liked the red dress best. Mother held up both dresses and asked, "Which do you like best?" Mary pointed to the red dress and said,
   a. "I want *that* dress."
   b. "I want that *dress*."

Though these strategies do not cover all the possible variations or present all possible modifications, they emphasize a major point: Every workbook page demands a distinct instructional strategy based on the format, structure, directions, and vocabulary on the page. It is important that teachers analyze each page, decide what modifications are necessary, and make the appropriate modifications.

The degree and type of modification depends on the group of children being instructed. High, average, and slow readers have very different abilities and needs, and instruction must be geared to their specific abilities and needs. Teachers must realize that regardless of how important *skill* instruction is, it is different from *reading* instruction, and the latter is significantly more important. It is imperative that children have an opportunity to interact with meaningful textual material every day.

Dictionary Clues

As children develop their reading skills and gain greater independence in reading, they invariably come upon more new words that they have difficulty pronouncing or defining. Often in such cases, children ask a peer, a parent, or a teacher for assistance. This option is sensible because adults and peers provide answers that are understandable and clear and that are delivered in meaningful, relevant, and familiar contexts, allowing children to gain a more thorough understanding of new words.

In many cases, however, this option is unavailable and children must be able to ascertain a meaning independently. In these situations children must be able to use a dictionary. The most common reasons for using a dictionary are to determine pronunciation and to determine meaning. But there are other, less obvious reasons, including to determine synonyms, plurals, parts of speech, verb tense, optional pronunciations, phonic respellings, syllables, and additional meanings. Before children are ready to use a dictionary, they must have certain skills, among them, knowledge of the letters in the alphabet, knowledge of the correct sequence of the letters in the alphabet, ability to recognize and identify initial letters of a word, and ability to recognize "before" and "after" concepts.

Many basal readers as early as second grade include a glossary of new words at the back. This is meant to give children an introduction to dictionaries and their use. Formal instruction in dictionary skills often begins in the third grade. Children are initially taught to use the dictionary for two main purposes: to determine pronunciation and to determine meaning.

Pronunciation Clues Dictionaries provide children with information about the pronunciation of words through the use of diacritical marks. These are marks placed above and beside the letters within words to indicate the appropriate sounds of the letters. Diacritical marks often vary from one book to another. It is therefore important for teachers to teach children the marking system used by their text or their classroom dictionary. Undertanding of the marking system does not ensure correct pronunciation, as the children must still use phonic knowledge to produce the word. Diacritical marks are often relatively difficult for many weak readers to learn.

Meaning Clues   In addition to providing pronunciation clues, the dictionary helps children assess word meanings. Undoubtedly, a dictionary is a very valuable tool to acquire meaning, with one caution. Teachers often use a dictionary to "teach" vocabulary. They have children look up lists of words in the dictionary, write out the definitions, and use them in sentences. This strategy is helpful only if children have a prior understanding of the words. If they do not, dictionary definitions tend to create more problems than they solve. Suppose children do not know the meaning of the word *island*. The teacher might send them to the dictionary to find the meaning. *The American Heritage Dictionary* defines an island as "a land mass smaller than a continent and surrounded by water." Children who initially did not understand the word *island* might now be faced with three more unknowns: *land mass, surrounded*, and *continent* — if indeed the child is even able to decode the definition. New vocabulary should be taught directly. Teachers should not depend on a dictionary for instruction. The dictionary can provide useful information only if children have attained a relatively high degree of vocabulary, word analysis, and cognitive skill development.

The danger in expecting young children to use the dictionary independently to define words and then to use those words is demonstrated by the following incident. In a third-grade classroom, the teacher gave children a list of words. Their assignment was to look up each word in the dictionary, write down the definition, and compose a short paragraph to demonstrate knowledge of the word. The exercise seems valid, and it would certainly be valid if it were given to the right group of children. Unfortunately, that was not the case, because in one student's notebook the following entry appeared:

Word	*frugal*
Meaning	to save
Paragraph	Sarah and I went walking by the lake. Sarah fell in the lake. "Frugal me, frugal me," she cried, so I jumped in and frugaled her.

The point should be adequately made.

A more useful way to reinforce dictionary skills is to have children create, keep, and constantly add to their own personal dictionaries. Each child might be given a spiral notebook. Such a notebook has two functions: to help children with word meanings and to help children with spelling. Left-hand pages can be designated "Meanings" and right-hand pages designated "Spelling." Each page can be used for one letter of the alphabet. As children meet unknown words, the teacher can provide the definitions and children can enter the words and the meanings in their personal dictionary.

In addition, as children engage in writing activities, words that they find difficult to spell can be provided by the teacher. Children can enter the spellings in their personal dictionaries, and the words can be available for future use. Teachers can remind children to use their dictionaries when they need assistance. This strategy not only assists vocabulary development but also reinforces spelling skills.

Summary

Several sources are available in graphic language from which readers can receive clues to word recognition. These sources are sight vocabulary, meaning, visual stimuli, word structure, phonics, and the dictionary. The sources provide overlapping information and work together to assist the reader. If readers are taught to use all sources of information, reading can progress very quickly and efficiently. If readers are taught to overrely on one or a few sources, efficiency is greatly reduced because information is significantly limited. This lack of information invariably results in slow, inefficient word calling and diminished comprehension. One of the major jobs of the teacher of reading is to expose children to a number of information sources and to encourage them to use more of the available clue systems in reading.

Basal series tend to overrely on phonics and to underutilize meaning and sight vocabulary clues. It is very important that teachers become competent at modifying reading series and at creating appropriate learning experiences for children at all levels of ability and need.

References

Bailey, M. H. "The Utility of Phonic Generalizations in Grades One Through Six." *Reading Teacher* (February 1967).

Berdiansky, B., B. Cronnell, and J. Koehler. *Spelling-Sound Relations and Primary Form-Class Descriptions for Speech-Comprehension Vocabularies of 6–9 Year Olds.* Tech. Rep. no. 15. Inglewood, Calif.: Southwest Regional Laboratory for Educational Research and Development, 1969.

Burmeister, Lou E. "Usefulness of Phonic Generalizations." *Reading Teacher* (January 1968).

Chall, J. *Learning to Read: The Great Debate.* New York: McGraw-Hill, 1967.

Chapman, L. J., and M. Hoffman. *Developing Fluent Reading.* Milton Keynes, England: Open University Press, 1977.

Clymer, J. L. "The Utility of Phonic Generalizations in the Primary Grades." *Reading Teacher* (January 1963).

Cronbach, L. J. *Educational Psychology.* 3rd ed. New York: Harcourt Brace Jovanovich, 1977.

DeCecco, J. P., and W. R. Crawford. *The Psychology of Learning and Instruction.* Englewood Cliffs, N.J.: Prentice-Hall, 1974.

Emans, R. "The Usefulness of Phonic Generalizations Above the Primary Grades." *Reading Teacher* (February 1967).

Fitzgerald, G. "Why Kids Can Read the Book but Not the Workbook." *Reading Teacher*, no. 32 (May 1979).

Houghton Mifflin Reading Series. Passport, fourth-grade text. Boston: Houghton Mifflin.

Johnson, D., and P. D. Pearson. *Teaching Reading Vocabulary*. New York: Holt, Rinehart and Winston, 1978.

LaBerge, D., and S. J. Samuels. "Toward a Theory of Automatic Information Processing in Reading." In *Theoretical Models and Processes of Reading*, edited by H. Singer and R. Riddell. Newark, Del.: International Reading Association, 1976.

Manning, J. D. *Reading: Learning and Instructional Processes*. Geneva, Ill.: Palidin House, 1980.

May, F. B., and S. B. Eliot. *To Help Children Read: Mastery Performance Modules for Teachers in Training*. Columbus, Ohio: Merrill, 1978.

Moskowitz, A. "On the Status of Vowel Shift in English." In *Cognitive Development and the Acquisition of Language*, edited by T. E. Moore, New York: Academic Press, 1973.

Oliver, M. E. *Making Readers of Everyone*. Dubuque, Iowa: Kendall/Hunt, 1976.

Perfetti, C. A., and A. M. Lesgold. "Discourse Comprehension and Sources of Individual Differences." In *Cognitive Processes in Comprehension*, edited by P. Carpenter and M. Just. Hillside, N.J.: Erlbaum, 1977.

Samuels, S. J. "Automatic Decoding and Reading Comprehension." *Language Arts*, no. 53 (1976).

Vaughn-Cook, A. F. "Phonological Rules and Reading." In *Linguistic Theory: What Can It Say About Reading?*, edited by R. Shuy. Newark, Del.: International Reading Association, 1977.

Venezky, R. L. "Regularity in Reading and Spelling." *Basic Studies on Reading*, edited by H. Levin and J. P. Williams. New York: Basic Books, 1970.

———. *The Structure of English Orthography*. The Hague: Mouton, 1970.

7

The Basal Reading Lesson

This chapter analyzes the traditional basal format. A basal reader series is based around one mode of instruction and stays closely within that mode. Consequently, a sameness permeates the way in which children are introduced to and relate to textual material even though the selections vary greatly in style, form, content, interest, and complexity.

Each selection of material needs to be treated differently based on two factors: the structure, content, and difficulty of the text and the interest, capability, and prior knowledge of the readers. The three activities to be emphasized in textual presentations are introductory activities, actual reading activities, and summation activities. But basal series contain so many elements — the reader, skill charts, workbooks, manual skill exercises and the like — that often the real importance of reading is minimized or lost entirely. Often teachers find it difficult to convey the impact of literature within the abundance of ancillary materials. This chapter answers the question "What is important in a reading lesson?"

☐ What are the different types of introductory activities teachers can use with textual material?

☐ Under what conditions is prereading vocabulary instruction necessary?

☐ When should conceptual organizers be used as introductory activities?

☐ What are some methods teachers can use to vary the actual reading of selections?

☐ What are some summation activities and what purpose do they serve?

Popularity of Basals

Basal series are textbooks used for reading instruction and organized by grade level. They came into widespread use beginning in the 1960s, and now are used to teach reading in about 85 to 95 percent of American schools (Chall, 1967; Staiger, 1969; Aukerman, 1981).

Reasons for Popularity

There are many reasons for the widespread use of basal reading series.

☐ Basal series are convenient. They provide what a publisher and a group of authors consider to be a relatively balanced reading experience in one package.

☐ Basal series are sensible for districtwide adoption, given the high mobility of families in many areas.

☐ Basal series are relatively self-contained. They represent all elementary grade levels — kindergarten through sixth grade — presumably fitting each child to a text within the series. Many series provide materials through junior high grades.

☐ Basal series seem somewhat teacher-independent because they standardize instruction by giving extensive and precise directions for their use. This undoubtedly makes it easier for beginning teachers or insecure teachers to cope with the instructional task.

☐ Basal series are part of a popular technology of learning that reduces instructional material to small hierarchically organized units. Children are instructed and progress in stepwise fashion from the beginning level to the final level. The teacher's role is to present the sequentially assigned skills, assess children's performance, diagnose deficiences, reteach unlearned skills, reassess children's performance, and move to the next level.

It is unfair to give the impression that basal systems are merely glorified skills packets. This is far from the case. Basal readers, particularly post-1970s series, contain a fine and varied selection of literature. Unfortunately, many teachers admit that more instructional time is consumed by mandatory skill instruction and less on actual reading instruction that could focus on exploration of meaning through comprehension. This emphasis on skills is particularly true in the instruction of poor readers. We use the phrase "actual reading instruction" to emphasize that skill instruction is essentially different from reading instruction (Pearson, 1980). Whereas skill instruction focuses on discrete parts of the reading process, reading instruction focuses on facilitating communication and interaction between the reader and the print.

Factors That Reduce Effectiveness

Maximum communication and interaction are often not achieved because the potential effectiveness of basal series is undermined by time constraints, sameness, and rigidity.

Time   The reading curriculum has become increasingly complex in the last few decades. The trend has been toward more skill instruction, more assessment of skills, more reteaching of skills, and more record keeping. In addition to the increasing demands of skill instruction, the number of children in individual classrooms continues to rise and the amount of time allotted to teaching reading has decreased or remained the same because of expanded curriculum offerings. These time constraints work most against poor readers, who need constant exposure to print but who often are locked into skill instruction that rarely is transferred to actual reading.

Sameness   Undoubtedly, the basal series of the post-1970s show great improvement over those of previous years (Moe and Johnson, 1980). More attention is given to sex-role, racial, and ethnic variety. Illustrations and artwork have become more varied. There is a more appropriate mix of fiction and nonfiction, narrative and expository forms, poetry and drama, and so on. Reading selections more accurately reflect the changing society and the information needs of the readers. But an obvious sameness often pervades these series. All workbooks within a series look the same and follow the same format throughout the grades, skills are introduced in the same basic ways in all the books, the selections are introduced with one strategy, the questions are asked in the same ways, and artwork and types of selections are strikingly similar throughout the grades. This sameness was expressed well by a child after the first month of second grade. Asked how he liked second grade, he replied, "It's okay. It's really exactly like first grade except they changed all the covers of all the books."

Rigidity   The format of basal series is very structured. The teaching directions are extremely detailed and are often followed closely by teachers. Some teachers depart from the mandates and devise their own modifications, but, as Pearson (1980) points out, these efforts are often carried on behind closed doors, as it were, and often result in a certain degree of defiance and guilt.

Time constraints, sameness, and rigidity often rob reading instruction of the chance to develop effectively communication and interaction between students and textual material.

Toward Effective Instruction

Three activities are critical to the effective instruction of any text selection: introductory activities, actual reading activities, and summation activities. Introductory activities consist of strategies to prepare students for the selection and enhance their comprehension, interest, and motivation. Reading activities include variations in the actual reading task. Summation activities consist of strategies used at the end of the selection to apply skills that were introduced earlier and to extend understanding of, interaction with, and appreciation of the textual material. The art of teaching reading as a communicative process rests in the ability of teachers to analyze each reading selection and to vary the teaching strategies to fit the demands of the selection itself and the needs and abilities of the children.

Introductory Activities

The selections in a reading text vary in difficulty of vocabulary, familiarity of concepts, complexity of ideas, and style of writing, but the same basic format is usually used to introduce all the selections. This often results in overpreparation or underpreparation of children for the reading task. Teachers must read each selection prior to instruction, analyze the demands of the story, weigh the demands against students' abilities, and choose the most suitable methods of instruction. Among the many activities that can be used to prepare children for reading are prediction/discussion, vocabulary preinstruction, overviews, conceptual organizers, prereading questions, listing, concept building through related media, and combination approaches. Most of these activities are discussed in more detail in Chapter 4, pages 76–90.

Prediction/Discussion   There are many clues to the content of a selection — title, pictures, major headings, boldface type, italicized type, charts, and graphs. Before reading the text, teachers can direct children to look at a number of these clues and to use them to predict what the text will be about. Children's predictions can be written down and used as a checklist as they read through the text. During reading, children should be encouraged frequently to make predictions and to validate or negate their previous predictions by further reading. If the vocabulary and conceptual familiarity are manageable for the children, prediction and checking may be sufficient to prepare and motivate children toward reading. If not, teachers should use vocabulary preinstruction strategies and conceptual organizers.

A modification of the prediction strategy is to give children the title and major headings of a selection prior to instruction and to ask them to generate predictions of what the selection might be about, record facts that they already know about the topic, or draw pictures of what they think the selection will be about. As they read the material, they can evaluate their predictions.

Vocabulary Preinstruction Some selections contain vocabulary items or expressions that are not in the meaning vocabulary of many children. Many texts suggest that unfamiliar vocabulary items be dealt with as children meet them in the context of their reading. This practice is often appropriate for children who have relatively strong vocabularies and who make good use of sentence and paragraph context to understand unknown words. For many other children, however, stopping during reading to identify and explain unfamiliar words may all but destroy the continuity of the text and ruin comprehension and interaction. In such cases, it is helpful to instruct children in new vocabulary items before they read the story (Thomas and Robinson, 1982). It is important that vocabulary instruction include discussion of the concepts and use of the words in realistic language as opposed to simply having children look up words in a dictionary and write down definitions. Teachers should be discriminating in choosing vocabulary for preinstruction. In vocabulary-heavy selections, with more difficult words than teachers have time to teach or than children have the ability to learn at one sitting, teachers should be pragmatic and choose the most important words — those most frequently used, those most essential to the comprehension of the selection, and those that are least well defined in context. It is also helpful to introduce the word in the context in which it is used in the selection (*twist* and "twist of the plot," *possessed* and "self-possessed person").

Overviews An overview is a summary of the major points within a selection. It gives children an outline as a guide for reading. An overview is completely text-bound, that is, it is limited to the information in the text. Though an overview is a useful strategy, it has one major limitation: It gives clues to the content of material only, not to the underlying concepts involved. Because of this, overviews should be used with selections for which children already have necessary conceptual knowledge. Otherwise overviews are not appropriate.

One way that teachers can help build concepts is to provide related visual materials that familiarize students with new topics prior to reading.

Conceptual Organizers   Some selections that do not have difficult vocabulary or plot may contain concepts and experiences that are unfamiliar to children. It is essential that teachers analyze selections, identify major concepts necessary for comprehension, and make children conceptually prepared prior to reading instruction. (Conceptual readiness was discussed in more detail in Chapters 4 and 5.) Teachers can use conceptual or advance organizers, which help students identify the relationships between the reading selection and what they already know, understand, and have experienced. This link is vital to comprehension (Smith, 1980; Strange, 1980). Conceptual organizers have been shown to be effective for all grade levels, content areas, and ability levels. We strongly suggest that the conceptual preparation be done orally, with much verbal interaction between the teacher and children. (Greenslade, 1980; Liuten, Ames, and Ackerson, 1980).

Prereading Questions   Research on the effectiveness of prereading questions has produced ambivalent results, although many teachers find such questions useful. Reading authorities who strongly endorse this strategy (Thomas and Robinson, 1972; Herber, 1978) claim that prequestions focus children's attention on significant information within the text and give children a framework and a purpose for reading. Prequestions also set up certain expectations of print that make prediction easier and more accurate. Other theorists find that prequestions may limit learning because children may look only for the information asked and ignore other important information (Rothkopf, 1966).

I believe that prequestioning can be a useful and important strategy if teachers use it sensibly. The crucial issue is the type of prequestions that should be asked. If teachers use narrow, literal, text-bound questions, chances are that children will indeed become adept at searching for the "one correct" answer and will ignore other important information. But if teachers ask broad questions (convergent, divergent, and evaluative) that require children to draw inferences, identify generalizations, and make judgments, children essentially are forced to process the material before they can answer the questions. Rather than asking questions like, Where did James go in the first section? Who was with Meg on the night of the fire? When did the war begin?, teachers can ask questions like, What are four words that you could use to describe James? Why did you choose those words? What is the major problem mentioned in the first chapter and how do you think it will be solved? How does the saying "The grass is always greener on the other side of the fence" relate to the information on the first page of the story?

Prequestions alone are usually not adequate introductory activities because they do not prepare children for new vocabulary or unfamiliar concepts. But when children have adequate vocabulary and appropriate concepts prior to reading, prequestions can be highly effective in guiding their reading, helping them to attend more closely to content, and giving them a purpose for reading.

Listing   Listing is designed to alert children to the knowledge they already have about a topic covered in their reading selection. The listing process provides children with useful information that forms the foundation for comprehension and further learning. Listing is most effective when applied to expository material. The strategy involves the following steps.

1.   Write the topic of the selection on the chalkboard.
2.   Ask children to tell *anything* they know that is related to the topic.

3. List their responses on the board.
4. When all responses have been listed, discuss each response, elaborate on it, modify it, and so on.
5. Lead children to identify any general categories that emerge.
6. Ask children to make predictions based on the discussion.
7. Have children read the material. As they do, the information in the list will be confirmed, modified, added to, and so on.

Concept Building Through Related Media   Children's appreciation of their reading can be enhanced by providing them with objects, pictures, music, films, and related materials that provide some experience with the new topic prior to reading. This experience is particularly helpful before reading expository material. Before reading an article on volcanoes, for example, children may be shown pictures or film of a recent volcanic eruption. Or before reading a selection about a desert, the teacher and children can view and discuss pictures of different deserts and desert plants and animals. These experiences serve several purposes. They expose children to new vocabulary, build necessary concepts, provide vicarious or firsthand experience with the topic, heighten motivation toward and interest in reading, encourage interaction, and aid prediction by providing background information and developing expectations of print.

Combination Approaches   Perhaps the most effective introductory activities will consist of combination of strategies. A relatively simple story may require only prediction activities with discussion and an overview. A more difficult selection may require vocabulary preinstruction, a concept organizer, and prediction exercises. An expository selection dealing with a relatively unfamiliar topic may require vocabulary preinstruction, background building with pictures and discussion, and prereading questions to provide guidance and set purposes for reading. Another expository selection dealing with a relatively familiar topic may require vocabulary preinstruction, listing, and prediction exercises.

Each reading selection requires a different kind of introduction depending on the demands of the selection and the knowledge of the readers. It is essential that teachers analyze each selection, identify the needs of the children who will read the selection, and then choose the appropriate strategy or combination or strategies to introduce the selection.

Reading Activities

Once children have been appropriately prepared for textual material, the actual reading of the selection begins. Most basal series use a single reading strategy: read silently, stop at designated segments and answer questions asked by the teacher, reread or read orally, stop and answer questions until the end of the selection. Certainly, this strategy is quite reasonable with some selections. But several other formats can also be used to maximize children's interaction with and appreciation of print, among them the following.

> Choral reading
> Readers' theater
> Paired reading
> Prepared reading
> Inquiry reading
> Flexible reading
> Echoic reading
> Combination approaches

Choral Reading   In choral reading, a group of children reads aloud a section of passage all together. Stories that have a refrain or repetitive sequence, such as "The Three Billy Goats Gruff" and "There Was an Old Lady Who Swallowed a Fly," are particularly suited to choral reading. In such instances, a group of children may read the repetitive segments and individual children may read the nonrepetitive text. The following excerpt from "The Grandmother" (Simpson, 1973) shows how choral reading can be used with verse.

(Individual)

The Grandmother was old and ready to die.
Death said I am here.
And the Grandmother answered,
Yes, I see you, Death.
So the Grandmother called
all of her children together,
saying,

(Group)

> My life has been long
> My sorrows few
> My joys many
> But now I am weary and ready to die.

(Individual)

But the oldest daughter of the Grandmother
began pulling her hair out, crying,
> Ayee, Mother, do not leave us,
> for we have formed a chain
> and you are the clasp that binds us.
And the Grandmother, who greatly loved her children,

told Death to wait a little while.
The Grandmother lived on and on.
Then again Death said, I am here,
and the Grandmother answered, Yes, I see you, Death.
So the Grandmother called
all of her children together,
saying

(Group)

My life has been long
My sorrows few
My joys many
But now I am weary and ready to die.

It is important that the group achieve proper expression and fluency, especially after the sequence has been repeated a few times. This strategy not only is motivating to all children, but it also gives poorer students a chance to hear, imitate, and practice good oral reading.

Readers' Theater   Stories that contain much conversation lend themselves to readers' theater. Using this strategy a teacher informally transforms a story into a play by assigning individual children specific speaking parts while the teacher or other students assume the role of narrator. The following excerpt from "Calvin" shows how a story easily can become a play.

Narrator

One day the Rays went to a pet store. They looked at many pets. Then they saw just the right pet — a furry yellow kitten.

Child 1

"May we have him, Mother?"

Narrator

asked Jane.

Child 2

"Please let us get him, Mother, Please,"

Narrator

said Mary.

Child 3

"He will be such a good pet,"

Narrator

added Mike.

Child 4

"Well,"

Narrator

said Mother.

Child 4

"If you take care of him, feed him, clean up after him, and play with him, we will get him."

Children 1, 2, 3

"We promise,"

Narrator

said the kids.

Child 1

"Let's call him Calvin,"

Narrator

said Jane.

This is a highly motivating strategy that can transform a relatively motionless story into a dramatic event. Teachers are encouraged to be as creative as possible with this strategy. If a group is particularly responsive to a story, informal sets and costumes can be created and the story can be practiced and performed by the group for the entire class.

Paired Reading   Paired reading is somewhat similar to choral reading. Children are selected in pairs to read sections of text together. Teachers can pair better readers with poorer ones so that the poorer readers are forced to read more fluently. In addition, poorer readers have the opportunity to hear and keep pace with good models. This strategy can effectively be interspersed with other forms of instructional reading.

Prepared Reading   Many nonfluent readers never have an opportunity to read a selection well. Prepared reading gives such children an opportunity to practice assigned sections of a selection to a level of fluency prior to group instruction. During the actual reading, these children can read their prepared sections and experience the pride of reading well before their peers. This strategy must be used with material that is written close to children's independent reading levels. Most vocabulary and most necessary concepts of the selection must be familiar to the children. As with all other reading strategies, prepared reading should be accompanied by an emphasis on comprehension and appropriate questioning strategies. (See the section Thinking Strategies in Chapter 4 on page 90.)

Inquiry Reading   Some selections are quite easy for some groups of children to read and understand because of the low vocabulary and concept demands. Teachers can assign such selections to children as independent reading activities. Children can read the selections on their own prior to the reading lesson. The teacher can also assign questions for children to answer after they have read the selection and before the reading lesson. The reading period can then be spent discussing the selection on interpretive and evaluative levels. High-level questions can be used to help enhance children's appreciation of the text. As children answer questions, they can be asked to justify or support their answers by referring to appropriate sections from the text. This strategy is excellent for developing analytic and critical reading skills.

Flexible Reading   Many selections in basal readers can be used to help children develop flexibility in their rate of reading. It is very important that children develop the ability to read different types of materials for different purposes and at different speeds. Early in their reading experiences, children should be taught the value of establishing reading speeds appropriate to their material. Reading instruction often forces children into the poor habit of slow, inefficient reading, which greatly hampers their comprehension of print. Carrillo (1973) points out: "Too much attention in the early stages of reading instruction to phonics, structural analysis, structural linguistics and/or oral reading will interfere later with flexibility of rate." Burmeister (1974) also suggests that early acceptance of slow, over-cautious reading reinforces excessive attention to the individual skills of reading and results in children's difficulty in coping with the demands of postelementary reading. The need for a flexible reading rate is emphasized by Parker (1970): "Good readers are like good drivers. They don't move at the same rate all the time. They are flexible."

Children can be taught flexibility through many strategies. Two of the most important are skimming and scanning.

Skimming is a quick strategy that helps readers get the gist of a selection without reading the entire text. The process involves reading the title, the first paragraph, the subheadings, possibly the first and last sentences of each paragraph, and the entire last paragraph of a selection. Skimming a book can include reading the index and table of contents. Skimming allows readers to get a general idea about a selection or book. It is a valuable strategy to use in deciding whether a book might be of particular interest or whether a selection is likely to contain a given type of information. Skimming is used mostly with expository writing.

Teachers can teach children to skim by choosing articles that are one to two pages long and directing children to read the title, the first paragraph, the subheadings, the first and last sentences in each paragraph, and the last paragraph. Then the teacher can ask questions to help children use the information to make judgments:

> What will the article be about?
> Is the article something that will interest you?
> Would the article be useful in writing a report on the history of modern jazz?
> Does the article deal primarily with facts or opinions?

Scanning involves moving one's eyes quickly across and down a page to obtain specific facts or isolated details. Adults scan material constantly. We scan a telephone directory to find a specific name, or we scan a recipe to find a specific ingredient. Thomas and Robinson (1982) suggest that there are three levels of scanning:

1. *Level 1:* Scanning for information that stands out easily (dates, names, numbers) to answer questions such as "In what year did the war begin?"
2. *Level 2:* Scanning for an answer that contains the same words as the question does, such as "Does the Ibu tribe depend on *fishing* or on *hunting* for its survival?"
3. *Level 3:* Scanning for an answer that requires different words from the question, such as "Can you find any support for the idea that the people were afraid?"

Teachers can develop scanning ability in children by asking them to find specific facts in a limited time in textual material. Many expository selections in textbooks lend themselves to practice with this strategy. Teachers should begin with level 1 activities and gradually move through level 3.

The importance of developing a flexible reading rate is summed up by Karlin (1972): "Good readers know how to shift gears when they read and let the nature of their material and their purposes for reading control their speed of reading."

Echoic Reading   Echoic reading is particularly useful for nonfluent readers. In this activity, the teacher reads a section of print and a child rereads the same section. The rationale is that poor readers seldom hear good models. What they hear daily is the poor oral reading of other children who read as badly as or worse than they do. In reading a section first, the teacher provides the proper word attack, fluency, and expression to be imitated, or echoed, by the student. Extended use of echoic reading helps the poor reader to read more fluently and with more appropriate expression (Manning, 1980). An important consideration is the length of the passage. It should be long enough to prevent the child from recalling it from memory and short enough to allow the child to hold the words and expression in memory and use that knowledge to decode the text well. The teacher will be able to decide on the appropriate length for individual children after some practice using the strategy.

Combination Approaches   As with introductory activities, reading activities can be combined. Flexible reading can be appropriately used in combination with all the strategies except inquiry and prepared reading. Echoic and paired reading can easily be used with the same selection. Choral reading and readers' theater can be used jointly by having individual children read speaking parts and groups of children narrate the story. In addition, the strategies can be combined with the typical basal format of silent reading, questioning, oral reading, questioning, and so on. Combinations are limited only by the creativity of the teacher.

The reasons for using these activities are not only to add greatly needed variety to the reading experience but also to heighten significantly children's communication with, interest in, and appreciation of print. It is necessary, therefore, to combine all strategies with a variety of questions that heighten comprehension and extend critical and creative thinking abilities.

Summation Activities

After children have read and comprehended a selection, the teacher can extend children's appreciation by engaging them in summation or extension activities. These activities can focus on any aspect of the selection and can guide children to in-depth analysis and discussion of the material. The strategies of story form, report form, semantic webbing, and fact analyzer (see Chapter 4, pages 104–114) are all appropriate summation activities. In addition are strategies that focus on character analysis, problem solving, plot analysis, and vocabulary development.

Character Analysis   Many activities can assist children in gaining further insight into characters. Individual characters can be identified and children can be asked to choose three to five words that best describe the character, supporting their choices with statements from the text:

Character

Character	Descriptive Words	Text Proof
Steven	honest	returned money he found
	shy	didn't like meeting new people
	responsible	did his chores rather than going to the movies

Similarly, children can analyze characters' emotions:

Character	Emotion	Situation
Elise	angry	kids teased her
	disappointed	she didn't get the job she wanted
	annoyed	she yelled at Janet
	sorry	she apologized

Teachers can help children draw inferences and think creatively about characters with activities like the following.

Which characters would appropriately sing the following songs and on what occasions?

Song	Sung By	When
"Walk on By"	_____	_____
"Bridge over Troubled Water"	_____	_____
"Lying Eyes"	_____	_____
"Don't Blame Me"	_____	_____
"You're So Vain"	_____	_____
"The Way We Were"	_____	_____

Which character or characters would most likely make each of the following comments? Give the reasons for your choices.

Comment	Character	Reason for Choice
"You made your bed; now lie in it."	_____	_____
"I'll make time to help you."	_____	_____
"I don't care what you think! I'll do it my way."	_____	_____
"I know the situation is bad, but let's look at the bright side."	_____	_____

Children can be encouraged to write poetry based on characters. Following is one motivating pattern for poetry about a character.

Poetry

Character Name
Verb, Verb (-*ing* ending)
Adverb, Adverb, Adverb
Adjective, Adjective
Character Name

The following poem was written in that pattern by a fourth grader.

Sarah,
Thinking, Questioning
Slowly, Cautiously, Quietly
Shy, Afraid
Sarah

2, **Problem Solving**   Many reading selections contain material that can be used to develop and reinforce problem-solving skills. Teachers can use various activities to train this skill, including the following.

Children can be provided with a problem posed in the selection, asked to brainstorm many possible solutions, and finally directed to choose the best solution based on the situation.

Problem	*Possible Solutions*	*Best Solution*
The early settlers had a serious shortage of food.		

Children can practice problem solving by starting with an answer and generating possible, appropriate questions:

Create two questions to match each of the following answers.

Answers	*Possible Questions*
Pollution	1.
	2.
Polyps	1.
	2.

Teachers can give children a problem or question posed in the text and ask them to generate a solution not mentioned in the selection. Children can then rewrite the ending of the selection based on the solution they have created.

3, **Plot Analysis**   In Chapter 4, we considered the story form as a strategy for plot analysis. Herber (1978) views a plot as consisting of five major segments:

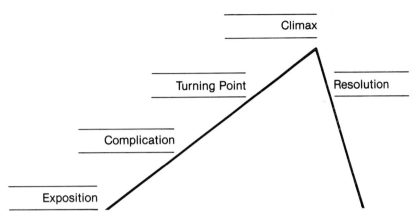

FIGURE 7–1
Five-point plot structure (Herber, 1978)

1. The *exposition*, the beginning, which explains the information necessary to understand the ensuing action
2. The *complication*, which presents the problem or conflict
3. The *turning point*, in which the plot takes a decisive turn
4. The *climax*, the point of highest suspense
5. The *resolution*, in which the complication is unraveled and solved

Herber uses a visual representation of these five points to help children further internalize plot structure (Figure 7–1). The terminology can be adjusted for younger children, in which case the steps could be labeled beginning, problem, turning point, high point, and solution.

It is not the learning of the labels that is important but the internalization of the usual parts of a plot and the ability to use that knowledge to comprehend a selection.

Vocabulary Development Most reading selections can be used to extend and develop children's vocabulary skills, which are critical language skills. Most basal series have heavy vocabulary loads, but often children are "exposed" to much vocabulary rather than "taught" or given adequate practice in vocabulary. Considerably more attention needs to be paid to vocabulary development. The following vocabulary exercises can be used to extend and reinforce children's vocabularies and to heighten their interaction with print:

Categorization

Find five words from the selection that fit into each of the following categories: emotions, natural resources, land forms.

Vocabulary exercises can be used with reading selections to extend and reinforce children's vocabularies.

2, *Word Finds*

Find the following words in the selection:
a. a word that means uncomfortable
b. a two-syllable word that is the opposite of nervous
c. a word that means someone from another country

3, *Word Building*

The word *understand* was used in your reading selection. How many words can you build using that word as a base?

4, *Analogies*

Finish the following analogies. All the answers are words used in your reading selection.
a. *Refrigerator* is to *food* as *briefcase* is to _____.
b. *Large* is to *huge* as *small* is to _____.
c. *Laughter* is to *happiness* as *tears* is to _____.

5. *Shades of Meaning*

Which of the following words have the (a) *same* meaning as, (b) a *close* meaning to, or (c) a *different* meaning from the word *happy*?

glad, overjoyed, pleased, fortunate, gratified, prosperous, harmonious, pleasant, joyous, gloomy, glamorous

6. *Synonyms*

Find a word from your reading selection that means the same as each of the following words.
a. order
b. yell
c. frighten
d. tolerate
e. dislike

7. *Antonyms*

Find a word from your reading selection that means the opposite of each of the following words.
a. afraid
b. admire
c. disease
d. adore
e. solid

Applying the Strategies

We have stressed that reading is an involving and interactive process. The teaching of reading is also an active decision-making process. Effective teaching of reading depends on the teacher's ability to analyze students' needs and the demands of the text and to provide instruction accordingly. This concept is illustrated in Figure 7–2.

Prior to instruction, teachers need to answer three important questions.

1. What do the students already know about the material?

   Key Concepts
   What pertinent vocabulary do the students know?
   With what concepts are they already familiar?
   What content do they have?

2. What does the material demand of the learners?

   Key Concepts
   What vocabulary is mandatory?
   Which concepts are vital?
   How extensive is the content?

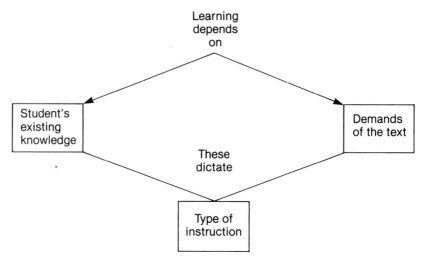

FIGURE 7–2
Elements of effective instructional decision making

3. Which instructional strategies will be most effective to move students from where they are to where they need to be to understand the material?

   Key Concepts
   The larger the distance between where learners are and where they need to be, the more extensive and intensive instruction must be.
   The smaller the distance between where learners are and where they need to be, the less extensive and intensive instruction should be.

Reflection on these three questions should lead to three important conclusions.

1. Different groups of readers (high, average, low) bring different levels of prior knowledge to textual material; therefore, instruction across different groups of children must vary.
2. Within any group of children, levels of prior knowledge will vary based on the demands of each selection. Instruction within any group, therefore, will vary from selection to selection.
3. Effective teaching of reading depends on teachers' awareness of the distance between the knowledge of learners and the demands of texts and their use of a wide variety of instruc-

tional strategies that can significantly lessen that distance and make learning successful.

Based on the selection "The Great Barrier Reef" (see page 90), the following model demonstrates how the strategies presented in this chapter can be applied to the instruction of different groups of children.

INSTRUCTION PLAN

GROUP 1: POOR READERS

Question 1:   What do students already know?

Answer: Sight and meaning vocabularies low
Unlikely to know the words *pollute, polyps, masses, surface.*
  Slow vocabulary acquisition
Unlikely to have much information on coral reefs, ocean life, and so on. Content of the text is likely to be foreign

Question 2:   What does the material demand?

Answer: Vocabulary relevant to coral reefs: *coral reef, polyps, pollute, masses, damage, surface, Pacific Ocean*
Basic knowledge of coral reefs: general location, formation, use, and so on
Basic concepts of time, space, formation, destruction

Question 3:   Which strategies will be most effective, given much distance between students' knowledge and the demands of the text?

Before Reading: Vocabulary preinstruction (*polyps, pollute, masses, surface, damage, coral*)
Concept building through experiences and discussion (pictures of coral, coral reefs; filmstrips; and so on)
Prediction and discussion (prediction based on title and vocabulary)

During Reading: Flexible reading: scanning (Where is the reef located? How long is the barrier reef?)
Echoic reading if necessary.
Questioning that focuses on factual recall, inference, visualization
Much discussion

After Reading: Fact analyzer
            Vocabulary extension
            Writing and art extensions

GROUP 2: GOOD READERS

Question 1:   What do students already know?

Answer: Strong sight vocabulary
        Strong meaning vocabulary
        Ability to use context
        Fast vocabulary acquisition
        Likely to have at least basic knowledge of coral reefs; content of the text likely to be somewhat familiar

Question 2:   What does the material demand?

Answer: Vocabulary relevant to coral reefs: *coral reef, polyps, pollute, masses, damage, surface, Pacific Ocean*
        Basic knowledge of coral reefs: general location, formation, use, and so on
        Basic concepts of time, space, formation, destruction

Question 3:   Which strategies are necessary, given little distance between students' knowledge and the demands of the text?

Before Reading: Listing to identify and clarify prior knowledge
            Vocabulary preinstruction if necessary
            Prediction and validation

During Reading: Traditional silent/oral reading, with discussion
            Questioning that focuses on factual information, inference, visualization

After Reading: Extension in social studies, such as reading more extensively about coral reefs
            Writing and art extensions
            Researching marine life

It should be clear that reading instruction is an active decision-making process. Teachers identify students' needs, analyze the demands of the text, and, using that information, make appropriate instructional decisions. The result of this strategy is that all children receive differentiated instruction that provides them with the tools necessary to learn. This strategy also eliminates the sameness and rigidity that characterize many instructional programs. Each reading period can be somewhat different because instruction is created specifically to facilitate learning.

Summary

Reading series contain many selections that vary in difficulty, familiarity of content, complexity of concepts, familiarity of vocabulary, and the like. Each selection requires different instructional strategies. It is necessary, therefore, that teachers become familiar with a wide variety of options for the instruction of textual material. The art of teaching reading lies in the ability and willingness of teachers to analyze reading selections and decide on appropriate strategies according to the demands of the selection and the needs of the children.

References

Aukerman, R. C. *The Basal Reader Approach to Reading.* New York: Wiley, 1981.

Burmeister, L. E. *Reading Strategies for Secondary School Teachers.* Reading, Mass.: Addison-Wesley, 1974.

Carrillo, L. W. "Developing Flexibility of Reading Rate." In *Reading and Related Skills,* edited by M. Clark and A. Milne. London: Ward Lock, 1973.

Chall, J. *Learning to Read: The Great Debate.* New York: McGraw-Hill, 1967.

Greenslade, D. C. "The Basics in Reading from the Perspective of the Learner." *Reading Teacher,* no. 34 (1980).

Herber, Harold. *Teaching Reading in Content Areas.* Englewood Cliffs, N.J.: Prentice-Hall, 1978.

Karlin, R. *Teaching Reading in the High School.* 2nd ed. Indianapolis, Ind.: Bobbs-Merrill, 1972.

Liuten, J., N. S. Ames, and G. Ackerson. "The Advance Organizer: A Review of Research Using Glass' Technique of Meta-analysis." Paper presented at the annual meeting of the National Reading Conference, San Antonio, Texas, 1979.

Manning, J. C. *Reading: Learning and Instructional Processes.* Geneva, Ill.: Paladin House, 1980.

Moe, A. J., and D. Johnson. "Current Approaches, Part One." In *Teaching Reading, Foundations and Strategies,* edited by P. Lamb and R. Arnold. Belmont, Calif.: Wadsworth, 1980.

Parker, D. H. "Reading Rate Is Multilevel." In *Teaching Reading Sills in Secondary Schools,* edited by A. V. Olson and W. S. Ames. Scranton, Pa.: International Textbook Company, 1970.

Pearson, C. "Reading vs. Reading Skills." *Learning* (November 1980).

Rothkopf, E. Z. "Learning from Written Instructive Materials: An Exploration of the Control of Inspection Behavior by Test-like Events." *American Educational Research Journal,* no. 3 (1966).

Simpson, J. "The Grandmother." In *Sounds of Jubilee,* edited by B. Martin and P. Brogan. New York: Holt, Rinehart and Winston, 1973.

Smith, F. *Understanding Reading.* New York: Holt, Rinehart and Winston, 1980.

Staiger, R. C. "Basal Reading Programs: How Do They Stand Today?" In *Current Issues in Reading,* edited by N. B. Smith. Newark, Del.: International Reading Association, 1969.

Strange, M. "Instructional Implications of a Conceptual Theory of Reading Comprehension." *Reading Teacher,* 33:4 (January 1980).

Thomas, E. L., and H. A. Robinson. *Improving Reading in Every Class: A Source Book for Teachers.* Boston: Allyn and Bacon, 1982.

8

Diagnosis and Remediation of the Remedial Reader

Diagnosis and remediation are concepts that must eventually concern all teachers of reading. Each classroom contains children who, for one reason or another, do not perform or progress adequately in reading. In such cases, teachers must be able to diagnose the children's problems and provide remediation to solve them.

This chapter analyzes the concepts of diagnosis and remediation. We make a distinction between formal and informal diagnosis and discuss the advantages and limitations of each. We analyze the prerequisites and effectiveness of remediation. Remediation is effective when it involves some kind of instructional change, either structural or process. We explain these two types of change, make recommendations about them, and provide specific models and methods of remediation.

□   What is a good working definition of diagnosis and what implications does that definition have for teaching?

□   What must teachers know about standardized tests to use their results to categorize children?

□   What advantage does informal diagnosis have over formal diagnosis?

□   What are some of the most important prerequisites of remediation?

□   What implications do structural and process changes have for classroom remediation?

□   What are the major principles on which the Basic Instructional Sequence is built? How can a teacher modify the sequence to meet the needs of different groups?

An Overview of Diagnosis

Diagnosis is often presented as a two-pronged concept that includes formal and informal assessment. Formal diagnosis refers to the administration of standardized diagnostic tests that focus on specific reading skills and that yield scores to be used in assessing students' performance in those skills. Informal diagnosis refers to continuous teacher-directed analysis of reading behavior based on observation of students' actual reading and their performance of specific tasks related to particular reading skills. The distinction can be seen in Figure 8–1.

The term *diagnosis* is closely linked in teachers' minds with formal diagnostic testing. Often when teachers speak of diagnosis, they refer to the process of sending children to a school psychologist, Chapter I teacher, or special education teacher to be given a standardized diagnostic test or battery of tests. The results of these tests are often interpreted and sent back to the classroom teacher along with recommendations regarding instructional treatment or placement in remedial programs. Indeed, standardized diagnostic tests are one form of diagnosis, but their use in no way should complete the diagnostic process. Although such tests are used widely across the United States, there is much confusion about what they are, what information they provide, and how they should be used. It is our position here that while standardized diagnostic tests fulfill some important functions, they are in no way adequate in pinpointing the specific problems faced by children or in solving these problems.

Formal Diagnostic Tests

Standardized diagnostic reading tests are constructed to assess strengths and weaknesses in particular skills and to provide a somewhat detailed analysis of children's skills. In addition, standardized diagnostic tests compare the individuals taking the test with a norm group. To determine the norm, test authors administer it to a sample group of children that represents the total group to which the test is intended to be given. For example, if test authors want to know the average achievement of second graders on a particular test, they may test a sample of between 300 and 500 second graders. The performance of that group yields the norms, or standard scores, against which the performance of any other child who takes the test is compared. Naturally, for norms to be valid, the number of children in the sample should be large enough (more than 200 individuals) and the group should include representative numbers of boys and girls of different races, living environments, and so on.

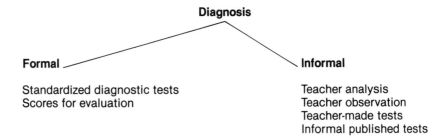

FIGURE 8–1
Differences between formal and informal diagnosis

Some standardized diagnostic tests focus on single facets of the reading task, such as oral reading or phonic analysis. Examples of such tests include the following:

Gray Oral Reading Test
The Psychological Corporation, 1967

Gilmore Oral Reading Test
The Psychological Corporation, 1968

Instant Word Recognition Test
Jamestown Publishers, 1971

McCullough Word Analysis Test
Ginn and Company, 1963

Reading Miscue Inventory
Macmillan, 1972

Other tests attempt to assess several key aspects of reading, such as comprehension, vocabulary, auditory discrimination, phonic knowledge, and phonic usage. Among such tests are:

Botel Reading Inventory
Follett, 1978

Spache Diagnostic Reading Scales
California Test Bureau, 1981

Durrell Analysis of Reading Difficulty
The Psychological Corporation, 1980

Gates-McKillop-Horowitz Reading Diagnostic Tests
Teachers College Press, 1981

Reading Diagnosis
Jamestown Press, 1981

Reporting Results   The results of diagnostic tests can be presented in any of four ways. Often more than one reporting method is used.

1.   *Raw scores.* Raw scores indicate the total number of items an individual gets correct on each section of the test (subtest). Also keep in mind that the raw score reflects the *number* of items correct, not the *specific items* answered correctly.
2.   *Grade scores.* Raw scores are usually converted to grade-level scores. A raw score of 15 might yield a grade score of 3.6. Grade scores are almost always incorrectly interpreted. If a child receives a grade score of 3.5, it is often assumed that the child should be reading at the mid-third-grade level. Diagnostic tests do not indicate exact reading levels. The test results simply are measures that compare the child to the sample norm. A score of 3.5 means that the child answered as many items correctly as did the average third grader in the fifth month of school in the original sample. The score of 3.5 represents the level at which the child's reading broke down; it indicates a frustration level for the child.
3.   *Percentiles.* Percentiles indicate the position of the individual's score compared to the distribution of scores in the original sample. If a child receives a percentile score of 75, that child's performance was as good as or better than 75 percent and poorer than 25 percent of the sample.
4.   *Stanines.* Stanine is an abbreviation for standard nine. Stanine scores have values ranging from one to nine, with one being the lowest score and nine the highest. Stanines are normalized standard scores with a mean of 5 and a standard deviation of 2. Most children (54%) fall within stanines 4, 5, and 6, with fewer children (23%) falling between stanines 1, 2, and 3 and stanines 7, 8, and 9 (23%).

Strengths   Standardized diagnostic tests can provide usable information and clearly have many strengths.

☐   They provide information on the comparative functioning of children.
☐   They provide a somewhat objective measure that can be used over time as a measure of growth.
☐   They provide a *general* profile of reading skill strengths.
☐   The provide a *general* profile of reading skill weaknesses.
☐   They provide teachers with *initial*, general directions for skill instruction.

Limitations   Standardized diagnostic tests also have serious limitations, of which teachers must be aware.

Diagnostic tests are of no assistance in remediation unless teachers analyze the actual responses of children and identify what information the children know and don't know. Of what value to the teacher is the fact that a child received a score of 1.8 on a consonant cluster test? The teacher has no idea of which clusters the child knows or doesn't know. How will the teacher know where remediation will begin? What clusters will the teacher teach? The only way the teacher can get that information is to acquire the child's actual test responses. Looking at the test, the teacher may find out that the child knows clusters *st*, *pr*, and *br* and does not know clusters *fl*, *gr*, and *dr*. Then the teacher has a clear point at which to start remediation. Simply knowing a grade score like 4.5, a percentile score like 65, a raw score like 6 or 9 correct, or a stanine like 4 does not assist a teacher in making appropriate instructional decisions.

Diagnostic tests often assess a *sample* of skills, not all skills or all language units demonstrating the skill. Of approximately thirty consonant combinations, a test may include ten or fifteen. The results, then, would relate to a child's knowledge of those ten combinations only and would indicate nothing about the remaining fifteen or twenty not tested. This is true for all areas, including sight vocabulary, meaning vocabulary, phonic skills, and the like.

Even when test results are analyzed, they provide only a starting point for remediation. Because tests can include only a sample of reading skills, formal or diagnostic testing must always be followed by more relevant, ongoing diagnosis.

Standardized tests predispose teachers to focus on children's weaknesses. The tests lure many teachers into accepting the medical model of diagnosis, which involves locating the illness and concentrating totally on eradicating the problem. The results of standardized tests are often used to identify specific skill deficiencies and to build entire remedial programs around those deficiencies. This approach not only ignores children's strengths but results in an unfortunate segmentation of reading that emphasizes isolated skill learning and provides little exposure to real reading.

Diagnostic tests are administered so seldom during the school year that they are of little assistance in providing necessary ongoing feedback.

Because formal diagnostic tests are administered in a "one-shot" fashion and often have no systematic follow-up analysis, many teachers tend to view diagnosis as a one-time procedure and fail to internalize its ongoing nature.

Informal Diagnosis

Informal diagnosis is the continuous analysis of children's reading behavior to identify strengths, weaknesses, and specific skill needs and to develop remediation activities to meet those needs. Informal diagnosis is the foundation of the view of diagnosis accepted and elaborated on in the rest of this chapter.

A Working Definition

Diagnosis can be described as a four-sided concept that places equal weight on analysis, measurement, evaluation, and change. (See Figure 8–2.)

Analysis is the careful and continuous observation of children's behavior to identify areas of progress and areas of weaknesses or failure. Measurement is the administration of a diagnostic test, formal or informal, to obtain a score or set of scores. Evaluation is the examination of the measurement scores to identify specific skill strengths, skill weaknesses, and patterns or trends of errors. Change is the modification of instructional strategies to bring about positive change in students' reading.

All four factors work together to constitute a complete diagnosis, which I define as follows.

> Diagnosis is an ongoing procedure that involves continuous analysis of students' behavior, measurement of samples of their behavior, careful evaluation of the measurement results, and change of instructional strategies that results in positive change of students' behavior.

This definition of diagnosis contains six important concepts:

1. *Ongoing Procedure.* To be effective, diagnosis must be a constant procedure. All reading behavior provides information that can be used to diagnose strengths and weaknesses. Teachers should view each reading session as an opportunity for diagnosis of needs and remediation of difficulties.
2. *Continuous Analysis.* Throughout each reading period, a teacher must listen to and observe children's reading behaviors and be aware of any general problems or weaknesses. Teachers need to analyze continually children's attitudes toward reading, their view of reading, the language clues children use or ignore, the integration of skills in actual reading, and similar reading behaviors.
3. *Sample Measurement.* Once a possible problem area has been identified, the teacher must be able to create an informal as-

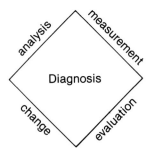

FIGURE 8–2
Diagnosis as a four-sided concept

sessment tool or to use a preconstructed test to measure the child's degree of weakness. The teacher should make an effort to test as large a sample of skills as possible to gain an accurate measure of what the child knows and what the child needs.

4. *Evaluation of Results*. Using the sample measurements, the teacher should analyze the results carefully to ascertain specific skill needs, specific skill strengths, specific error trends or error patterns, and seriousness or urgency of errors and error patterns.

5. *Change in Instructional Strategies*. If a child has failed in one instructional setting, the failure must be due at least in part to the instructional strategies used. For remediation to be successful, the instructional strategies used in the past *must be changed*. The way in which the material was originally presented must be modified to meet more closely the needs of the child.

6. *Change in Student's Behavior*. If instruction is modified to meet more closely the needs of the child, instruction will be more successful and the child's pattern of failure will be changed to one of success.

This definition of diagnosis has clear implications for any classroom setting. The following example shows how the definition can be translated in practical use.

Eian is a seven-year-old boy in the first semester of first grade. He repeated his kindergarten year because he showed no progress in reading readiness. Ms. Payne is his first-grade teacher.

Ongoing Procedure

During the first month of first grade, Ms. Payne noted that Eian still had difficulty instantly recognizing several letters and letter sounds. It was generally difficult for him to identify beginning sounds, to rhyme, and to blend isolated sounds into whole words.

Continuous Analysis

Once actual reading instruction began, Ms. Payne noted that Eian had great difficulty learning letter sounds and used no phonic knowledge to guess at words. For example, Eian would see the word *will* and say "go," or he would see the word *the* and say "she." However, Eian could easily recognize his name in print and knew the words *school*, *McDonald's*, and *street* by memory. Eian had a great zest for learning, but after the first month of school be began to be more quiet and withdrawn.

Sample Measurement

After the first month of phonic instruction, Eian still experienced no success. At this point Ms. Payne decided to test Eian. She constructed the following very simple tests.

   Naming the letters of the alphabet
   Producing the letter sounds
   Auditory discrimination test (For this test she took pairs of words like *hat/hate*, *bed/bad*, *press/dress*, *mitt/met*. She said them to Eian and asked him to indicate whether the pairs were the same or different.)
   Auditory segmentation and blending (For this test she segmented words, such as /h/-/a/-/t/ and /st/-/o/-/p/, and asked Eian to blend the sounds into a whole word.)
   Visual-form memory (For this test she taught Eian five meaningful words by sight: *boy*, *cat*, *dog*, *girl*, and *chair*.)

Evaluation of Results

The results showed that
   Eian knew 20 letter names.
   Eian knew the sounds represented by the letters *b*, *d*, *f*, *g*, *c*, *k*, *m*, *n*, *p*, *r*, and *s*.
   Eian's auditory discrimination was weak, particularly for the vowel sounds.
   Eian could not blend any segmented words.
   Eian learned four of five sight words and retained the words over an instructional session.
Based on the results, Ms. Payne concluded that Eian had very weak or underdeveloped auditory skills, but his visual skills were quite good. She realized that she was using a strong phonic-based reading program and since phonics demands strong auditory abilities, she knew that Eian would not be successful unless she made some adjustments.

Change in Instructional Strategies

Ms. Payne made some necessary modifications in her reading program. Although Eian still received practice in letters and letter sounds, he also received strong sight-vocabulary instruction. The sight words were always high in meaning, and when high-frequency structure words were introduced they were always paired with meaningful words, such as "*the* man" or "*in* a house" or "*my* name." In addition, once a week Ms. Payne taught a language experience lesson to Eian's reading group, and after the lesson each child received a copy of the story to take home and practice each weekend.

Change in Student's Behavior

Eian is now in the fourth month of first grade. He still does not know all his sounds, particularly the vowel sounds. He still has great difficulty with auditory discrimination and segmentation. But Eian is reading well in his reading group. He has a strong sight vocabulary. He loves to read, and once in a while he will correctly sound out a word and grin from ear to ear at his success.

His teacher has exemplified the definition of diagnosis in her treatment of Eian.

Informal diagnosis is highly dependent on teacher observation and analysis of pupils' reading performance. This process must be a continuous part of reading instruction. As children read daily in their reading groups or in content-area settings, teachers should analyze their reading, diagnose strengths and weaknesses, and use this information to plan appropriate instructional and remedial activities.

The Informal Reading Inventory

One of the most effective informal diagnostic tools is the informal reading inventory (IRI). Informal inventories are often used to determine where children should be placed initially in graded reading series and to analyze children's general reading strategies. Informal inventories are composed of reading passages of between fifty and two hundred words taken from graded reading series. Sets of between six and ten comprehension questions follow each passage. The questions generally address details, main ideas, inferences, evaluation, cause and effect, and vocabulary. These inventories often include word lists of between ten and twenty sight words that accompany each graded passage. Typically, children read the vocabulary items and passages and answer the assigned questions. Teachers keep a record of the errors children make, analyze the errors, and deter-

Informal reading inventories are useful in helping teachers initially to place children within a reading series.

mine children's placement within the series. Many basal series provide an IRI for placing children in the series.

There are also many published informal reading inventories that can be used to ascertain children's general reading levels and to provide information relevant to initial group placement. Some informal inventories are:

Analytical Reading Inventory
Charles E. Merrill, 1981

Silvaroli Classroom Reading Inventory
William C. Brown, 1979

Ekwall Reading Inventory
Allyn and Bacon, 1979

Sucher-Allred Reading Placement Inventory
Economy Company, 1973

Basic Reading Inventory
Kendall/Hunt, 1978

Contemporary Classroom Inventory
Gorsuch, Scarisbrick, 1980

Informal Reading Assessment Tests
Houghton Mifflin, 1980

Although published inventories are available, many teachers prefer to prepare their own tests for use with their specific basal or content-area series. This can easily be done using the following steps.

Preparing an Informal Reading Inventory

To prepare an IRI, you need a series of graded texts. Try to obtain texts two grade levels above and below your current grade assignment because you will most likely have a wide range of readers in your classroom.

Step 1. Choose a reading selection of between fifty (for grade 1) and two hundred (for grade 6) words from the middle of each text. The passage should make sense in isolation. You will need one copy of each selection for each student and as many copies for yourself as there are students so you can record each child's reading.

Step 2. Count and record the number of words in each sample.

Step 3. Prepare between six and ten comprehension questions for each selection. Include a variety of questions to assess different levels of comprehension (factual, inferential, vocabulary, cause and effect, evaluative).

Administering the Informal Reading Inventory

The Informal Reading Inventory is administered to each child individually. To administer the IRI, start the child reading in a passage approximately two years below his or her estimated reading level. This ensures success at the start of the test. Then take the following steps.

Step 1. Briefly provide a context for reading the selection. For example, you might say to the child, "The passage you are about to read is about a young boy with a problem. Read to find out what his problem is."

Step 2. Have each child read the selection orally.

Step 3. As the child reads, accurately record the errors on your copy. If the child encounters an unknown word, encourage him or her to try it out. Wait a few seconds and then provide the word. It is helpful to have a clear and consistent marking system to record oral reading errors. A suggested recording system is as follows.

Substitutions: Write the substituted word above the correct word.

can
The man lifted his cane.

Omissions: Circle the omitted word.

The man lifted (his) cane.

Additions: Insert a caret and write the word.

long
The man lifted his ∧cane.

Hesitations: Place a slash mark before the word in question.

The man lifted his / cane.

Unknown word: Place a *P* above the word you had to pronounce for the child.

P
The man lifted his cane.

Repetitions: Underline the repeated word or phrase.

The man lifted <u>his cane.</u>

Self-corrections: Mark original error then place a (c) above the error.

©
The man lifted (his) <u>cane.</u>

Mispronunciations of names of people and places or pronunciations that reflect the child's dialect are not usually counted as errors.

Step 4. After the child has read the passage and you have recorded the errors, ask comprehension questions and record the child's responses.

Analyzing Oral Reading

The IRI places a child at one of three reading levels:

1. The independent reading level, at which the child scores

    98% or above on vocabulary
    90% or above on comprehension

2. The instructional reading level, at which the child scores

    90% to 97% on vocabulary
    70% to 89% on comprehension

3. The frustration reading level, at which the child scores

89% and below on vocabulary
50% and below on comprehension

The passage on which the child scores at the instructional level indicates the appropriate level for placement within the series.

Miscue Analysis Not only does the IRI provide information useful in placing children in texts at appropriate levels, but it also provides valuable insights into children's reading strategies. These insights are gained by analyzing children's oral reading errors and ascertaining their areas of strength and weakness. Such an analysis of errors is commonly referred to as *miscue analysis*, a term made popular by Goodman and Burke (1972) and one that assumes a prominent role in psycholinguistic applications in reading. One of the most important contributions that miscue analysis has made to the field of reading instruction is the concept that not all miscues are qualitatively the same; some are more significant than others. A miscue is viewed as significant if it results in loss of meaning. It is not significant if it retains the meaning of the passage. Given the sentence "The boy ran quickly down the road," the child who reads "The boy ran quickly down the *street*" has certainly made a miscue; but the meaning of the sentence is intact and the miscue therefore is not significant. It indicates that the child is attending to the meaning of the text. On the other hand, the child who reads "The boy ran quickly down the *rad*" has made a significant miscue because it has destroyed the meaning of the sentence. If the child does not correct the miscue, the child is probably not attending to meaning. Miscue analysis provides teachers with a valuable tool for evaluating the quality of students' errors.

In analyzing miscues, there are four important questions teachers should ask.

1. How well does the child use phonic information during reading? If the child said /rid/ for *ride* and /fum/ for *fume*, he or she knows initial and final consonants and uses them appropriately. But he or she does not use the final *e* construction.
2. How well does the child use syntactic information during reading? The text says, "The boy looked sadly to the right." The child reads, "The boy looked *slowly* to the right." In this case, the miscue is syntactically acceptable because it is syntactically similar to the text (both words are adverbs). If the child reads "The boy looked *sound* to the right," not only does the sentence lose meaning but the miscue is syntactically unacceptable because it is grammatically different from the text.

3. How well does the child use semantic information during reading? The text reads, "The day was very cold." The child reads, "The day was *quite* cold." In this instance, the miscue has not significantly changed the meaning of the text. On the other hand, if the child reads, "The day *wasn't* very cold," the meaning of the text has been dramatically changed.

4. How well does the child monitor reading and correct miscues without being prompted? If a child corrects his or her errors, the child is attending to meaning.

Analysis of miscues helps teachers determine the type of instructional and remedial work each child needs. The child who uses some phonic information but little syntactic and semantic information could benefit from extensive work in using context clues in conjunction with phonic information. The child who uses syntactic and semantic information well but ignores phonic information may need phonic instruction in whole-language settings. The child who fails to correct errors needs to be continually asked the question "Does that make sense?" and needs to be encouraged to use context and phonics to make sense of print.

Analyzing Comprehension

As the child answers the questions at the end of each passage, the teacher should analyze the type of questions answered correctly and incorrectly. Does the child tend to fail on vocabulary, factual, inferential, predictive, evaluative, or cause-and-effect questions? Does the child establish a success or failure pattern in comprehension? This information can be used to guide specific instruction in the strategies the child lacks.

Strange (1980) proposed one useful scheme for understanding possible causes for children's miscomprehension. He identifies seven major classes of errors:

1. *No existing schemata*. Children lack appropriate schemata (concepts) for understanding content.
2. *Naive schemata*. Children have underdeveloped or insufficient schemata for understanding.
3. *No new information*. The text provided no new information, and consequently the child is bored and inattentive.
4. *Poor story or passage*. The passage was poorly written and thus failed to activate children's existing schemata.
5. *Many schemata appropriate*. The material may be ambiguous or open to several interpretations.

6. *Schemata intrusion.* Children's existing schemata block compre-hension, resulting in responses that have little or no relation to the text.
7. *Textual intrusion.* Children focus on irrelevant, incidental, or unimportant segments of the text and fail to attend to critical elements.

When teachers have identified the sources of miscomprehension, they can assist children in acquiring the schemata necessary for understanding.

Children and Reading Difficulties

Classifications

Although principles of diagnosis can be applied in varying degrees to every child, children who are experiencing difficulty in reading are most dependent on the teacher's expertise in diagnosing their problems. Such children are often identified as fitting into one of four basic categories: (1) reading disabled, (2) underachiever in reading, (3) specific reading deficiency, or (4) limited reading ability.

Reading Disabled   Many children whose performance in reading is significantly below their capacity for learning to read often have average or above-average intelligence and perform adequately in other school subjects. Despite what seems to be appropriate instruction and often long-term remediation in reading, they fail to make expected progress in reading and continue reading two or more years below grade level. These children are often viewed as reading disabled.

Underachievers   Underachievers in reading are children who read adequately according to their age and grade placement but whose performance is below their reading capacity. Reading capacity is a measure of the level of reading performance one can expect from a child given his or her chronological age and mental and intellectual development. Among the formulas for calculating reading capacity or expectancy, perhaps the best known is the Harris formula (Harris and Sipay, 1980). In the following formula, MA = mental age and CA = chronological age.

$$\text{Reading expectancy age} = \frac{2(\text{MA}) + \text{CA}}{3}.$$

Mental age is calculated by the formula

$$MA = \frac{IQ \times CA}{100}.$$

For example, a child who is ten years old, beginning fifth grade, with an IQ of 120 would be said to have a mental age of

$$\frac{120 \times 10}{100} = \frac{1200}{100} = 12.0 \text{ years.}$$

In turn, that child's reading expectancy would be

$$\frac{2(MA) + CA}{3} = \frac{2(12) + 10}{3} = \frac{24 + 10}{3} = \frac{34}{3} = 11.3 \text{ years.}$$

Some educators suggest that to transform the reading expectancy age to a grade level, one should subtract 5.2, because children usually start kindergarten at about five years and two or three months. The reading expectancy age of 11.3, therefore, would yield a grade level of 11.3 − 5.2 = 6.1. This child would be expected to be reading at the sixth-grade level even though she or he is currently in the fifth grade. If the child is reading at the fifth-grade level, one could label such a child an underachiever in reading.

The Harris formula is one of many expectancy formulas, and results will vary from formula to formula. It is important that teacheres be aware of this variation and realize that reading capacity is simply a score derived from a formula and should not be a tool used to categorize or label children. (Teachers are urged to view the concept of reading capacity in a very flexible manner since it is doubtful that a formula can accurately indicate the true potential of the human mind.)

Specific Reading Deficiencies   This term refers to children who have relatively well developed overall or general reading skills but who experience marked difficulty in one or more specific skills. Often, for example, children may have average word recognition and word analysis skills for their grade placement but are noticeably weak in comprehension skills. They may not require the intensive intervention programs that the disabled reader does, but their deficiencies need to be identified and systematically remediated by the teacher.

Limited Reading Ability   Some children demonstrate poor reading skills because they have slow learning rates. They may have limited intellectual capacity, which results in a reading level below their grade placement. They often require significantly more practice and re-teaching than other children of their chronological age.

Regardless of the category in which children with reading problems fall, one fact is clear — they all require ongoing diagnosis and thoughtful, effective remediation. Teachers are urged not to place too much emphasis on fitting children into categories. If a child is not making appropriate progress in reading, for whatever reason, the most important response is not to categorize or label the child but to modify instruction immediately to establish and maintain progress.

The single most important characteristic of an effective reading program is the ability to promote progress in children. It matters little where the child performs at the onset of reading instruction. What matters is that day by day and session by session each child becomes slightly more proficient at learning to read.

Causes of Reading Difficulties

Learning to read is a very complex process, and many factors contribute to its success. Similarly, failure in reading is often a result of several contributing factors. Some of the factors we discussed in Chapter 5 as contributing to reading readiness are also relevant to our discussion here of reading difficulties.

We can visualize a child's learning as being affected by constitutional, intellectual, environmental, emotional, and educational factors (see Figure 8–3). Each factor can both positively and negatively affect learning to read. As these factors are discussed, remember that they have direct implications for both prevention and remediation of problems.

Constitutional Factors Constitutional factors are factors within the physiological functioning of the child. They include auditory, visual, and language factors.

1. *Auditory Factors.* Auditory discrimination is the ability to hear similarities and differences among sounds. This skill is vital to reading because the learning of phonics focuses on the ability to associate letters and combinations of letters with sounds and to distinguish differences between sounds. Discrimination is of even greater importance in learning isolated phonics, that is, phonic information outside the flow of connected discourse. If children are weak in auditory discrimination skills and they are expected to learn to read primarily through phonic analysis, they can be expected to fail.

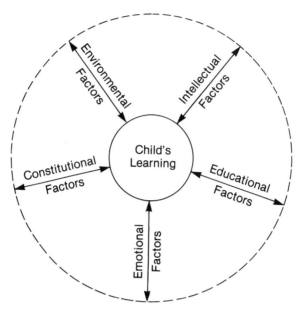

FIGURE 8–3
Factors that affect a child's learning

Auditory segmentation is the ability to segment speech — /m/ + /a/ + /t/; feed each segment in order into memory; blend the segments into a whole — /m/ + /a/ + /t/ = *mat*; and retrieve the whole word from memory. Auditory segmentation abilities are essential to the task of blending, a major skill in phonic instruction. Children who are unable to segment auditorally will probably fail in a strict phonic approach to reading.

Auditory acuity refers to the keenness of a person's hearing. Reading is somewhat dependent on the ability to hear differences and similarities among sounds. Children who experience severe hearing losses may encounter serious difficulty in learning to read, particularly in an auditory-dependent program such as phonics. It is important that children be given a thorough auditory acuity check before they enter school.

2. *Visual Factors.* Visual discrimination is the ability to recognize and identify differences and similarities among visual stimuli such as letters, words, and phrases. Visual discrimination is necessary to differentiate between forms like *b* and *d*, *p* and *q*, *c* and *o*, *bat* and *bad*, or *tell* and *tall*. Children with visual discrimination problems may need one or a combination of the following strategies:

Training in left-to-right directionality: *d* and *b*

Training in tracing words and letters

A strong kinesthetic component added to the reading program, such as writing, tracing, using sandpaper letters and words

Emphasis on meaning and using context to facilitate reading

Instruction in phonic analysis if auditory skills are strong

Instruction in structural analysis

Focus on larger language units like words rather than on smaller units like letters and sounds because more meaningful units are more easily processed than less meaningful ones

It would probably make sense to stay away from programs that demand strong visual skills, such as linguistic programs.

Visual acuity refers to the keenness of a person's vision. Since reading is somewhat of a visual art, undetected visual problems can certainly create difficulties in reading. Prior to entering school and periodically throughout their school years, children should have thorough vision checks.

3. *Language Factors.* Historically, research has shown a relationship between language development and reading (DeHirsch, Jansky, and Lanford, 1966; Monroe, 1951). Children who are slow in language development or who have difficulty in speech production, sentence structure, or vocabulary often experience difficulty in reading, particularly in reading with comprehension. Such children often need exposure to reading material that is highly meaningful and relevant to their own experiences. They also require instruction that focuses on vocabulary, experience, and concept building prior to reading, and they need much verbal interaction as they learn.

Intellectual Factors   Discussions about the relationship between intelligence and reading can be most frustrating. Research into this relationship has produced inconclusive results. One reason for the lack of clear results is that the extent of the relationship is highly dependent on the definition of reading one uses. If one defines reading as the decoding of combinations of letters into sounds, then the relationship to intelligence is not significant because individuals who have significantly below-average IQ's have successfully been taught to "read" relatively well this way. If, however, reading is defined as interaction with print through critical, creative, and evaluative thinking, then the relationship with intelligence is unquestionable. This in no way means that children with below-average IQ

To ensure that undetected visual problems are not the source of reading difficulties, children should have their vision checked before they enter school and periodically throughout their school years.

scores should not be expected to think critically, creatively, and evaluatively. These skills can and should be taught to all children.

In addition, the entire notion of intelligence must be kept in perspective. Children vary in their intellectual abilities, and some are obviously more talented than others. But it would be wise for teachers to internalize the statement made more than fifty years ago by Boring (1923): "Intelligence as a measurable capacity must at the start be defined as the capacity to do well on an intelligence test." Green (1975) sums up the IQ controversy well: "First of all, I.Q. is not a synonym for intelligence. The I.Q., intelligence quotient, simply represents a numerical score earned on a test. That test does not measure the broad range of experience encompassed by all intellectual functions." It is a well-accepted fact that one's IQ score can be affected by training. Low IQ scores, therefore, may not necessarily reflect inability to learn but rather deficits in knowledge and reasoning that may be positively affected by experience, exposure, and instruction.

Children with below-average IQ scores may need more thorough instruction, more practice, and more attention to vocabulary and concept building. They also require more exposure to and training in critical thinking, problem solving, prediction making, creative thinking, and inferential thinking skills. Reading must be taught as an active thinking process.

Environmental Factors   Many factors within the environment of children can contribute to reading failure. Some of the factors are socioeconomic background, high mobility, and parents' attitude.

Some children who live in economically deprived environments fail in reading. In many of these homes there may not be adequate financial resources to provide material such as books, reading games, magazines, or experiences such as visits to the library, the zoo, museums, and so on. Such experiences heighten children's interest in reading and provide needed exposure to experiences valued by schools. When economically disadvantaged children enter school, therefore, they may not possess the experiences or knowledge vital to reading readiness.

Many families change their residences frequently. The children in such families must adjust to different locations, different peers, different teachers, different reading texts, and different instructional strategies. For children who are quick to adjust, who have relatively fast learning rates, and who find learning to read manageable, high mobility may not negatively affect their reading performance. For children who adjust slowly, who have moderate-to-slow learning rates, and who experience difficulty in learning to read, high mobility may be a contributing factor in reading failure.

The attitudes of parents can affect children's learning. If parents do not value learning and reading, chances are that they will not encourage and motivate their children. If children are not read to at home, are not provided with books or reading material, are not given school-valued experiences, and are not encouraged to learn, they may not value reading and may not be motivated to learn. Likewise, parents who are overanxious about their children's academic achievements and who constantly pressure them to excel in school may foster negative responses in their children and cause them to underachieve or to fail in reading.

Emotional Factors   Emotional factors can affect children's reading performance. Reading is an interactive process that involves communication between a writer and a reader. As in all communication, emotional factors, such as fear of making an error or tension and anxiety, can inhibit performance.

If a child is overconcerned about making errors in reading, he or she will focus attention on the accurate pronunciation of print and will not attend sufficiently to comprehension. Over time this will result in "word calling," not meaning acquisition.

Many children experience tension when faced with the reading task. The tension may stem from fear of failure, frustration at inappropriate material, knowledge of inferior reading skills, feelings of inadequacy stemming from slow progress, or embarrassment at poor reading before peers. This tension can easily be detected by a sensitive teacher. When such children are asked to read orally, they tend to assume rigid postures, constantly move their hands or legs nervously, move uncomfortably in their chairs, read either laboriously slowly or too quickly, paying little attention to meaning, or get progressively louder and higher in pitch as they read. The longer children are allowed to read orally while displaying these symptoms, the more likely that reading failure, particularly in comprehension, will occur. It is important that teachers be sensitive to children's emotions during reading. If they notice symptoms of tension, they should reassure the children that they can succeed, model reading for the children, give them practice in real reading, and provide successful reading experiences.

Educational Factors   Often reading failure has its origins in inappropriate instructional strategies. Many children become failures in reading because for extended periods of time they are exposed to teaching strategies from which they could not learn, and instruction was not modified to meet their needs. These are the only factors over which teachers have total control. Six important factors are given below.

1. *Beginning reading instruction before children are ready to learn.* Chapters 4 and 5 considered the importance of conceptual readiness. Before any skill or content is taught, children must be conceptually reading for learning. Each skill, story, article, and so on demands a certain level of prior knowledge. Before children learn the skill of syllabication, for example, they need to be able to hear and respond to the rhythm of oral language; prior to learning sequencing skills, they must internalize concepts such as "first," "next," "then," and "last." Similarly, before children read a story set on an Indian reservation, they must be exposed to concepts related to Indian life, values, and so on. Attempting to instruct children in skills or content before they are conceptually ready is a major cause of reading failure.

2. *Failure to adapt existing programs to the needs of children.* It has been argued throughout this text that modification is imperative in reading instruction. Each instructional packet was designed with a particular audience in mind. Each series has a specific set of prerequisites. If material is used with children who do not have the prerequisites, then the failure of those children is certain. Teachers who insist on teaching programs rather than on teaching children force many children into failure. If a teacher instructs children using a strong phonic program, children who have underdeveloped auditory discrimination or auditory segmentation and blending skills will no doubt fail unless the teacher modifies the program by using sight vocabulary instruction or language immersion strategies. Failure to modify programs to meet children's needs results in the failure of many children to learn to read.

3. *Failure to use material of an appropriate level of difficulty.* Often children are instructed in reading with material that is too difficult for them. This results in frustration and failure. On the other hand, instructing children with material that is too easy perpetrates failure because it does not allow their reading skills to grow. It is important that teachers use material written on children's instructional levels, which means that the material is neither simple enough to be read well independently nor difficult enough to cause frustration. The instructional level assumes that prior to instruction children will not know all the words or ideas necessary for total success; but the teacher's instruction will compensate for what the children do not know and will fill in the gaps in their knowledge, thus making learning successful. Manning (1980) views the instructional level as that level at which children, with the assistance of the teacher, continue to respond aggressively to print using all learned phonic, semantic, and syntactic decoding strategies, in spite of the fact that they occasionally meet with failure.

4. *Failure to acknowledge the difference between skill instruction and reading instruction.* Throughout this text we have argued that skill instruction and reading instruction are not identical. Certainly, they overlap a great deal; but it is a mistake to assume that when isolated skills are being taught, "reading" is being taught. Skill instruction focuses on the weaknesses of children — what they do not know. Reading instruction focuses on children's strengths and on their acquaintance with multiple clues in language, that is, with semantics, syntax, and phonics. Skill instruction helps children *learn* skills. Reading instruction helps children *use* skills. There is no other reason for children to learn skills but to use them in actual reading. Programs that lock children in a spiraling pattern of skill instruction and underplay actual reading invariably force children who have difficulty

learning skills into a pattern of failure. Some children will simply not learn isolated skills until they have been taught to read.

5. *Failure to differentiate between qualitative and quantitative errors.* One of the most unfortunate and detrimental practices in reading instruction is the habit of viewing all errors as negative. Errors must happen in all learning. They indicate both strengths and weaknesses. A child who sees the word *bench* and says "bent" certainly has made an error. That error tells us that the child does *not* know the word *bench* as a sight word and the /ch/ sound; but it also tells us that the child *does* know the beginning consonant sound /b/, the vowel sound /e/, the sound /n/, and the syllable *ben*. The child has a significant knowledge base on which to build in remediation.

In addition, teachers often wrongly focus on the *number* of errors rather than the *quality* of errors. When we discussed diagnostic testing, we made the point that simply knowing the number of errors tells us nothing of diagnostic or remedial value. Two children may have taken the same word recognition test and received the same score: 5 of 10 correct. The words tested were *break, many, start, them, plate, wouldn't, between, rest,* and *fact.* Child 1 made the following errors:

"beck" for *break*
"sat" for *start*
"pate" for *plate*
"ret" for *rest*
"fat" for *fact*

Child 2 made the following errors:

"man" for *many*
"breck" for *break*
"then" for *them*
"plat" for *plate*
"fas" for *fact*

Although both children made the same quantity of errors, the quality of those errors is significantly different, and the two kinds of errors require totally different interpretations. Child 1 knows beginning and ending single consonants but does not know single vowels, vowel combinations, or consonant combinations. Child 2 knows initial single consonants, initial consonant combinations, and short vowel sounds but needs practice with ending sounds, vowel combinations, and long vowels. Categorizing these children as the same based on the number of errors and providing the same remediation would result in little growth and, ultimately, failure.

6. *Failure to view reading as a thinking process.* Many reading programs not only focus on isolated skill instruction but also emphasize factual, literal comprehension and minimize critical thinking, creative thinking, inferential thinking, and problem-solving skills. Such programs produce children with minimal comprehension skills. Focusing on memorization of details rather than on thinking and comprehension from the earliest stages of reading instruction will result in failure in processing and understanding print.

Remediation Techniques

Many factors contribute to children's failure in reading. Becoming aware of these factors and constantly modifying techniques to meet the needs of children can change failure patterns to success. This text has presented and explained instructional strategies, most of which are important in remediation. The term *remediation* often makes teachers think of a formalized prescription of skills based on a formal diagnosis. *Actually, remediation is simply the systematic modification of instruction based on ongoing observation and analysis of reading behavior.* This process necessarily involves the discontinuation of strategies that do not work and the implementation of strategies that do work to ensure children's progress in reading.

Basic Principles

Five principles are essential to the success of remedial efforts:

1. *Remediation must focus on the individual.* To be effective, remediation must begin with the specific needs of each student. Often teachers concentrate so intently on teaching a program or a set of instructional materials that they try to modify the child's learning style to meet the demands of the materials. Remediation must focus on modifying the materials to meet the needs of the child. It is the child's needs that should dictate the type of material to be used. The child with weak auditory skills needs sight-word and visual patterning materials. The child with low visual discrimination needs auditory analysis and meaning-oriented programs.

2. *Skill instruction must be child specific.* We have seen that children whose performance looks the same based on numbers of errors may actually have totally different skill needs. Remedial programs

that insist that all children progress together through a given skill sequence ignore the needs of many children, forcing some to repeat previously learned skills and to receive no instruction in skills they need. Remediation must respond to the specific needs of each child and focus on meeting individual needs.

3. *Remediation should involve much actual reading of connected discourse.* The goal of all remedial instruction must be helping children to actually read realistic material more proficiently. Real reading, therefore, must be the foundation of all remediation. Children who read poorly need to read more, not less. The more they practice reading, the better they will learn to read.

4. *Remediation must be provided on each child's instructional level.* If the material is too difficult, children will be too frustrated to learn and will fail. If the material is too easy, their reading skills cannot grow, but they will continue to read at their existing level. Teaching at the child's instructional level requires direct teaching and teacher-pupil interaction. Because of the high interaction demands, it is unlikely that remedial programs will be successful if the reading component is individualized and children spend most of their time working independently without the instruction of the teacher. In an individualized situation teachers do not have sufficient time to instruct each child. As a result, children in these programs are often placed below their instructional levels because material must be easy enough to be handled independently. It is more productive for teachers to arrange small groups for the actual interactive instruction and to place children in groups according to their levels. The skills component of a reading program requires individualization because it is unlikely that all children will have identical skill needs.

5. *Remediation must be carried out at an appropriate pace.* Teachers of remedial reading programs often make the mistake of believing that, because children have somewhat slow learning rates, instruction should be given slowly and methodically. Consequently, they often choose one skill and teach it slowly in the same way for one instructional period. If it were possble to stand back and objectively view such a lesson, we would see it as a repetitive, boring, routinized, and motionless time frame in which the attention and interest of children is lost almost immediately. Interestingly enough, the worst thing for a slow child is slow instruction. Slow children need motivating, fast-paced instruction that captures their attention and forces interaction. The alternative to slow teaching is not superficial, rushed teaching, however. It is thorough but diversified instruction; teaching the same skill, in several different ways, using visual, auditory, and kinesthetic modalities in one instructional setting.

Components for Success

The strategies we have presented for effective reading instruction, although essential to the instruction of all children, are mandatory for the success of remedial readers. An effective reading lesson for remedial readers should include the following components.

I. Preparation for and motivation toward reading (see Chapter 4)
   A. Vocabulary preinstruction
      1. Necessary sight words
      2. Necessary meaning vocabulary
   B. Concept preparation
      1. Alerting children to essential concepts
      2. Relating essential concepts to children's experiences
   C. Content preparation
      1. Overviews
      2. Predicting content, listing the predictions, and reading to check predictions
      3. Prereading questions

II. Reading and interacting (see Chapter 7)
   A. Varied forms of oral reading
      1. Echoic reading
      2. Paired reading
      3. Readers' theater
      4. Choral reading
      5. Prepared reading
   B. Silent reading
      1. Silent reading passages matched to individual children; weaker children assigned shorter, less complicated passages
      2. As competence in reading increases, silent reading increases
   C. Emphasis on questioning
      1. All children encouraged to interact verbally
      2. Questions used to teach children thinking skills, not to test children on content
      3. Variety of questions used to build skills in critical thinking, creative thinking, inferential thinking, problem solving, and prediction (see Chapter 4)
      4. Questions placed at varying points during reading — before reading to guide comprehension, during reading to encourage thinking, after reading to extend appreciation and comprehension

       5. Children encouraged to support their responses with specific information from the text

III. Skill instruction
  A. Skills individual-specific; skills should reflect the needs of each child
  B. Skills taken from children's actual reading errors, not as prescribed by the materials
  C. Children first conceptually prepared for skills; skills introduced in whole, meaningful language (see Chapter 6)
  D. Children given immediate practice in skills using real reading material so skill instruction transfers to reading situations

IV. Extension of reading
  A. Vocabulary extension (see Chapter 7)
  B. Plot analysis (see Chapters 4 and 7)
  C. Character analysis (see Chapter 7)
  D. Brainstorming for building critical thinking and problem solving (see Chapter 4)

It should be clear how closely diagnosis and remediation are interrelated. Diagnosis must direct remediation and remediation must involve constant diagnosis. In addition, remediation is an ongoing procedure that is difficult to separate from instruction. The aim in all reading instruction should be to extend and develop children's competence in reading and to remediate their problems continually. Diagnosis and remediation, therefore, should be permanent and ongoing activities within all classrooms.

An Instructional Model

One instructional model that incorporates all the components of a successful remediation lesson is the Basic Instructional Sequence, created by John Manning (1980).

The Basic Instructional Sequence is an eight-step teaching sequence designed to provide thorough reading instruction for children who need remediation. The sequence is intended to be applied to self-contained material, such as a story or an article.

The purposes of the sequence are to provide thorough instruction in vocabulary and phrase units, ensure the success of children, ensure the growth of children's reading skills, provide for trimodal instruction, and provide instructional directions for teachers.

The eight steps are as follows.

1. Review
2. Introduction to new vocabulary
3. Introduction to new phrases
4. Preparation for reading
5. Oral reading

> For diagnosis
> For instruction
> For practice

6. Silent reading with an emphasis on comprehension
7. Skill instruction
8. Enrichment

Step 1: Review. Rationale: Children forget rapidly. They need repeated review. In addition, because learning to read is an accumulation of skills, insights, and knowledge, some information taught yesterday is important to today's learning.

Before starting a new lesson, children need to be reminded of prior knowledge that may be important, in the form of words, phrases, vocabulary, skills, or concepts. A review provides for children a frame of reference from which to begin new learning. It also orients children's attention to a new learning task.

Step 2: Introduction to New Vocabulary. Rationale: If children are being instructed on their instructional level, the teacher can assume that the children will not know certain vocabulary items in the text. Success at the instructional level depends on the teacher's providing instruction in new vocabulary before reading begins.

Before presenting a lesson, teachers should read the selection and identify the vocabulary that should be pretaught to the children. Care must be taken to choose the most useful and essential vocabulary and to identify an appropriate number of items so as not to go beyond the children's learning rate. Vocabulary should be presented trimodally — orally, visually, and kinesthetically — and children should be able to identify each word automatically before they proceed to step 3. A detailed explanation of Manning's vocabulary presentation was provided in Chapter 6, pages 147–148.

Step 3: Introduction to New Phrases. Rationale: One predictable reading pattern of poor readers is word-by-word reading. Teachers often teach children, particularly poorer readers, word by word, or worse, word part by word part. In addition, teachers often accept children's word-by-word reading and make no effort to correct the children's reading style and help them read more fluently.

Phrase instruction requires that teachers identify in the text the phrases that include the vocabulary items from step 2. If the word *basement* was chosen for instruction in step 2, the phrase that contains it in the text — say, "to the basement door" — should be identified and taught. Phrase instruction fulfills many purposes. It builds fluency, it provides additional practice in vocabulary, it provides for incidental learning, it provides more language from which to build anticipation or predictions from print, and it provides children with confidence as they meet prelearned phrases in the text.

Step 4: Preparation for Reading. Rationale: Reading is interaction between the reader and the print. It is dependent on the interest the reader has in the text and the prior knowledge the reader has about the concepts and content of the text.

Before reading instruction takes place, the teacher must conceptually prepare children for the text and encourage them to predict and anticipate meaning from the text. The title, pictures, subheadings, and phrases can all be used to help children predict the content of the material. In addition, a combination of introductory activities (see Chapter 7) can be used to prepare children for reading.

Step 5: Oral Reading. Rationale: Particularly in the early stages of reading, oral reading is essential for identifying children's reading strengths and weaknesses and for assessing the skills that the children are using or not using in their reading. Oral reading is often grossly misused and, as a result, it reinforces children's bad habits and develops patterns of reading failure. Oral reading should be used for diagnosis, instruction, and practice.

Teachers should use children's oral reading as a tool for assessing their skill needs. As children read, the teacher should record and analyze their errors. Teachers may wish to keep a small notebook for each group and to record errors in some way. Following is one simple method.

Date _____

Child	*Word*	*Child Said*	*Analysis*
John	in	on	sight vocab.
	them	then	sight — endings
	stop	sop	*st* comb.
	ride	rid	silent *e*
	drive	div	*dr*, silent *e*
Mary	them	the	sight vocab.
	enough	(no response)	sight vocab.
	even	(no response)	sight vocab.
	through	the	sight vocab.
	great	gret	*ea* comb.

This tool is indispensable for diagnosing and identifying children's skill needs. If oral reading for diagnosis is used daily, teachers will be able to identify patterns of errors for individual children and to provide skill instruction specific to their needs.

It is suggested that children be allowed to read orally for diagnosis only for short periods of time because this strategy allows them to read aloud poorly, thus reinforcing bad reading habits. The chart on page 242 is an example of an oral reading report form that can be used to record and analyze oral reading errors.

Once diagnostic reading is completed, oral instructional reading should begin. For children to read better, they must be instructed in appropriate reading skills, one of which is echoic reading (see Chapter 7). Echoic reading provides children with a model of good oral reading and allows them to improve their reading skills.

Children who are poor readers need much practice in reading, but the practice must reinforce good reading habits. Oral reading for practice assumes that children are reading smoothly with appropriate vocabulary and expression. If this is not the case, then oral reading for practice should be discontinued and oral instructional reading reinstated.

Step 6: Silent Reading. Rationale: The goal of all reading instruction should be to develop independent reading skills. Silent reading is therefore vital from the very early stages of reading. For remedial reading, however, silent reading should begin with short segments of one or two sentences and should be followed by questions that require children both to restate and to comprehend material. As children develop skill in silent reading, the length and complexity of the silent reading passages should be increased. Naturally, comprehension and attention to higher-level thinking skills should be the focus of silent reading.

Step 7: Skill Instruction. Rationale: As children read, they will demonstrate the skills they are not using in reading. Such skills must be identified and taught or retaught to them.

An emphasis must be placed on helping children understand skills and in ensuring transfer of skills to actual reading. For an extensive discussion of appropriate skill instruction, see Chapter 6. If the diagnostic reading segment identifies skills that are needed by entire groups of children, group skill instruction is justified. If not, individual children should be instructed in the skills they need most.

Step 8: Enrichment. Rationale: Reading involves interaction and communication. After children have read a selection, the teacher can use various strategies to extend children's comprehension and appreciation of textual material.

Any individual strategy or combination of strategies presented

ORAL READING DIAGNOSTIC REPORT

Name _____ Page(s) Read _____

Date	Word	Child Said	Oral Reading Behavior

ERROR ANALYSIS RECORD

Sight Vocabulary	Phonic Needs					Structural Analysis	
	Initial Consonants	Final Consonants	Consonant Clusters	Vowels	Base Words	Compounds Contractions	Affixes

in the section Summation Activities in Chapter 7 is appropriate as enrichment. In addition, the strategies of story form, report form, fact analyzer, and semantic webbing (Chapter 4) could all be considered enrichment activities.

The Basic Instructional Sequence provides an excellent structure for the effective instruction of a remedial reading lesson. If a reading selection is too long to be completed in one instructional period, the sequence can be divided over two class periods. The teacher can stop after step 3, step 4, step 6, or step 7. The only rule related to breaking the sequence is that each class period must begin with the review phase.

Summary

Diagnosis and remediation are overlapping concepts. Both are ongoing and continuous parts of all reading instruction. Some children will fail in reading, but failure will not persist if teachers continually monitor children's progress and immediately modify instruction to meet their needs. Teaching reading requires systematic changes in teaching strategies. Remediation is successful when teachers abandon strategies that fail children and change programs to fit children's needs rather than attempting to change children to fit existing programs.

References

Boring, E. G. "Intelligence as the Tests Measure It." *New Republic*, no. 35 (1923).

DeHirsch, K. J., J. Jansky, and W. Lanford. *Predicting Reading Failure*. New York: Harper & Row, 1966.

Goodman, K. S., Ed. *Miscue Analysis: Applications to Reading Instruction*. Champaign, Ill.: National Council of Teachers of English, 1973.

Goodman, Y., and C. Burke. *Reading Miscue Inventory: Manual-Procedure for Diagnosis and Evaluation*. New York: Macmillan, 1972.

Green, R. "Tips on Educational Testing: What Teachers and Parents Should Know." *Phi Delta Kappan*, no. 57 (October 1975).

Harris, A., and E. Sipay. *How to Increase Reading Ability*. 7th ed. New York: Longman, 1980.

Manning, J. C. *Reading: Learning and Instructional Processes*. Geneva, Ill.: Paladin House, 1980.

Monroe, M. *Growing and Reading*. Chicago: Scott, Foresman, 1951.

Strange, M. "Instructional Implications of a Conceptual Theory of Reading Comprehension." *Reading Teacher*, no. 33 (January 1980).

9

Reading and the Gifted and Creative Reader

The topic of gifted education has generated tremendous interest, particularly during the past fifteen years. There is a growing societal mandate for schools to plan adequate accelerated programs for gifted and creative learners. This trend seems to be gaining momentum in the 1980s.

We will look at gifted education in a historical perspective and then examine the teacher's role in classroom instruction of the gifted reader. Although many school districts are moving toward separate programs for the gifted and talented, we still place the major responsibility for the reading development of *all* children on the classroom teacher. Effective reading instruction of gifted readers — indeed, of all readers — rests with the teacher's ability to modify existing programs. This chapter presents several modification strategies, including content deletion, substitution, compression, and extension, as well as the AIME model, which was created to help teachers extend any basal reader into an effective program for gifted readers. Although we focus specifically on the reading instruction of gifted and creative readers, we hope to show that effective pedagogy leads to good instruction for all groups of children.

FOCUS QUESTIONS

☐   What are some characteristics of gifted readers?

☐   What are the basic differences between gifted learners and creative learners?

☐   What are some of the basic principles vital to the instruction of gifted and creative readers?

☐   What are the major methods of content modification? How is each method relevant to the reading instruction of gifted and creative readers?

☐   What are four instructional models that can be used for teaching reading to gifted learners?

Giftedness and Gifted Education

Historical Perspective

Interest in giftedness is not new. As early as 1892, Galton attracted much attention to the topic in his landmark study "Hereditary Genius: An Inquiry into Its Laws and Consequences." This was followed by Terman's renowned longitudinal study in 1947, *Genetic Studies of Genius.* As these early titles imply, the initial concern with the topic was in investigating genius, which was defined as the possession of an IQ of 170 or above. Because this early view of giftedness focused primarily on intellectual genius, IQ was the single determining factor.

By the early 1920s the overriding concern with IQ was the cause of much criticism. As a result, the concept was qualified by additions such as mentally gifted, to denote intellectual abilities; aesthetically gifted, to denote ability in the performing and fine arts; and physically gifted, to denote ability in sports and physical endeavor.

In 1958 the National Society for the Study of Education broadened the definition of the gifted child to be "one who shows superior performance in any worthwhile line of endeavor including intellectual, academic, creative, music, graphic arts, dramatics, mechanical skills and social leadership" (Getzels and Dillon, 1973).

In the 1950s a related term was introduced: *creativity.* Concern with creativity came about primarily as a result of the work of Guilford (1950). Through Guilford's efforts, creativity was seen as an extremely important trait that was somewhat related to giftedness but that contained some elements not necessarily included in intellectual giftedness. Whereas giftedness referred to superior performance in academics, arts, or leadership, creativity referred to superior divergent thinking ability, that is, thinking that is unique, flexible, unconventional, and fluent.

The 1960s and 1970s saw a heightened interest in the investigation of the home environments that produced gifted and creative children. Gordon (1970) identified the following factors as contributing to giftedness:

Parents provided many learning activities.
Parents encouraged problem-solving behaviors.
Parents provided many cultural activities.
Parents taught children how to perform tasks.
Parents placed high value on education.
Parents involved children in external learning activities such as day camp, library visits, and the like.
Parents had many books around the home.

Many homes of gifted readers provide from very early years a variety of interesting and motivating print for children. Children surrounded early by a strong print environment have a head start on becoming gifted readers.

Parents discussed many things with children.
Parents used effective vocabulary with children.

Interest in giftedness and creativity has shown consistent growth during the past decade and has steadily accelerated during the past five years (Cassidy, 1981; Polette, 1982; Swaby, 1982).

Definitions and Characteristics

For the purposes of this text, the gifted child is defined as one who shows outstanding academic abilities and/or demonstrates a high level of performance in school subjects. The creative child is defined as one who responds to problems and reacts to issues in novel, unconventional, and creative ways. For teachers to identify and meet the needs of these children, the teachers must be familiar with some dominant characteristics of each group. Renzulli, Hartman, and Callahan (1971) state that gifted children exhibit a number of the following learning characteristics.

Unusually advanced vocabulary
A large storehouse of information about a variety of topics
Quick mastery and recall of factual information
Rapid insight into cause-and-effect relationships
Provocative and constant questioning
Eagerness to find out why and how people and things tick
Ready grasp of underlying principles and ability to make valid
    generalizations
Keen and alert observation
Much independent reading
Ability to understand complicated material by separating it
    into its parts

Torrance (1969) has identified several characteristics of creative students. Among them are the following.

Intense absorption in listening, observing, or doing
Intense animation in physical involvement
Use of analogies in speech
Tendency to challenge ideas of authority
Habit of taking a close look at things
Continuing in creative activities after scheduled time for stop-
    ping
Ability to show relationships among apparently unrelated
    ideas
Intense curiosity
Habit of guessing at and testing outcomes

Ability to concentrate
Penetrating questioning
Tendency to see many alternatives and to explore new possi-
bilities

Although there are strong similarities between intellectually
gifted and creative children, they are not necessarily identical. Many
gifted children are indeed creative and many creative children are
indeed gifted. However, some gifted children are not particularly
creative thinkers and some highly creative children are not intellectually gifted. Most of the strategies presented in this chapter can be
applied to both groups of children, but it is important that teachers
recognize that the two groups do not toally overlap. The most significant feature of gifted children is their strong intellectual performance. These children must be challenged intellectually and can be
expected to read and comprehend textual material written on advanced grade levels. They should also be encouraged to develop their
creative abilities. The most significant features of creative children
are their flexibility of thought and their ability to generate unique
alternatives and novel possibilities. These children *may* not be reading
above grade level, but they must be challenged creatively and encouraged to extend their experiences and build their conceptual
backgrounds. Many creative children are misunderstood in school
settings because their intense curiosity and unusual responses are
often mistaken for willful disruptive behavior. Awareness of the characteristics of these children will help teachers to identify them better
and to assist them in the development of their creative abilities.

Key Factors in the Reading Program

Because of the learning abilities and traits of gifted and creative
children, the reading program for these children should capitalize
on the gifts they possess and expand and challenge their abilities.
Polette (1982) suggests that such a reading program should place
heavy emphasis on the following factors.

Higher cognitive levels of thought
Critical reading
Vocabulary development
Wide exposure to literature
Productive thinking
Imaginative thinking
Visualization
Exploration of values
Language arts approach

The following discussion shows how each of these factors can be applied in an actual reading program.

Higher Cognitive Levels of Thought   The most famous cognitive thinking model was created by Bloom (1956), who identified six hierarchially arranged levels of thought: knowledge, the recall of previously learned factual material; comprehension, the understanding of material; application, the ability to use information; analysis, the ability to break down material into its components; synthesis, the ability to put the parts back together to form a new whole; and evaluation, the ability to judge the value of material based on internal or external standards. A reading program for gifted and creative children should emphasize the last four levels of thought:

1. *Application:* Children should be guided to use, try, apply, diagram, operate, make, and demonstrate.
2. *Analysis:* Children should be assisted to take apart, analyze, compare and contrast, organize, simplify, categorize, and unravel material.
3. *Synthesis:* Children should be given many opportunities to improve on, compose, imagine, create, hypothesize, solve problems, brainstorm alternatives, elaborate on, and create options.
4. *Evaluation:* Children should be encouraged to make decisions, judge, justify their responses, make recommendations, criticize positions, rate material, debate issues, appraise, rank, and give and support opinions.

These four levels of thinking are encouraged primarily by exposing children to questions such as the following.

What would happen if _____?
How might the situation change if _____?
How might this have been different if _____?
If you were _____, how would you _____?
How many ways can you think of to _____?
Suppose _____. What would be the result?
What might happen next?
What if _____?
What do you predict?
How do you know that?
What in the passage leads you to believe that?
What do you think?
Do you agree? Why?
What is your opinion of _____?
How would you feel if _____?
How would you have reacted to _____?

Was _____ justified in this action? Why or why not?
What might have accounted for this reaction?

Such questions as these enable children to develop their abilities of
application, analysis, synthesis, and evaluation. Remember that principles of reading instruction are applicable to all subject areas. Reading is not a subject; reading is involved in literature or science or
social studies or math or civics or values clarification. The strategies
and ideas discussed in this chapter can and should be applied across
all teaching areas.

Critical Reading   The reading program should provide many opportunities for critical reading. Children should frequently engage
in activities that develop skills in reading and interpreting charts,
cartoons, graphs, scales, and diagrams; recognizing and making generalizations; making distinctions between literal and nonliteral information; drawing conclusions and making inferences; judging au-
thenticity, relevance, or clarity of information; recognizing fact from
fantasy; recognizing humor; recognizing fact from fiction; identifying
similarities and differences in texts; identifying and reacting to bias
or propaganda; justifying or expanding on author's choice of vocabulary; understanding figurative language; and analyzing character
traits. Many of these skills are appropriately developed in the content
areas.

Vocabulary Development   An intentional effort should be made to
expand children's listening, speaking, writing, and reading vocabularies. Vocabulary growth can be achieved by expanding word use
through vocabulary development exercises; increasing knowledge of
synonyms and antonyms; outlawing "tired" words such as *good, bad,
nice, big, funny,* and the like; building a personal thesaurus; developing fluency of word use; attending to subtle differences in word
meaning.

Wide Exposure to Literature   It is very important that gifted children be exposed to a wide variety of literature, including fiction,
nonfiction, narrative, exposition, drama, poetry, biography, humor,
myth, legend, fable, and folk tale.

   The tendency to separate reading and the other areas of the
curriculum must be avoided in all reading contexts but primarily in
the education of the gifted. Reading texts predominantly consist of
fictional, narrative material. Teachers must make a conscious effort
to broaden that base. A narrative selection about Abraham Lincoln,
for example, can lead to extended reading of a biography of Lincoln.

A story set in Haiti can lead to an extended social studies unit on the West Indies. A funny story may lead to a study of humor using many sources. The reading of a myth may lead to a unit on mythology in which students both read about and create myths.

In addition, many works of literature are particularly effective in expanding children's knowledge of the content areas. Some titles useful in social studies are the following.

> *And Then What Happened, Paul Revere?* by Jean Fritz, Coward, 1973
> *Ben and Me* by Robert Lawson, Little, Brown, 1939
> *The Cabin Faced West* by Jean Fritz, Coward, 1958
> *A Gathering of Days* by Joan W. Blos, Scribner's, 1979
> *Tituba of Salem Village* by Ann Petry, Crowell, 1964
> *The Witch of Blackbird Pond* by Elizabeth Speare, Houghton Mifflin, 1958
> *Brady* by Jean Fritz, Coward, 1960
> *A Pocket Full of Seeds* by Marilyn Sacks, Doubleday, 1973

Some trade books are available even in mathematics: *Think Metric* by Franklyn Branley, Harper and Row, 1973, and *Meter Means Measure* by Carl Hirsch, Viking Press, 1973.

Teachers should form alliances with librarians, who are strong resources for literature that is essential to a creative program in reading.

Productive Thinking   Productive thinking is made up of several separate abilities. Four of these are of particular importance to the reading instruction of gifted and creative children: fluency, flexibility, originality, and elaboration. The following section provides suggestions for developing these abilities in reading as well as in other content areas.

1.   *Fluency* is the ability to make *many* responses quickly. Teachers can ask questions such as "How many synonyms can you think of for the word *tell?*" or "How many different kinds of houses can you think of?" There are many trade books that can be used to develop fluency. Some suggestions for activities related to them, are given below.

Children can be encouraged to fill in the blanks in paragraphs taken from a real book such as in the following example from *The Man Whose Name Was Not Thomas* by Jean Craig:

> Once, a good many years ago, there was a man whose name was not Thomas. His name was not _____, either, nor _____ nor _____ nor _____. His name was not _____ or _____ or _____.

A-B-C Bunny by Wanda Gag is a study in alliteration; "B is for Bunny bouncing backwards"; "D is for dog digging in dumps." Children can create their own alliteration using each letter.

In *A for the Ark* by Roger Duvoisin, Noah calls animals into the Ark alphabetically. Children can be encouraged to think of as many animals as they can that begin with certain letters.

One effective strategy for the development of fluency is brainstorming. This activity can be used in any content area. Some suggestions for brainstorming topics in different content areas follow.

Social Studies
What might be the consequences of America's dependence on
    the Arab nations for oil?
List as many reasons for war as you can.
List as many effects of the invention of the telephone as you
    can.
Think of as many advantages of TV as you can.
Think of as many disadvantages of TV as you can.
List changes in the environment and society over which you
    have no control.

Science
Think of a variety of energy sources.
List as many things that endanger the environment as you
    can.
List living creatures that change their form from childhood to
    adulthood.
List animals that hibernate.

Literature
List many different forms of literature.
List many fairytale characters.
"A stitch in time saves nine." List alternative ways of express-
    ing this statement.
List many villains from literature.
List mythical characters.

2. *Flexibility* is the ability to switch one's thinking quickly and to look at one object or idea in several different ways. For example: Into how many different categories can you fit the word *apple*? Flexibility allows children to see many alternatives for one object or issue and to view one thing, action, or element in many different ways. Flexibility can be developed by the use of activities such as the following.

Placing single objects, individuals, and so on in as many cate-
    gories as possible

Listing many possible uses for a single object
Listing many ways to do one thing
Thinking of many reasons for a single action or response
Listing many results of the same action or decision

3. *Originality* is the ability to respond in unique ways. In fostering and developing originality, teachers should give children opportunities to respond to questions and engage in activities such as the following.

Complete the following sentence in as many unusual ways as you can: The reason the giraffe has such a long neck is _____.

How many unusual ways can you think of to solve the following problem?

Write another ending to this story. Your ending should be possible but atypical.

An apple is like a house because _____. How many reasons can you think of? Stay away from obvious comparisons.

_____ is to home as _____ is to _____. Finish this analogy in as many ways as you can.

Create an original poem, story, art project, experiment, and so on.

Think of unique reasons for an alliance between the United States and the Arab nations.

List ways to eliminate poverty in the United States. Do not mention solutions that you know have already been tried.

What are some original uses of the gas helium?

The ability to camouflage oneself automatically would be helpful because _____. Finish the sentence in as many unusual ways as you can.

Before the invention of the telephone and telegraph, what unique forms of communication might have existed?

Finish the following similes and be able to explain your comparisons: The view was as breathtaking as _____. The explosion was as frightening as _____. After the flood the city looked as devastated as _____.

Creative children are very adept at such activities; their talents make it easy for them to generate original responses and to see options and alternatives that are not obvious.

4. *Elaboration* is the ability to build on an existing structure and create a new, expanded one. This skill is easily developed through literature. Children can be encouraged to imitate the structure of a piece of writing, using their own words and ideas. Consider,

for example, the structure of *Brown Bear, Brown Bear, What Do You See?* (Martin, 1974):

> Brown Bear, Brown Bear
> what do you see?
> I see Red Bird
> looking at me.
>
> Red Bird, Red Bird
> what do you see?
> I see Yellow Duck
> looking at me.

Elaboration expects children to abstract the structure and then to create an original product based on that structure:

> *Noun, Noun,* what do you see?
> I see *Noun* looking at me.

Mark, a seven-year-old student, came up with the following verse.

> Seed, seed, what do you see?
> I see the dirt looking at me.
>
> Dirt, dirt, what do you see?
> I see roots looking at me.
>
> Roots, roots, what do you see?
> I see a stem looking at me.
>
> Stem, stem, what do you see?
> I see leaves looking at me.
>
> Leaves, leaves, what do you see?
> I see huge trees looking at me.
>
> Huge trees, huge trees, what do you see?
> I see the clouds looking at me.
>
> Clouds, clouds, what do you see?
> I see the sky looking at me.
>
> Sky, sky, what do you see?
> I see angels looking at me.

Books that are particularly suitable for practicing elaboration are *Fortunately* by Remy Charlip, *Who Wants a Cheap Rhinoceros?* by Shel Silverstein, *A Little Worm Book* by Janet and Allan Ahlberg, *One, Two, Three, Four* by Kate Considine and Ruby Schuler, and *What Is Pink?* by C. G. Rossetti.

Imaginative Thinking The reading program must provide many opportunities for children to develop their powers of imagination.

This can be done by involving them in activities and by asking such questions as the following.

How many ways can you think of to _____?
What if _____?
Suppose _____.
How many uses are there for _____?
Create a different ending for the story.
Solve the problem in another way.
Rewrite the story with a different outcome.

Visualization   The importance of visualization, or mental imagery, to reading comprehension has been solidly established in research (Anderson and Kulhavy, 1972; Kulhavy and Swenson, 1975; Lesgold, McCormick, and Golinkoff, 1975; Levin, 1973). The ability to create visual images and to describe details of those images has been shown to enhance comprehension of and involvement in print. Visualization abilities can be developed by activities such as the following.

Expanding the knowledge and use of descriptive words
Describing in detail scenes, events, pictures, and characters
Brainstorming descriptions of single objects, pictures, or characters
Reading descriptive scenes and drawing detailed pictures of them
Finding pictures and photos that capture a character's facial expressions at particular times
Describing in detail what is seen in the mind's eye after reading descriptive passages
Reading a description and creating a detailed diorama of it

Exploration of Values   One trait that characterizes gifted and creative children is their avid need to understand motivations, actions, and responses of themselves and others. One responsibility of the reading program is to expose such children to a variety of situations and experiences that will give them an opportunity to refine, clarify, expand, and modify their own values and become aware of the values of others. Teachers often wish to play it safe and expose children only to conventional issues. For gifted and creative children it is necessary to break away from the narrow boundaries and discuss issues, reactions, decisions, traditions, and opinions that will help children clarify and extend their value systems. This can be done by discussing values with children; exposing children to literature dealing with different races, cultures and points of view; and emphasizing evaluative questioning and demanding support for responses.

One useful strategy in helping children identify, analyze, evaluate, and challenge values is the use of Kohlberg's stages of moral development (1969) as a discussion tool. Kohlberg described six stages of moral development, which he said have a formal and identifiable cognitive base. Although the stages are somewhat related to age, we cannot delineate specific ages at which each stage is acquired. Progression through the stages is a result of interaction between individuals and their environment, discussion of unlike values, analysis of differences in value systems, and finally the acceptance or rejection of a new stage of development.

The following is Kohlberg's identification of each stage.

Stage 1: Individual responds to cultural rules to avoid pain or punishment.

Stage 2: Individual responds to cultural rules to obtain rewards or favors, not out of any feelings of loyalty, justice, and so on.

Stage 3: Individual obeys rules to be liked or accepted by others or to gain their approval. No real moral commitment exists.

Stage 4: Individual obeys rules because doing so maintains the social order of things. One does right because it is one's duty. Legal or religious rules govern behavior.

Stage 5: Individual's prime concern is with the welfare of others — individuals, nation, community, family. "Right" consists of placing the good of others ahead of one's personal good.

Stage 6: Individual formulates a personal, conscious, self-chosen set of ethical principles that take precedence over the laws of others.

Kohlberg found that ten-year-olds often exhibit stages 1, 2, and 3. At thirteen, children primarily reason at stages 3 and 4. He also concluded that children prefer that adults reason with them at one stage above their present stage. In this way, they can analyze, criticize, and possibly change their values.

Literature provides an excellent avenue for the development of children's moral thinking and values. A teacher can use literature to identify moral dilemmas, discuss the motivations underlying moral dilemmas, evaluate the moral decisions characters make, and help the children judge the decision against their own moral code.

Some excellent trade books that can be effectively used to develop children's moral sense are the following.

The Giving Tree by Shel Silverstein, Harper and Row, 1964
Crow Boy by Taro Yashima, Viking, 1955

Both creative and structured writing ought to be a planned part of the language arts curriculum for gifted and creative readers.

> *Stevie* by John Steptoe, Harper, 1969
> *A Big Fat Enormous Lie* by Marjorie Sharmat, Dutton, 1978
> *A Certain Small Shepherd* by Rebecca Caudill, Holt, 1965
> *Annie and the Old One* by Miska Miles, Little, Brown, 1971
> *Charlotte's Web* by E. B. White, Harper, 1952
> *Grandma Didn't Wave Back* by Rose Blue, Watts, 1972
> *Sounder* by William Armstrong, Harper, 1969
> *Maxie* by Mildred Kantrowitz, Four Winds, 1970
> *Bridge to Terabithia* by Katherine Paterson, Crowell, 1977
> *Then Again, Maybe I Won't* by Judy Blume, Bradbury, 1971
> *A Figure of Speech* by Norma Fox Mazer, Delacorte, 1973
> *Mrs. Frisby and the Rats of NIMH* by Robert O'Brien, Atheneum, 1971

In addition to trade books, basal readers are filled with stories that present moral problems that can be analyzed; alternative solutions can be brainstormed and discussed.

Language Arts Approach Reading is not an isolated subject. It is part of the language arts system, which consists of reading, writing, listening, and speaking. Efforts should be made to integrate reading with writing, discussion, and listening to reactions and responses of others.

Creating a Dynamic Reading Program

Teachers of gifted and creative children should create a program based on the factors just discussed. With the guidelines presented here, it is relatively easy for teachers to collect literature, build experiences, create questions and activities, and combine them into a reading program. Unfortunately, most teachers in the United States do not have the option of independently creating their reading curriculum. Many teachers are convinced that they should try to meet the needs of gifted children, but classroom realities make it very difficult to do so. Most teachers find themselves having to satisfy the very different needs of several groups of children and operating under the constraints of time, material, space, money, and energy. The reading program produces particular difficulties because the differences in performance across a class of children are so acute, the range of reading ability is so wide, and the materials and time to vary instruction are so limited. In addition, most teachers find themselves instructionally locked into a basal format that specifies a list of competencies and presents a particular body of literature that all children are expected to complete in a predetermined time span. Analysis of traditional basal texts often shows that the content of many texts is inadequate for the appropriate instruction of gifted children. Smith and Dechant (1961) stated that "it is extremely difficult to help the gifted achieve maximum growth if one limits oneself to a system that must frequently be geared to the needs of the average or even the dull child."

Reading instruction for gifted children often is viewed as too mammoth a task that would require either abandoning the basal series and creating an entirely new curriculum or teaching the entire basal text first and then finding additional material for gifted learners.

The remainder of this chapter demonstrates how teachers can use regular instructional materials to their greatest advantage and modify them to meet the needs of gifted children.

Curriculum Modification Strategies

If teachers are expected to teach children a well-defined curriculum presented in a basal text, they must modify that curriculum to teach gifted children effectively. Keeley (1981) suggests four basic strategies for curriculum modification: compression, deletion/substitution, addition, and expansion. In creating an effective program for gifted children, segments of the existing curriculum must be compressed, deleted, added to, or expanded to become a creative, intellectually stimulating reading program.

Compression   Compression is the process of pulling together information that is repetitive or simple and presenting it in a single block in a shorter time than usual. Inherent in the term is the concept of acceleration because it is assumed that a certain body of information can be completed in a shorter time.

The area of the reading curriculum most conducive to compression is the skills component. Basal reader skills are usually presented in a workbook, with each skill repeated about three to five times at intervals throughout the workbook. Gifted children are often familiar with many skills prior to workbook instruction, or they learn the skills very quickly and do not need the repetitive instruction. In such cases, skill instruction can be compressed. In a second-grade workbook, the skill "Finding Syllables" may be introduced on page 19 and reinforced on pages 29, 40, 46, 64, and 82. The teacher could present the skill on page 19, and children who achieve 90 percent mastery can be assumed to know the skill. Pages 29, 40, 46, and 64 can be compressed into one unit that children can complete independently. The last page can remain as a review.

It is always advisable to give such children a chance to apply their skills to actual reading situations. A follow-up activity, for example, might be to find in the reading selections four words containing one, two, and three syllables.

This model for compression, then, consists of the following steps.

1. Teach the skill initially.
2. If children achieve 90 percent mastery, most of the remaining similar exercises can be compressed.
3. Use in actual reading situations.
4. One or two exercises remain for review and practice later.

Compression lends itself well to contractual learning. Learning contracts are an excellent way of organizing children's time outside of group instructional time, of developing responsibility for completing tasks, and of fostering independence. The philosophy underlying learning contracts is that children's time in school is divided into two categories: instructional time and independent time. Instructional time always precedes independent time. Independent time is spent in activities that are preplanned and preassigned. They should be completed independently or in small groups within a given amount of time, depending on the task and on the age and abilities of the children.

Figures 9–1 through 9–6 demonstrate the variety of learning contracts.

Deletion/Substitution Some segments of basal texts are inappropriate for gifted and creative children because the children already know the information, the selection has little value because of the ability level of the children, the material is too simple, or the teacher feels unwilling or unable to teach the selection. Such selections can be deleted for gifted and creative children. Segments of both the skill sequence and the literature strand can be deleted. But when segments are deleted, more appropriate ones should be substituted. This is an ideal way to modify the existing program to include some of the essential components discussed earlier. Traditional dictionary skills can be deleted, for example, and the making of a thesaurus substituted. Alphabetizing exercises can be deleted, and a vocabulary strand can be substituted. Simple narrative selections can be deleted and biographies, myths, or factual selections substituted.

FIGURE 9–1
Independent reading contract: reading bingo

Name ————————————————————————————————————

Date ————————————————————————————————————

Read the story ———————————————————— and complete three
assignments to form a winning Bingo pattern.

Make up five interview questions, with answers, for the main character.	Collect ten pictures that describe the story. Explain how they relate to the story.	Make a map of the story. Provide a key.
Choose two characters. Give five ways in which they are alike and five ways in which they are different. Support your answers.	FREE FREE Create your own assignment.	Pretend you are the author of the story. Explain why you chose the title and tell five more titles you had considered.
Explain what you think happened to the main character after the story ended.	Describe an experience you have had that was similar to an experience of one of the characters.	Write out your title decoratively, and for each letter write a sentence or phrase that tells about the story.

Portions of the questioning segment of typical basal programs almost always need deletion. Basal texts include an abundance of lower-level questions and only a few higher-level questions. Almost without exception, traditional questions should be deleted and questions that draw on higher levels of thought should be substituted.

Addition   Often new skill units need to be added to the basal reading curriculum. The teacher can add units in areas such as structural analysis, critical reading, productive thinking, vocabulary, mental imagery, values clarification, figurative language, listening, or parts of speech.

Expansion   Expansion refers to the horizontal spiraling of the literature component of the basal text. Often literature lends itself to introducing new, related material. A story set in Paris, for example, may lead to a geography study of France. An article on butterflies

FIGURE 9–2
Daily reading contract

Name _____

Date _____

Complete the following tasks by 2 p.m.

Reading

1. Read pages 40–44 in your text and answer the following questions.

    a. _____
    b. _____
    c. _____
    d. _____

2. Find the meaning of the following words and use each in a sentence.

    a. _____
    b. _____
    c. _____
    d. _____

Writing

1. Rewrite your favorite section of the story in your own words.
2. Create two alternative endings to the story. Which of the three endings do you prefer? Why?

Skills

1. Complete workbook pages 24, 32, 64, 82, and 92. Check your answers with someone in your group and do corrections on a separate sheet of paper.

---

may lead to a unit on metamorphosis. A selection illustrated by McDermott may lead to a comparative study of art. The process of expansion answers the following questions.

> What ideas could be used to elaborate on a given selection?
> How can each selection be enriched?
> What activities could be added to the passage?
> What pieces of literature could be added to extend the passage?
> What community resources can be utilized to extend a selection?
> What activities can the children be involved in to expand comprehension of the material?

This is a perfect opportunity to add selections of a variety of literature types that extend and expand the literature base.

FIGURE 9–3
Weekly reading contract

Name _____

Date _____

Complete the following assignments by Thursday at 2 p.m.

Reading

  1. Read the story _____.
    a. Write a review of the story.
    b. Create a poster of your favorite scene.
    c. Choose ten words that best explain your favorite character. Find and write
       phrases or sentences from the story that justify your choice of each word.
  2. Read a story of your choice. Be prepared to tell the story to the group.

Skills

  1. Do workbook pages _____.
  2. Find four examples of each of the following in your story.

    a. Compound words
    b. Two-syllable words
    c. Three-syllable words
    d. Descriptive words

Research

  1. Your story is set in California. Do some research in the library and find out
     ten important facts about California. Be ready to share your findings with the
     group.

Creative Thinking

  1. Your reading selection described how a butterfly eats. How many synonyms
     for the word *eat* can you think of (minimum 15)? Look for possible synonyms
     as you read and listen throughout the week.
  2. How many things can you think of that change their form from birth to
     adulthood?

A reading program for gifted students should include specific skills and traits that are often not found sufficiently in traditional basal reading series. Teachers of gifted students have two options: (1) They may abandon the basal and create a reading program independently, or (2) they may begin with the basal and modify it to meet the needs of the students. Option 1 is not feasible for most teachers. Option 2 is well within the grasp of all teachers. Implementation requires a great deal of time and preparation, but the results are well worth it. The process can be made easier if groups of teachers assigned to the same grade level team their efforts and share their activities.

FIGURE 9–4
Reading contract

Name _____

Date _____

1. Read pages 122–148.
2. Workbook assignments: Do pages 29, 49, 56, 57, 61, 66, and 94.
3. Answer the following questions, using complete sentences.
   a. _____
   b. _____
   c. _____
4. Put the following words from your story in alphabetical order.

   _____
   _____
   _____
   _____
   _____
   _____

   Without looking back at the story, try to remember how and why each word was used.
5. Design a cover for the story. Cut words and pictures from old magazines and make a collage or an advertisement for the story. Be prepared to discuss your advertisement.

Models of Teaching Reading to Gifted Readers

In addition to general curriculum modification strategies, instructional models are available to vary the reading program to help reorganize the curriculum structurally. Following are four such models.

Inquiry Reading   In 1981 Cassidy described inquiry reading as a four-week research activity created to provide a focus for children's attention, to expose children to a wide variety of material, and to provide situations in which children can share information. The strategy is divided into four one-week segments.

Week 1

1. Teachers define and discuss inquiry and research.
2. Children are told that
   a. each child will investigate a question he or she has always wanted to find out about.
   b. it will be a four-week endeavor.
   c. the results will be shared.
3. Possible areas of interest are brainstormed and discussed.

FIGURE 9–5
Daily reading contract

```
┌─────────────────────────────────────────────────────────────────┐
│                                                                   │
│   Name _____   │
│                                                                   │
│   Date _____   │
│                                                                   │
│   1. In your workbook do pages 16, 25, 29, 32, and 40.            │
│   2. Put the following words in ABC order.                        │
│                                                                   │
│         _____                            │
│         _____                            │
│         _____                            │
│                                                                   │
│   3. Find two words that rhyme with the following words.          │
│       a. pat      _____   _____   │
│       b. ten      _____   _____   │
│       c. same     _____   _____   │
│       d. hop      _____   _____   │
│   4. Read pages 21–25 in your reading book. Answer the following questions. │
│       a. _____       │
│       b. _____       │
│       c. _____       │
│   5. Finish these sentences.                                      │
│       a. I liked this story because _____. │
│       b. I did not like the story because _____. │
│       c. My favorite character was _____. │
│       d. I liked that character because _____.│
│                                                                   │
└─────────────────────────────────────────────────────────────────┘
```

4. For each topic decided on, three questions are developed for investigation.

5. Resources, authorities, and mentors are discussed.

6. Interviewing techniques are discussed. Students should make an initial phone call or write a letter to mentors or authorities. Lists of questions are generated.

7. Possible methods of sharing information are discussed: tape recording, mural, newspaper, diorama, skit, model, newspaper, and so on.

8. Deadlines are set.

Weeks 2 and 3

1. Students work independently and discuss their progress daily in the group.

2. Teachers
   a. review note taking.
   b. assist students in locating references.
   c. suggest that students keep a folder with references and the like.

FIGURE 9–6
Reading contract

Name _____

Date _____

Skills

Work with a partner and complete the following workbook pages: 64, 68, 75, 82, 87, 94. Check and correct your own work.

Comprehension Activities

Yesterday we completed the story _____ in the group. Work with a partner and answer the following questions. Check your grammar and spelling.

a. _____

b. _____

c. _____

Small-Group Project

Work with your group and research the following topic: _____. Find ten facts about the topic. You must use at least three sources. Material you may need is on reserve in the library.

Free Reading

Read independently for at least twenty minutes a day and fill in the information below.

	Book Title	Pages	Time	Reading
Monday				
Tuesday				
Wednesday				
Thursday				
Friday				

Rate each day's selection on a 1-to-3 scale.
1 = Great   2 = Fair   3 = Boring

---

d. encourage students to share problems and successes.

e. overview the construction of projects.

f. meet with individual students to check progress.

Week 4

1. Students complete the project.

2. A first-run presentation is made to the group and other group members make suggestions for improvement.

3. Students present final products to an outside audience of parents, other students, or another class.

4. Students evaluate the process and the final products.

The strategy teaches many valuable skills, including research methods, critical analysis, note taking, organization, and presentation skills.

Renzulli Enrichment Triad   The Renzulli triad (1971) is a three-part enrichment strategy based on the following assumptions.

Enrichment is an experience above and beyond the regular curriculum.

Enrichment should show respect for students' interests.

The time and place of the activities is not important.

1. *General Exploratory Activities.* Exploratory activities are designed to bring students in touch with topics, such as volcanoes, prehistoric animals, astronomy, musical instruments, or weather, that might interest them. Activities might include interest centers, visitations, presentations, field trips, or a combination. The activities are meant to stimulate students; they should provide students with the opportunity to manipulate objects, interact with presenters, ask questions, and become actively involved in many processes. Children who are interested in doing further research into any aspect of the topic are encouraged to participate in the next phase.

2. *Group Training.* In this phase interested students are involved in activities geared toward developing thinking and feeling processes. These activities analyze and discuss the experiences in the previous section. They may involve brainstorming issues, interpreting elements, comparing processes, elaborating on aspects of the topic, clarifying values, or heightening awareness of segments of the presentations. An effort is made to provide a wide range of thinking, feelings, experiences, and options.

3. *Individual Projects.* In this phase students choose a specific question to research. They pose questions, discuss sources, and research to find answers. The teacher provides guidance, checks progress, and makes suggestions. Students' research projects are displayed, published, and shared, as appropriate.

The Reading-Strategy Lesson   In 1980 Goodman, Burke, and Sherman described a reading-strategy lesson that has implications for the instruction of gifted learners. It is a four-step process that gives students the opportunity to develop higher-level cognitive thinking skills. Before applying this model, the teacher chooses a strategy used in literature that students should learn more about. Such a strategy might be plot, theme, generalization, propaganda, bias, humor, or point of view. The teacher chooses appropriate material to teach students about that strategy.

The lesson takes place in four phases.

1. *Initiating.* In this phase the interest of the student is heightened. Students are presented with material that stimulates discussion of the strategy. In a strategy lesson on propaganda, the teacher might choose some ads from a newspaper. Students can read the ads and discuss aspects that are true, false, questionable, biased, misleading, and so on.

2. *Interacting.* Students discuss issues about the topic in the group. The teacher provides many opportunities for students to explore the material and discuss each other's responses. In the case of the advertisement, students might brainstorm questions such as the following:

> Why did the author write the ad?
> What is the purpose of the ad?
> What facts do you believe and why?
> What do you question and why?
> Would you buy this item? Why?
> What language makes the ad believable and what language
>   seems questionable?
> How can you find out more information about the product?
>   Do you have to purchase it to find that information?

Once discussion is completed, students should find examples of similar strategies. In this case they would find other ads that make similar claims, question people about the advertised product, or buy the item and formulate their own opinions.

3. *Applying.* Students apply their new knowledge of the strategy to new material and situations. They can consider articles presenting conflicting views on the same issue, analyze each article, identify propaganda and questionable statements, recognize factual information, and respond critically to the strategy.

4. *Expanding.* In this phase students extend the strategy to other areas of the curriculum. The strategy can be expanded in writing by writing sentences or phrases that give facts and opinions, in reading by collecting newspaper articles that contain similar elements, in language by setting up classroom debates about the topic, and in social studies by comparing and contrasting people's reactions to products and to advertisers' claims.

The AIME The AIME (analysis, identification, modification, and extension) is a model for modifying and extending existing reading material to challenge, motivate, and heighten the learning of gifted students (Swaby, 1982).

The model consists of four steps that the teacher uses to plan instructional strategy. The steps are given first in outline form and then explained in detail.

STEP 1: ANALYSIS

Decision: What selections are included in the text? What are the general categories?

STEP 2: IDENTIFICATION

Decision: Which selections in the text fit into one of the following categories: instructional modification, general extension, and specific extension?

STEP 3: MODIFICATION

Decision: How can I modify the regular instructional framework to maximize learning, motivation, and achievement?

Options:

1. Guided reading
2. Independent reading followed by group discussion
3. Comparative reading
4. Critical reading
5. Enrichment reading

STEP 4: EXTENSION

Decision: Which extension strategy shall I use for each selection?

General Options:

1. Art
2. Literature
3. Drama
4. Writing
5. Community resources

Specific Options:

1. Social studies
2. Science/health
3. Math

STEP 1: ANALYSIS

The teacher's first step is to analyze the text and to become sensitive to general information. The teacher attempts to answer the following questions.

What selections are included?

What are the general categories? (Fantasy, poetry, drama, social studies, science, fiction, nonfiction, exposition, narration, biography, and so on.)
What selections have particular personal appeal?

STEP 2: IDENTIFICATION

The teacher identifies the selections that fit into one of three categories.

Instructional modification. The teacher identifies selections that, because of their content, are least likely to lend themselves to instructional extension or enrichment. Such selections would not suggest further reading, in-depth analysis, or creative reading or writing activities. The only modification the teacher could give such selections would be in presentation of the material.

General extension. The teacher identifies selections whose content is most likely to lend itself to instructional branching or enrichment. The teacher can easily envision instructional activities that could emerge from the basic selections. The extended learning might consist of further exploration of literature; experiences in art, drama, music, or writing; exposure to people and places in the community, and so on. The teacher begins with the material in the text and ends with information outside of the text.

Specific extension. The teacher identifies selections that are most easily integrated with or directly related to the content areas of social studies, science/health, and math. The selections can be used as extenders or elaborators in those other areas. The teacher thus integrates the reading curriculum with other major curriculum areas.

STEP 3: MODIFICATION

Selections in the category Instructional Modification are somewhat uncomplicated and are not particularly interesting or stimulating to the teacher or the children. Nevertheless, the teacher can use various instructional modifications to maximize interest, motivation, and learning.

Guided reading. Begin with prediction. Look at title, pictures, boldface type, illustrations, graphs, and so on. Ask children what they think the story is about. Read the story and check predictions. Predict and check predictions throughout. Introduce and elaborate on any new vocabulary items. As children read, ask a variety of questions. Concentrate on questions that tap Bloom's levels of application, analysis, synthesis, and evaluation. (See Chapter 4.)

Independent reading followed by group discussion. Selections within the independent reading level of gifted readers, which contain little or no unknown vocabulary or concepts, can be read by children independently. In the group, the teacher guides discussion of the selection, emphasizing higher-level questions. Students are asked to use the text to support their responses, as in the following example.

> *Question*
>
> *Question:* What kind of a person do you think Jane's mother is?
> *Response:* Mean and selfish.
>
> *Support*
>
> *Question:* What in the text makes you feel that way about her?
> *Response:* She abused her child and would never listen to anyone with a different opinion from her own.

Comparative reading.   Some selections might share distinct and identifiable features. Such selections can be studied simultaneously or as a mini-unit in comparing and contrasting. Such selections might be two selections written by the same author, two selections dealing with the same theme, or two selections with similar major characters.

Critical reading.   Certain selections may be particularly suited to concentration on critical reading skills, including reading and interpreting charts, cartoons, graphs, scales, and diagrams; recognizing and making generalizations; making distinctions between literal and nonliteral information; drawing conclusions or inferences; and recognizing fact from fantasy.

Enrichment reading.   As a change of pace from individual oral and silent reading, teachers can use various enrichment strategies, such as choral reading and readers' theater. If a selection has repeated fragments, refrains, choruses, and the like, the entire group can read those segments aloud and individuals can read nonrepetitive sections. If the selection has much dialogue, individuals can be assigned character parts and other students or the teacher can read the narrative (nonconversational) material. In effect, the selection can be changed to a play with very little effort. Both strategies were discussed in Chapter 7. Teachers should be as creative as possible with these strategies. They are in no way mutually exclusive. For example, comparative and critical reading or guided and critical reading can be paired.

STEP 4: EXTENSION

General extension covers the areas of literature, the arts, and the humanities. Specific extension spans the areas of social studies, science/health, and math.

General extension.   For each selection identified as appropriate for general extension, the teacher must decide what particular extension or extensions to use.

Some activities in art might be the following.

Awareness:

Analyze illustrations to discover how artists use them to enrich the text. Analyze the type of art used (watercolor, pen and ink, black-and-white prints, color prints, abstracts).

Activities:

Draw your favorite character. Pay particular attention to expression, feeling, and other emotional aspects. Look through pictures and find one that best portrays your favorite character and one that portrays your least favorite character.

Comparison:

Look at a number of books illustrated by the same illustrator. What is similar? What is different? Analyze illustrations of different types of literature (fantasy, folk tales, mystery, and so on).

Some literature activities might be the following.

Related/Thematic:

Read additional selections on similar themes. Compare and contrast them in terms of plot development, major characters, outcomes, treatment, setting, and so on. Read additional selections by the same author. Compare and contrast. Are there any striking similarities? Is there any way one could identify the author without seeing his or her name?

Comparative:

Read different versions of the same story. Compare and contrast them in terms of plot, language variations, illustrations, and so on. Read the whole work from which excerpts have been taken. Analyze the author's use of figurative language, symbolism, and so on.

Mental Imagery:

Describe in detail how a character or a setting looks based on the text. Create sound effects for the text.

Affective Expansion:

Retell stories from different characters' points of view. Analyze outcomes in the text. Come up with possible alternative outcomes and show how the plot would have changed with each outcome.

In drama, students might read a particularly graphic selection and create a set for a specific scene. Students must decide what material and what furniture to use. They can find pictures in magazines that exemplify scenes in the selection. Or students can focus on one scene from a selection and write it as a scene for a play. They must decide what words, expressions, clothing, and so on are appropriate.

For creative writing students might do some of the following activities.

Personal:

Write your personal reaction to the selection.

Write a character sketch of your favorite character.

Write ten words that best describe your favorite or least favorite character. Support choices from lines or phrases from the text.

Journal:

Pretend you are the major character. Write three journal entries of your experiences: one at the start of the story, one in the middle, and one toward the end.

Journalistic:

Imagine that the main character is now an adult. What kind of job would she or he want? Write a résumé of his or her experiences.

You are an interviewer for a new TV program. Interview your favorite character. What questions would be most important to ask?

Students can make use of community resources by identifying selections that relate to groups of people or places in the community. Invite individuals to class or take children into the community. Discuss relevant issues with the children before and after the visits.

Specific extension.   Some selections can be integrated into the areas of social studies, science/health, and math. These selections can be treated as part of those curriculum areas and used to lead into content-area units. A reading selection about the brain, for example, might lead to a science unit on the brain and appropriate experiments on brain functions. Or a selection set in early England might lead to a history unit on the feudal system. Specific extensions are treated as extensions of the content areas and are used as catapults into further content development.

A word of caution. The activities mentioned in the extension section need to be taught and guided by the teacher. Teachers of gifted children often fail to provide the structure and guidance children need to achieve the most out of enrichment activities. These children certainly can work on their own, but only after the teacher has presented the structure, given examples, and begun the procedure with the group. The activities presented in the extension section are meant to be done primarily *with* the group. Also remember that groups of gifted readers represent a range of abilities and interests. In planning for instruction, therefore, teachers are urged to prepare two levels of material: one for whole-group involvement and another for a smaller group of children who may desire to go beyond the activities of the group. This individualization within the group is invaluable.

Structural Considerations in the AIME Once teachers have analyzed the basal material, categorized the selections, and planned for extensions of the appropriate selections, they need to make some structural arrangements. They must plan the presentation of the material to accommodate the mandatory material to be covered in a reading period as well as any new material. It is useful for teachers to begin by mapping out the school week and deciding what activities to carry out on each day. One possible plan follows.

Mondays: Skill Instruction/Practice. Compress weekly workbook skills into one day. Treat skills in two different ways:

1. Skills that are being introduced for the first time or that are difficult can be instructed and practiced in the group and reinforced in the reading material throughout the week.
2. Skills that are being repeated and that children have mastered can be introduced in groups and completed independently or in small groups, or skills can be assigned as a contract and children can be given a time frame in which to complete and hand them in.

Tuesdays: Basal Reading. One day per week should be devoted to reading selections that fall into the instructional modification category. These are selections for which the teacher needs only moderate preparation. It might be that children read the entire selection in the group *or* read sections before coming to the group and complete the selection in the group *or* read the entire selection independently and discuss the content in the group. Teachers should vary presentations based on the demands of the material.

Wednesdays: Day 1 of Extension. Teachers will introduce the initial extension selection, with the same variations as under instructional modification. For example, they may initially teach this material by using guided reading, critical reading, enrichment reading, independent reading followed by discussion, or comparative reading. In all cases, they should ask a variety of questions geared toward a subtle introduction to the second extension.

Thursdays: Day 2 of Extension. This day is devoted to the actual planned extension. A variety of formats can be used: whole group, pairs, small groups, or individuals, depending on the nature of the extension.

Fridays: Day 3 of Extension — Enrichment/Sharing. Depending on how elaborate the extension is, a third day may be required. If not, the final day of the week can be used as a general enrichment day in which children share information, perform for others, or participate in some whole-group learning activity. Interclassroom enrichment can take place, in which groups of children from different classrooms share information. Interclassroom enrichment can be most effective if a number of classrooms at the same grade level have participated in different extensions of the same material and then come together to share their varied perspectives of the material. It can also be effective to share among different grade levels that may be researching different aspects of the same topic.

Summary

Teaching reading to gifted children is indeed a challenge. Because of the restrictions of traditional basal series, teachers are compelled to modify the curriculum significantly to meet the needs of gifted and creative students. Strategies of curriculum modification assist teachers in analyzing and changing the existing reading program. In addition, teachers can use certain models of instruction to extend the material and to provide some structural variety. Although teaching gifted students demands much preparation, the learning, motivation, and achievement it affords gifted and creative students are well worth the extra effort. Many strategies that are effective for gifted students can be modified to meet the needs of all children.

References

Anderson, R. D., and R. W. Kulhavy, "Imagery and Prose Learning." *Journal of Education Psychology*, no. 63 (1972).

Bloom, B. S. *Taxonomy of Education Objectives: Handbook 7, Cognitive Domain.* New York: David McKay, 1956.

Cassidy, Jack. "Inquiry Reading for the Gifted." *Reading Teacher*, 35:1 (October 1981).

Galton, Sir Francis. *Hereditary Genius: An Inquiry into Its Laws and Consequences.* New York: Macmillan, 1892.

Guilford, J. P. "Creativity." *American Psychologist*, no. 5 (1950).

———. "Creativity: Yesterday, Today, Tomorrow." *Journal of Creative Behavior*, no. 1 (1967).

Gordon, J. R. *Parent Involvement in Compensatory Education.* Urbana: University of Illinois Press, 1970.

Goodman, Y., C. Burke, and B. Sherman. *Reading Strategies: Focus on Comprehension.* New York: Holt, Rinehart and Winston, 1980.

Keeley, J. "Curriculum Working Paper." Colorado Springs, Colo.: School District 11, 1981.

Kohlberg, L. "Stage and Sequence: The Cognitive Development Approach to Socialization." In *Handbook on Socialization Theory and Research*, edited by David A. Goslin.

Kulhavy, R. W., and I. Swenson. "Imagery Instruction and the Comprehension of Text." *British Journal of Educational Psychology*, no. 45 (1975).

Lesgold, A. M., C. McCormick, and R. M. Golinkoff. "Imagery Training and Children's Prose Learning." *Journal of Educational Psychology*, no. 67 (1975).

Levin, J. R. "Inducing Comprehension in Poor Readers: A Test of a Recent Model." *Journal of Educational Psychology*, no. 65 (1973).

Polette, N. *Reading, Writing, Research with Gifted Children K–8.* Englewood, Colo.: Educational Consulting Associates, I.W.C., 1982.

Renzulli, Joseph S. "The Enrichment Triad Model: A Guide for Developing Defensible Programs for the Gifted and Talented." *Gifted Child Quarterly*, 20:3 (February 1976).

Renzulli, J. S., R. K. Hartman, and C. M. Callahan. "Teacher Identification of Superior Students." *Exceptional Children* (November 1971).

Smith, H. P., and E. Dechant. *Psychology in Teaching Reading*. Englewood Cliffs, N.J.: Prentice-Hall, 1961.

Swaby, B. "The A.I.M.E.: A Classroom Model for the Reading Instruction of Gifted Readers." *Indiana Reading Quarterly* (Fall 1982).

Terman, L., and P. Oden. *Genetic Studies of Genius: The Gifted Child Grows Up*. Vol. 4. Stanford, Calif.: Stanford University Press, 1947.

Torrance, E. P. *Creativity*. Belmont, Calif.: Dimensions Publishing Company, 1969.

10

Oral Language and Reading Development

Undoubtedly, children's oral language development has an effect on their reading. Reading is a language process, and while there are significant differences between the acquisition of language and the acquisition of reading and between speech and print, there are also some striking similarities. Both oral language and reading are affected by similar aspects of syntax or grammar, semantics or meaning, and phonology or sound. The wealth of children's experiences adds significantly to the information and understanding they bring to the reading task.

Many children who have difficulty reading need more elaborate experiences with language, both oral and written, and need to be shown how to use familiar language clues in reading. This chapter considers the nature of oral language development and the ways teachers can encourage oral language interaction in the classroom.

□   What are the three major theories of language acquisition?

□   What major language functions should children internalize by school age?

□   What are some linguistic problems that stand in the way of appropriate language development?

□   What strategies can classroom teachers use to facilitate oral language growth in school?

□   How can teachers increase oral language interaction during reading instruction?

The Study of Language

Language is indeed one of the most complex of human behaviors. Language is learned so naturally that most adults take the magnitude of the task for granted. Only when we observe that something has gone wrong in the language development of an individual do we even attend to or consciously remember indexes of language development. Actually, children's initial learning of language has fascinated scholars since the eighteenth century, although most of the research into language acquisition and development has been done within the last twenty years. In the attempt to explain how children acquire primary language, theorists have developed three major theories of language acquisition: the behaviorist theory, the nativist theory, and the cognitive theory. Although no one theory has been able to explain fully the process of language acquisition, each one has added to our understanding of how language is initially learned.

Behaviorist Theory

Individuals adhering to the behaviorist theory view language learning as beginning with children's instinctive effort to imitate the sounds they hear in their given linguistic environments. As children attempt to imitate the speech sounds, adults in their environments respond to and reinforce their efforts. That reinforcement causes children to produce more sounds of language. As children learn new language forms, they add them to previously learned elements. A child may learn naming words such as *mama*, *milk*, and *dada*, and then may learn a relationship word like *allgone* or *my*. The child then adds the new form *allgone* to the already existing elements to form a more complex unit, such as "allgone milk" or "allgone mama." As the child learns more units, he or she puts them all together to form more complex phrases and sentences. This process of learning individual elements and then linking them together is referred to in behaviorist theory as *chaining*. As children grow, adults reinforce closer and closer approximations to adult speech, thus shaping children's language production into progressively more adult forms. The principles of imitation and reinforcement, chaining and shaping, then, are major factors in behaviorist theory (Skinner, 1957; Staats, 1968, 1974).

Nativist Theory

The nativist theory of language acquisition views language as biologically based. Language is species-specific; that is, human beings are born to acquire and develop language. We are born with innate, latent language structures that are biologically founded. As children mature physiologically, their language structures also mature. This creates a readiness for language. Adult language begins to be meaningful and stimulating to children, and the combined effect of maturation, readiness, and stimulation makes children begin to learn, practice, and develop their language skills.

Those adhering to the nativist theory use the following facts to support the theory's biological emphasis.

1. Language development is tied to general maturation.
2. Milestones in language development are reached in a fixed order and are normally not able to be speeded up or retarded.
3. There seems to be a critical period (between ages two and four) beyond which initial learning of language becomes significantly more difficult.
4. All languages share the universal principles of syntax, semantics, and phonology (Lenneberg, 1967).

Cognitive Theory

The cognitive theory views language as being acquired within the larger context of human learning. Human beings are born with the ability to process cognitive information, which includes language. As children grow, they pass through various developmental stages that allow them to attend particularly to and learn from certain aspects of their environment. Shortly after the first year of life, children enter the developmental stage, during which language becomes particularly important. They begin to attend to language and apply to language their already emerging cognitive skills. This allows them to start to process language and to abstract from language the rules necessary to build their own language. The interplay between emerging language and thinking abilities allows them to produce increasingly complex language (McNeill, 1970; Wadsworth, 1971; Vygotsky, 1973).

Some Implications for Reading Instruction

Throughout this text, the relationships between spoken language and written language have been stressed. Many of the strategies children use to make sense of oral language are also used to make sense of written language. If such a strong tie exists between these two forms of language, it may very well be that the acquisition of oral language has strong implications for the acquisition of written language. In other words, the questions How does a child acquire oral language?

and How does a child acquire written language (reading)? might be quite interrelated. As we have seen, the three major theories of language acquisition provide three different answers to the question How does a child acquire oral language? From each answer, we can draw different implications for reading acquisition.

If language was acquired as the behaviorist model prescribes and if reading was acquired in a somewhat similar manner, then the following implications for initial reading instruction might apply.

- ☐ The reading task may need to be broken down into small, sequentially arranged segments so that the chaining process can occur easily. This would be consistent with the phonic methodology.
- ☐ Children may need to be consistently reinforced in learning to read, particularly at the beginning stage.
- ☐ Children's reading behavior should be shaped by rewarding reading performance that is closer and closer to adult models.

The implications for reading acquisition based on the nativist theory would be quite different. They might include the following.

- ☐ Reading acquisition might be tied to maturation. There might be a biologically determined time during which the child may be ready to read.
- ☐ Children may need to hear a great deal of interesting and motivating "print" (children's literature) prior to reading instruction to be appropriately stimulated and motivated toward reading.
- ☐ Immersion in written language and multiple opportunities for practicing, sharing, and using reading skills may be essential.

Another set of implications emerges when we analyze reading acquisition according to the cognitive theory.

- ☐ There may be a specific developmental stage in which acquisition of reading fits.
- ☐ Children may need to see and hear a great deal of print prior to and during reading instruction to begin to abstract the rules of reading and to build their own system.
- ☐ Children may need to interact with adults as they are read to and as they read to help them apply their already emerging thinking abilities to the comprehension of print.

These different implications for reading acquisition make us more aware of the variety of interpretations of the reading process. Although there are strong relationships between oral and written language and although theories of oral language acquisition provide us with insights into a variety of options for reading acquisition, there are some very important differences between oral language acquisition and reading acquisition. Some of the more important differences are as follows.

- ☐ Oral language is acquired in a predominantly tension-free environment in that children are given relative freedom to learn language at their own pace using their own techniques. This is often not true of reading acquisition.
- ☐ Language learning is a very gradual process, whereas reading instruction begins quite abruptly in kindergarten or first grade.
- ☐ Many children have significantly stronger natural reinforcement and motivation attached to oral language learning than to learning to read.
- ☐ Relatively few children have to be "taught" to speak. The reverse is true for reading.

Acquiring Language

Oral Language Acquisition

All three theories of language acquisition have increased our understanding of how humans learn their primary language. Regardless of which theory or theories we accept, there are certain important facts we know about children and their involvement with language based on our observation of children as they acquire and use language.

Language acquisition is an active process. From birth, children are active processors of information. They are constantly affected by and they respond to their linguistic environment. They react to language and produce its sounds. Long before they speak in clear, adultlike speech, they understand that language is used for specific purposes, such as communication and meeting one's needs. As they begin to build their language, they do so through active involvement in the language experience. Children are constantly acting on and reacting to language. Language learning is in no way a passive process.

Language is used for a variety of purposes. As children develop their language, they use it in a variety of ways: to communicate with others, to get their needs met, to investigate unclear or unfamiliar concepts, and to please themselves or others. Children learn to vary their vocabulary, tone, and so on according to the purpose they choose.

Children pass through clearly identifiable language stages. Children progress gradually through linguistic stages. Some of the more well defined stages are as follows.

1. Babbling stage (birth to approximately one year). Babbling represents the first sounds made by the infant. During the first few months of life, the sounds produced by babbling are the same in all languages. By approximately three months of age, however, the sounds that are not present in the child's linguistic environment start to atrophy, and the child continues to practice the sounds in his or her present environment (Norton, 1980).

2. Holophrastic stage (approximately one to two years). During this stage, children begin to use single words, called *holophrases*, to communicate the meaning of entire sentences. A child may say "wa-wa" to mean "I want some water" or "jacket" to mean "Put on my jacket and take me outside." Holophrastic speech allows children to begin to use language for special, social reasons. During this time, children's naming vocabulary develops quickly.

3. Telegraphic stage (approximately two to three years). During this stage, syntax or grammar develops as children begin to use combinations of two or more words. Language at this stage often sounds like the language adults use when they send a telegram: function words are omitted. Children may say sentences like "Allgone milk," "Mary dress," "Gimme juice," or "No want night-night." As children mature linguistically, telegraphic language develops into more complete sentence structure.

Table 10–1 shows the further development of language through the more complex linguistic stages.

Children learn the vocabulary and the conventions of language. Children learn that words carry meaning and that certain words fit into specific language slots and serve specific purposes. They learn that words represent things (*table*), actions (*run*), descriptions (*big*), explanations (*slowly*), or connectors (*and*). They also learn that language conventions must be observed. For example, specific words are used to open and close conversation; one maintains one's turn in conversations; and one requests information in specific ways. Conventions and forms are learned through observation of role models in the linguistic environment.

Children learn by being immersed in language. From birth, children are surrounded by language. They hear language, they see people responding to language, and they hear the different tones of language and the variety of emotions expressed by language. Through this immersion in language, they start to abstract certain consistencies or regularities (rules) and gradually solve the problem of how to use and understand language.

TABLE 10.1
General language characteristics

3 months	The young child starts with possible language sounds and gradually eliminates sounds that are not used around him or her.
1 year	Many children speak single words (such as "ma-ma"). Infants use single words to express entire sentences. Complex meanings may underlie single words.
1½ years	Many children use two- or three-word phrases ("see baby"). Children begin to develop their own language rule systems. Children may have a vocabulary of about 300 words.
2–3 years	Children use such grammatical morphemes as plural suffix /s/, auxiliary verb *is*, and irregular past tense. They use simple and compound sentences and understand tense and numerical concepts such as "many" and "few." Vocabulary is about 900 words.
3–4 years	The past tense appears, but children may overgeneralize the *-ed* and *-s* markers. Negative transformation appears. Children understand numerical concepts such as "one," "two," and "three." Speech becomes more complex, with more adjectives, adverbs, pronouns, and prepositions. Vocabulary is about 1,500 words.
4–5 years	Language is more abstract, and more basic rules of language are mastered. Children produce grammatically correct sentences. Vocabulary includes approximately 2,500 words.
5–6 years	Most children use complex sentences quite frequently. They use correct pronouns and verbs in the present tense. The average number of words per oral sentence is 6.8. It has been estimated that the child understands approximately 6,000 words.
6–7 years	Children speak complex sentences that use adjectival clauses: conditional clauses beginning with *if* appear. Language becomes more symbolic. Children begin to read about, write about, and understand concepts of time and seasons. The average sentence is 7.5 words long.
7–8 years	Children use relative pronouns as objects in subordinate adjectival clauses ("I have a cat that I feed every day"). Subordinate clauses beginning with *when*, *if*, and *because* appear frequently. The average number of words per oral sentence is 7.6.
8–10 years	Children begin to relate concepts to general ideas through use of such connectors as *meanwhile* and *unless*. The subordinating connector *although* is used correctly by 50 percent of children. The active present participle and perfect participle appear. The average number of words in an oral sentence is 9.0.
10–12 years	Children use complex sentences with subordinate clauses of concession introduced by *nevertheless* and *in spite of*. The auxiliary verbs *might*, *could*, and *should* appear frequently. Children have difficulties distinguishing among past, past perfect, and present perfect tenses. The average number of words in an oral sentence is 9.5.

Reading Acquisition

Just as theorists have attempted to explain how children acquire oral language, researchers have attempted to create models of how children acquire written language, that is, learn to read. Some theorists view reading acquisition as a result of children's learning the smallest units of the task (letters, sounds), putting the parts together (blending), memorizing the units that cannot easily be broken into isolated parts (sight vocabulary), and, finally, learning the complexities of higher-level symbol-sound relationships (rules) (Samuels, 1976). If this model of reading acquisition were related to theories of language acquisition, it would be somewhat similar to the behaviorist school of thought. Segments of both oral and written language are isolated, repeated, reinforced, and added to, segment by segment, until they approximate adult models.

Other theorists view reading acquisition as the result of children's immersion in print. Children are exposed to print, they hear and understand print, they start to see correspondences between print and speech, they begin to recognize relationships between written and oral language, and finally they start to abstract rules that govern the way sounds are represented by combinations of letters. In this view, oral language is the most important aid to the acquisition of reading. Reading is successful when readers use the familiar skills of understanding speech and apply those skills to understanding an author's message (Goodman, 1974). This view is reminiscent of the nativist theory.

As is true with theories of language acquisition, no theory of reading acquisition completely describes the phenomenon of reading. However, reading acquisition theories do add to our understanding of how reading is acquired.

Throughout this text, reading has been referred to as a language process. Print represents in graphic form many of the vocabulary items, phrases, experiences, ideas, and structural patterns that children have heard and used in oral language. Just as children use meaning (semantics), word order (syntax), and sound (phonology) to decode and to understand oral language, so should those three factors aid them in the decoding and understanding of print. A major responsibility of the teacher of reading is to help new readers to make these important links.

Language and the School-Age Child

By the time the typical six-year-old enters school, he or she is a relatively proficient user and comprehender of the language. Be-

Reading acquisition is fostered when teachers of very young children read to them often, discuss what is read, and assist them in making the link between oral and written language.

tween 6,000 and 8,000 word forms have been mastered. These words fit in one or more of the following vocabularies.

The *listening vocabulary* consists of words that children can understand when they hear them. They may not use the words, but they comprehend them when they are spoken by others. This vocabulary is usually the largest.

The *speaking vocabulary* consists of words children can recognize, understand, and produce orally. This vocabulary is constantly growing but is smaller than the listening vocabulary.

The *reading vocabulary* consists of words that children can decode and comprehend. Most children entering first grade have at least a minimal reading vocabulary. Most recognize their name, signs for restaurants like McDonald's, names of cereals, and the like. Others recognize much more. This vocabulary is often very small but becomes greatly expanded when reading instruction begins.

The *writing vocabulary* consists of words children can under-stand, produce orally, read, and spell. Because of the multiple de-mands on this vocabulary, it usually is the smallest for many school years.

Insights into Language Use   In addition to possessing several words, most children have also internalized several key insights into language and its use. They know that language is used to communicate with others. This communication allows them to share their ideas and experiences with others. They have also learned that specialized, accepted forms of communication must be observed. Special lan-guage must be used to begin and end conversations, greet individuals, take one's leave, meet new people, answer the telephone, and so on. They know that language is used to get things done and that they can use language to fulfill their needs and desires. They know that language is used for personal reasons. Children use language to learn more about themselves and to see how they compare to others. They know that language is used to find out about the world. They use language to gather information by asking questions about their en-vironment. And they know that language is used for imagination and play. They use language to stretch their imaginations, to pretend, and to explore.

Most children enter first grade with the ability to use language in each of these ways. They have learned language skills through constant interaction with others in their linguistic environment. They have been exposed to a variety of models and have learned slightly different forms from each. They have heard language from adult family members, child family members, peers, adult neighbors and friends, television characters, book characters, and so on. Language has developed in a context predominantly free from stress, tension, or punishment. Language, for the most part, has been highly moti-vating and reinforcing.

Based on these factors, most children's language experiences have been varied, positive, and reinforcing. If reading instruction is to be effective maximally, teachers must extend this language base through discussion and verbal communication and must show chil-dren how to apply this wealth of language skills to the decoding and comprehension of print.

Role of the Teacher

Though most children enter school with appropriately developed linguistic abilities, many children do not. It is important that teachers become aware of possible linguistic problems to provide assistance for such children. Often children who are weak in their language development demonstrate problems in two major areas: the development of receptive language skills and the development of productive language skills.

Fostering Receptive Language   Receptive language is incoming language. If children have underdeveloped receptive language skills, they do not appropriately comprehend oral (and often written) language. Difficulty in this area might be demonstrated in one or more of the following ways.

1.   Children may not understand many commonly used words; they may have inadequate vocabulary development. Often they have particular difficulty understanding abstract words. Many children have simply not been exposed to a sufficient variety of adult models of oral language. They may not have had adequate conversations or been read to. They might need more direct discussion of and instruction in vocabulary.

Children who have difficulty with vocabulary development have specific needs in classroom instruction, both in and outside of the reading group. The following are some strategies to extend vocabulary.

☐   Provide vocabulary preinstruction prior to reading instruction.
☐   Provide experience (real or vicarious) for all vocabulary instruction.
☐   Expose children to a variety of interesting words.
☐   Match words to pictures or actual objects.
☐   Classify words into categories, such as people, food, animals, sports, emotions, and so on.
☐   Show pictures and have children use a variety of words to describe them.
☐   Focus on synonyms and antonyms.
☐   Develop a special vocabulary program to focus directly on vocabulary growth. Spend more time learning vocabulary automatically.
☐   Talk about words constantly in the classroom to make children word conscious.
☐   Read to children daily and discuss the material with them.

2.   Children may not understand common sentence forms. Some children have difficulty processing relatively familiar sentences, particularly when they are asked to draw inferences based on what they hear. Such children tend to perform very poorly on reading comprehension or language comprehension tasks. Some strategies that may be used to help these children are the following.

□   Have children draw inferences based on simple sentences. For example, "Up in the mountains the wildflowers were in full bloom." Ask "What season might it be?" "What makes you think that?"

□   Read sentences and have children identify "who," "when," "where," "why," and "how."

□   Read sentences with words or phrases left out and have children complete the sentences appropriately.

□   Play the "I'm thinking of a word" game. Have a word in mind and give clues until someone guesses the word.

□   Ask questions that develop thinking skills, like "How are a turtle and a fish alike?" "How would a blind person know when food on a stove is burning?"

□   Provide practice in analogies, such as ring is to _____ as bracelet is to wrist; banana is to apple as carrot is to _____.

□   Use divergent questions during and after reading. (See Chapter 4.)

3.   Children may have difficulty following directions, because of underdeveloped auditory skills or simply because of a failure to attend or focus their attention. Since much of school experience involves following directions, teachers must provide practice in the skill. Some strategies follow.

□   Pass out a number of objects and direct students to respond if they have a specific object. For example, "Stand if you have a blue plastic object." "Put your hand up if you have something you can use for cutting."

□   Call children to order or dismiss them, using specific directions. For example, "Boys with blond hair may go." "Girls who have sneakers on may go."

□   Provide children with a blank piece of paper and a pencil. Give directions that result in a specific design. For example, "Draw a circle in the top right-hand corner. Draw a triangle in the bottom left-hand corner. Write a number seven in the circle."

□   Read directions that will result in a usable product, such as a kite.

□   Have children respond to workbook directions that require skill knowledge: "Circle the word *through*. Put an X on the word that starts like *play*. Draw a line under the word that means 'little.' Put a number 1 beside the word that rhymes with *pin*.

4.   Children may have difficulty listening critically and making judgments. This may be the result of difficulty in appropriate listening, critical thinking, or a combination. Many children have not been

exposed to purposeful listening in their home environments. They have not been questioned on levels that develop critical thought. In addition, many children have not been listened to enough to develop good listening skills from adult models. Listening skills are vital to the development of appropriate comprehension. Some examples of activities that develop listening skills are the following.

☐ Model good listening skills for children. Be an active listener by maintaining eye contact with children who speak to you, responding fully to their questions, asking appropriate questions, and encouraging discussion.

☐ Read daily to children. Encourage discussion of the material and use a variety of questions.

☐ Expand the use of questions that develop critical thinking skills, such as questions that ask children to predict, identify facts or opinions, identify factual or fictional material, respond to truth or falsehood, and the like.

☐ Read a variety of print forms to children — stories, articles, poetry, newspaper clippings, content-area material, and so on.

☐ Read to children and have them listen for specific reasons, such as for synonyms of a given word, for antonyms of a given word, for specific facts, for descriptions, for reasons for behaviors or emotions, for rhyming words, for facts and opinions.

Fostering Expressive Language Expressive language is language produced by an individual. Children who have underdeveloped expressive language skills have difficulty communicating effectively with oral (and often written) language. Some of the more frequent areas of difficulty are the following.

1.   Children may have difficulty formulating expressive sentences. Such children often speak in sentence fragments and use few words. They may seem hesitant to communicate orally or participate in discussions. Some sociolinguists, such as Bernstein (1961), attempt to relate language production to social-class variables. Bernstein refers to two basic categories of speakers: those who use an "elaborated code" and those who use a "restricted code." Elaborated-code speakers usually come from the higher social classes, in which play, language activity, discussion, and interaction are encouraged. Problem solving and exploration are also expected. These children tend to use language as a tool to communicate, solve problems, analyze, synthesize, gain information, and meet their needs. They use complex language structures, varied vocabulary, and expressive language.

Restricted-code speakers, according to Bernstein, usually come from the lower social classes. Their environments tend to discourage exploration (often due to limited play space), to contain more controlling and disapproving language, and to emphasize the "correct," thus blocking exploration of alternatives. Such children often do not engage in much discussion with adults and are more accustomed to linguistically passive activities (watching TV) than to linguistically active ones (reading and discussion). Their language usually includes simple sentences, a restricted range of grammatical forms, few subordinate clauses, few abstract words, and a limited range of words.

Bernstein points out that the use of restricted code does not mean linguistic deficiency or inability. It simply means those children have a different language experience than elaborated-code children. They hear restricted-code speakers in their social environments and model that code.

There are many strategies that teachers can use to extend children's oral language production, among them the following.

☐ Model elaborated language for children. Don't speak down to them.

☐ Read a variety of literature to children and provide opportunities for discussion.

☐ Expand on "show and tell" by asking questions about objects and having children respond.

☐ Give children objects and have them describe them in as much detail as possible. Lead them to pay attention to all aspects — size, color, texture, use, weight, and so on.

☐ Have children describe pictures, using as much detail as possible.

☐ Use wordless storybooks and have children create texts to go along with the pictures.

☐ Help children memorize familiar poems, rhymes, jingles, and the like.

☐ Provide puppets for role playing.

☐ Use questions that encourage language, such as "What would happen if?" "Suppose" "How many ways?" "How do you know that?" "What do you think?"

☐ Use sentence expansion techniques. For the sentence "The man ran down the street," ask "What kind of man?" (Fat, thin, with the brown hat.) "How did he run?" (Quickly, slowly, with a limp.) "Why did he run?" (To catch the bus, to get to his house, because he was late for an appointment.)

☐ Use sentence combining techniques, such as "I have a dog. The dog is fluffy" = "I have a fluffy dog."

☐ Provide children with phrases such as "in the house," "over the bridge," and "loud and clear," and have them use the phrases in sentences.

2. Children may have inadequate speaking vocabularies. Many children use a few words over and over and do not introduce new words into their conversations. It is important that teachers help children to expand their speaking vocabularies. Some suggestions follow.

☐ Provide incentives for word use. Use the "Word of the Week" idea, in which you choose one word to reinforce each week. Teach that word on Monday and throughout the week have children use the word. If they use it correctly in speaking, they receive 1 point. If they use it in writing, they gain 2 points. They can earn a maximum of 4 points per day. If by the end of the week they earn 12 or more points, reward them.

☐ Provide activities that stimulate language use.

☐ Have children build words from single root words, such as *man / postman, mailman, man-of-war, love / loving, loves, lover, lovely, loved.*

☐ List synonyms and antonyms of words.

☐ Provide words with multiple meanings (such as *run*) and have children use the words in as many ways as possible.

☐ Provide opportunities for storytelling or retelling of stories that have been read.

☐ Outlaw "tired" words from the classroom, such as *bad, good, big, little, happy, sad.*

☐ Have children keep personal notebooks of favorite words or new words.

☐ Have a "Favorite Words" display each week and provide time to discuss new words daily.

☐ Encourage, recognize, and reinforce the use of new words.

3. Children may not display appropriate language skills in school because they perceive school as a threatening environment. Some children feel rejection, hostility, or fear in school, and these feelings cause them to withhold their language. They simply choose not to share their language any more than is mandatory. Thus, in school, they do not practice their language normally and it does not seem to develop appropriately. Teachers can take steps to create a classroom environment that is conducive to the production and development of language, following some of the suggestions below.

☐ Create a warm and open atmosphere in the classroom.

☐ Provide opportunities for nonverbal activities such as music, art, dance, and play.

☐ Enhance children's self-concept and self-image.

☐ Provide nonthreatening situations in which language can be practiced (learning centers, story time, and the like).

☐   Be accepting of children's dialects.
☐   Provide meaningful experiences with language.
☐   Praise children when they communicate orally.
☐   Expose children to literature that deals with a variety of sex-role, racial, ethnic, and linguistic models.
☐   Spend time conversing individually with children. Encourage and praise verbal interaction.

Language Stimulation in the Classroom

No teacher would deny the importance of developing language skills in the classroom. We have seen that reading is part of the language arts system, which includes reading, writing, listening, and speaking. A well-rounded language arts experience must incorporate exposure to and growth in all areas. Furthermore, teachers must have as a primary objective the integration of the language arts. Reading cannot be separated from speaking (discussion), listening, or writing. Reading to children, conversing with them, and listening to them must be continuous goals of any language arts program.

Language development should be a major goal at all grade levels, but it is an absolute necessity at the primary level (K–3). Teachers should not only encourage language in the classroom but also plan ongoing activities specifically designed to stimulate language.

Conversation and Discussion

Conversation and discussion should be constant parts of the classroom environment. Children should be exposed daily to a sharing time in which issues of common interest are discussed. This time can sometimes be loosely structured, thus allowing children to share personal information. At other times it can be teacher-directed for the purpose of discussing future class projects, school issues, class programs, progress, school, community, or national news.

In addition to a daily chatting time, teachers can institute a weekly purposeful discussion period. Such a period would be designed to develop critical thinking, reasoning, problem solving, and rational thinking skills. During this session, a specific topic would be chosen and a specific goal set. Topics could vary weekly, as could goals. Possible topics might include classroom behavior, playground behavior, helping substitute teachers, reading and discussing a story, discussing a television program, raising money, a possible field trip, putting out a class newsletter, or class responsibility. The overriding

Having a daily informal chatting time in the classroom promotes oral language development and provides added concept learning for children.

goal of these discussion periods should be use of language to extend thinking and problem-solving skills. It is very important that all children be encouraged to participate.

In addition to discussion and conversation periods, teachers can use a variety of language centers that can be rotated each week or two. Children can be scheduled into these centers or allowed to participate when their work is completed. Such centers can include the following activities.

Telephoning. Most telephone companies have kits or materials, including model telephones, for school use. Children can be led to converse about specific issues in the classroom, scenes from stories they have read, or topics of their own choice.

Interviewing. Children can interview other children or teachers. Their interviewers can be tape-recorded and later written up for the class. Children can also assume roles based on stories they have read and interview each other.

Storytelling. Children can compose or retell stories. Their stories can be tape-recorded and written down later. Older children can also be asked to work with younger children to transcribe the stories.

Jokes and riddles. These can be read by the teacher on tape and groups of children can work together to compose their own jokes and riddles.

Creative dramatics. Children can be assisted in acting out stories or writing their own plays.

Imagining. Children can be involved in creative writing and sharing of their stories.

Manipulation. This center would include things to touch, see, feel, and do. The objects would be related to content being studied in reading, social studies, or science. Children would be encouraged to experience and discuss the objects.

Brainstorming. In this center particular problems may be posed (on tape or in writing). Children work in pairs or small groups and brainstorm many solutions or alternatives and the feasibility or consequence of each.

Integrating Oral Language Development with Reading Instruction

The reading lesson provides a very appropriate place in which to focus on language development. This focus serves a twofold purpose: It encourages interactive teaching by heightening communication between teachers and children and between children and print, and it develops both oral language and understanding of written material.

With a few modifications, the reading period can be used to extend oral language skills. Both the workbook and the text can be used to stimulate expressive language. Following are examples of how the workbook and the text can be used.

Use of the Workbook   A workbook page usually provides print and pictures, both of which can be used to stimulate language. To use the print as a language stimulus, teachers can have children perform four basic tasks during reading instruction:

1. Read words, phrases, or sentences.
2. Use words or phrases in sentences.
3. Manipulate the print. This requires children to give words that begin with a particular letter or sound; give synonyms for

words; give antonyms for words; identify why two words or ideas are alike or different; state locations where words would be found, such as *fish/ocean, lion/jungle*; state where action words would be done, such as *swim/pool, skate/rink*; and give rhyming words.

4. Follow directions. This requires children to circle special words; place an X through a word with a particular meaning; underline a word that begins with a particular letter or sound; and place a number beside a word that rhymes with some other word.

To use the pictures as stimuli, teachers can discuss them according to color, shape, use, emotions, locations, identification, or classification.

The actual instruction of a workbook page on the application of skill activities from Houghton Mifflin's *Honeycomb* might be carried out as on page 299.

Use of the Texts Reading texts provide many opportunities for language expression. The strategies for extending language fall into three specific categories: introductory language activities, concurrent language activities, and follow-up language activities.

Introductory activities, used before reading, are designed to stimulate language, to help children focus on important aspects of the story, to help children become aware of visual clues, and to help children use initial material for making appropriate predictions. The strategies involve asking questions such as the following.

☐ Look at the title. What do you think it means?

☐ Do you think the selection is true or make-believe? Why?

☐ Where do you think the story takes place? Why?

☐ What season is it? How do you know?

☐ What characters are in the pictures? What part do you think they play in the story?

☐ Describe the settings, specific characters, scenes, and so on.

☐ Isolate appropriate words from the title or headings and give another word that has the same meaning.

☐ How do you think this person feels? What in the picture makes you think that?

☐ What is the format of the selection? (Poetry, story, play.)

☐ What do you think is the emotional content of the story? (Happy, sad, fearful.) What clues lead you to believe that?

Once the stage has been set both linguistically and conceptually, children are ready to read the material.

1. The girl is too little to walk.

   She just ___crawls___ .

   crumbs   (crawls)   cooks

2. Carla was in a play.

   She had on a ___crown___ .

   (crown)   rack   crack

3. I will make a picture.

   I want some ___crayons___ .

   (crayons)   crackers   cookies

4. Andy was sick.

   He wanted to ___cry___ .

   camp   (cry)   crust

5. I can see them working.

   There is a ___crack___ in the fence.

   crash   cold   (crack)

ACTIVITIES WITH THE PRINT

1. Have children read each set of word choices first (*crumbs*, *crawls*, *cooks*).
2. Discuss each word and have children use each word in a sentence.
3. Ask questions that require that children demonstrate comprehension, such as the following.

   Give me three things that leave crumbs.
   Give me two things you would cook.
   Give me another word for "sick."
   How are the words *crayons* and *crackers* alike and different?

4. Give directions such as the following.

   Put a number 1 beside the word *crumbs*.
   Circle the word *rock*.
   Cross out the word that means "ill."
   Underline a word that rhymes with *down*.

5. Have students read the sentences and supply the correct answers.

ACTIVITIES WITH THE PICTURES

Ask questions such as the following.

   What part in the play did Carla get? How do you know? What play do you think it was?
   How many crayons are in the box?
   What is the shape of the box?
   What does the boy have in his mouth?
   Why does he have it in his mouth?
   Where is the picture of the infant?

Concurrent activities, used during reading, are designed to encourage oral discussion on all levels of thought during reading, to foster higher levels of comprehension, to develop expressive language abilities, and to expose children to varied points of view and forms of expression.

As children read, teachers can stop them at appropriate points in the text and require them to perform tasks such as the following.

- □   Give synonyms or antonyms of specific words.
- □   Anticipate outcomes of situations.
- □   Predict what will happen next.
- □   Identify feelings and emotions of characters.
- □   Give opinions about the reasons for the actions and behavior of characters.
- □   Compare and contrast characters, scenes, reactions, feelings, and so on.
- □   Identify and explain unstated assumptions.
- □   Predict final words or phrases in sentences and then verify predictions: "John closed the _____." "It was late at night so Jane went _____."
- □   Generate alternative actions.
- □   Generate alternative solutions to problems.

Once the selection has been concluded, teachers can use further strategies to extend comprehension, appreciation, and interaction. Such follow-up activities foster understanding of material by expanding both oral expression and textual comprehension, further develop expressive language, develop memory skills, provide practice in skills of sequence, categorization, and problem solving, integrate the language arts, and provide experiences with formalized and functional language.

Teachers can provide children with opportunities to get involved in activities such as the following.

- □   Retell the story from memory.
- □   Retell the story using picture clues.
- □   Look at two or three pictures and place them in proper sequence.
- □   Play classification games using specific words in the story.
- □   Ask and answer specific questions from the story that fall into the categories "why," "how," "when," "where," and "who."
- □   Role-play various situations from the text, such as meeting a new friend, answering the door, inviting a friend to play.
- □   Act out selected scenes from the text.

Application of Activities

We can see how these strategies can be used in actual instruction by considering the story "Can a Mouse Really Help?" (*Houghton Mifflin Reading Series*, 1976). The story is about a little mouse who is very unhappy; none of the animals will play with him because he is too small. Rabbit, Squirrel, Tiger, and Lion all ignore him until he helps Lion out of a dangerous trap. Then all the animals realize that, although he is small, Mouse really can help.

Introductory activities could include the following.

Describe Mouse in detail. (Picture clue)

What season do you think it is? How do you know? (Picture clue)

Where is Mouse? (Picture clue)

Is this a real or a make-believe story? How do you know? (Experience)

Read the title. What do you think Mouse can help do? (Experience; prediction)

How does Mouse feel? How do you know? (Picture clue)

Concurrent activities might include questions like those below.

Sample Text	*Activities*
Mouse was not happy.	Give me other words for *happy*.
"No one will play with me," said Mouse.	Why won't anyone play with him? (Prediction)
"Hi, Rabbit!" said Mouse. "Can you play?"	What do you think the answer will be? (Prediction)
"No," said Rabbit. "I want to see how far I can jump. You'll get in my way. You're too little. Go away, Mouse!"	Describe Rabbit. (Picture clue) What is Rabbit getting ready to do? (Picture clue) Give other words for *little*. How do you think Mouse feels now? Why? Have you ever been in a situation like this? How did you feel?
"Wait, Squirrel!" said Mouse. "Where are you going?" "I have to go to work," Squirrel said.	What work does Squirrel do? How do you know? Why do you think he does that work? (Picture clue)
"I could help you," said Mouse. "You couldn't help me," said Squirrel. You're too little."	What do you think Squirrel will say? Why? Describe Squirrel. (Picture clue) What is another word for little?

One method of developing expressive oral language is to have children retell stories and act out specific characters in the plot. These roles may then be performed for the reading group, the class, or for children in lower grades.

"You aren't *that* big, you know" said Mouse.

What is another word for *big*?

"I don't want to be seen with a mouse," said Squirrel.

Why doesn't Squirrel want to be seen with Mouse? What do you think about that?

Follow-up activities can be conducted by the teacher, an aide, or an older student.

Retell the story from memory.
Retell the story using only the pictures.
Do a sequence activity based on the text.
Play classification games, such as finding words in the text that fall into the categories of "animals," "things we do," and "ways we feel."
Have children ask and answer questions from the story that deal with who, why, when, where, or how.
Have children role-play a favorite scene.
Have children change the conclusion of the story.
Have children create three-line riddles about characters and ask each other the riddles.

These activities can help teachers use the traditional reading period not only to develop reading skills but also to stimulate oral language expression and extend comprehension.

This intensive attention to language development need not be applied to all children. Some children have highly developed language and comprehension skills and do not need such focused instruction. Some children have obviously weak language skills and require more direct attention, exposure, and instruction. Teachers are urged to vary their level of instruction based on the needs of the children.

Summary

The development of language is one of the most fascinating and complex areas of study. Most adults acquired language so automatically and effortlessly that they are unaware of the magnitude of the task. By the time most children arrive at school, they have learned a great deal about their language. They have a remarkable knowledge of vocabulary and know how to use elements of word order (syntax), meaning (semantics), and sound (phonology) to understand and use language easily and rapidly. This knowledge is vital and most helpful in the acquisition and development of reading skills.

Some children, however, have inadequate language skills. This inadequacy negatively affects not only language but reading development. Teachers must help children develop their linguistic abilities, both oral and written. Reading instruction should not be divorced from the other language arts. All the language arts are mutually dependent and can be used to extend each other. The reading period is an ideal place in which to develop language skills that will enhance not only oral language but also reading development.

References

Bernstein, B. "Social Class and Linguistic Development: A Theory of Social Learning." In *Education, Economy and Society*, edited by A. H. Halsey, J. Floud, C. A. Anderson. New York: Free Press, 1961.

Goodman, K. *The Psycholinguistic Nature of the Reading Process*. Detroit, Mich.: Wayne State University Press, 1974.

Houghton Mifflin Reading Series. Honeycomb, first-grade text. Boston: Houghton Mifflin, 1976.

Houghton Mifflin Reading Series. Honeycomb, first-grade workbook. Boston: Houghton Mifflin, 1976.

Lenneberg, E. H. *Biological Foundations of Language*. New York: Wiley, 1967.

McNeill, D. *The Acquisition of Language*. New York: Harper & Row, 1970.

Norton, D. *The Effective Teaching of Language Arts*. Columbus, Ohio: 1980.

Samuels, S. J. "Hierarchical Subskills in the Reading Acquisition Process." In *Aspects of Reading Acquisition*, edited by T. J. Guthrie. Baltimore: Johns Hopkins University Press, 1976.

Skinner, B. F. *Verbal Behavior*. New York: Appleton, 1957.

Staats, A. W. "Behaviorism and Cognitive Theory in the Study of Language: A Neopsycholinguistics." In *Language Perspectives: Acquisition, Retardation, and Intervention*, edited by R. L. Schiefelbusch and L. L. Lloyd. Baltimore: University Press, 1974.

———. *Learning, Language and Cognition*. New York: Holt, Rinehart and Winston, 1968.

Vygotsky, L. S. *Thought and Language*. Cambridge: M.I.T. Press, 1973.

Wadsworth, B. J. *Piaget's Theory of Cognitive Development*. New York: David McKay, 1971.

11

Developing Interest in and Motivation Toward Reading

Few teachers would deny the importance of motivation in learning to read. Reading instruction should not neglect motivation, but it often does, with tragic results. Many children possess the skills to read but never learn to read simply because they are not motivated to pick up a book and read other than assigned material. Other children have never even been motivated enough to learn the basic skills. Such children see reading as nonmotivating and even aversive. Many poor readers fit in this category and remain poor readers because they don't read enough to change their status.

One of the most important goals of reading instruction must be the development and fostering of motivation toward reading. Although teachers can provide a great deal of motivation in the teaching environment, the most effective way to achieve this goal is for both parents and teachers to combine their efforts and expose children to the pleasure of reading in the total home-school environment.

□   What is the teacher's role in the development of motivation toward and interest in reading?

□   What are some factors that contribute to motivation toward reading?

□   What is the role of computers in the teaching of reading?

□   How can computers be used to motivate children to read?

□   What are some strategies that teachers can use to motivate children toward reading?

□   How can writing be used to motivate children to read?

□   What is the role of the parent in children's reading experiences? How can teachers help parents to get involved?

Motivation for Reading

Several decades ago, the need to motivate children toward reading was not as important as it is today. Reading was one of the two major ways of finding out about the world. People either listened to the radio or read newspapers and magazines. Forms of family entertainment were limited, and reading to and with the family, conversation, and interaction were established parts of growing up. Adults recognized the necessity of reading and encouraged children to read. Children often saw adults reading and developed a sense of the importance of reading.

Today our society has drastically changed. The family structure is more flexible. Entertainment options are very diverse. Most homes have not only radios but one or more televisions. People are much more mobile, and it is possible to find out a great deal of information about one's neighborhood, town, state, or country without ever reading. Television has been used to pacify many children from a very young age; before they reach the first grade, children have already been exposed to thousands of hours of TV watching. The structure of the family is changing drastically as well. In most cases, both parents or the single parent work, and time is limited. There is often no time to sit down, read to, discuss with, and interact with children. In most homes, adults do not often read for pleasure, and children are not accustomed to owning books. The recent emphasis on video games, not only in the arcades but also for home use on television sets, has further decreased the actual time that many children are exposed to the pleasure and power of print.

Consequently, educators must realize that today, attention to motivation is more imperative than ever. We must also understand that, while some children will successfully learn how to read without any overt effort on the part of the teacher to motivate them, some children will learn to read only if the teacher first creates a desire to read and an interest in print.

Factors That Affect Motivation

Many factors affect children's motivation toward reading, both in the home and in the school.

Home Environment   Children begin very early to form impressions about the value of reading. Many factors within the home contribute to the motivation children have toward reading, including the following.

☐ There is a variety of printed material around the home. Children are exposed early to newspapers, magazines, picture books, storybooks, and the like. Printed material is available to them and is familiar to them.

☐ Adults read often to gather information and for pleasure. Children see the adults in their family reading print, sharing what they read, laughing at print, and enjoying reading.

☐ Children have their own collection of books. They have favorite books and are encouraged to use them.

☐ Children are read to at home. From early years, parents have read and reread children's favorite stories, poems, and so on, and have discussed the stories, talked about feelings, outcomes, events, and characters. Reading to children is a stable part of the home environment.

☐ Parents take children to the public library and choose books with them. They also give books as gifts.

☐ Parents encourage children to participate in reading. They encourage children to "read" the pictures, join in with reading of familiar passages, words, and so on.

☐ Reading is seen as a tool for gathering information. Often, when children ask questions, parents go to books to find the answers. Children thus see that print can give them information they need.

☐ Print is often used as a reward. It is a treat to hear "just one more" story or a favorite story. If they have done something well, reading to them is often used as a reward.

☐ As children grow up, they are encouraged to write, to learn words, and to read on their own. Their successes are encouraged, praised, reinforced, and rewarded.

☐ Parents take time to answer children's questions about print. They expose children to books that emphasize the alphabet, sounds, rhymes, and so on. When children have a problem, parents take time to help and guide them.

Children who grow up in such an environment come to school not only with a great deal of usable information about reading but also with natural curiosity and motivation toward further learning.

School Environment   Once children come to school, factors within the school environment add to their motivation toward reading and toward learning to read. Some of these factors are the following.

☐ Teachers extend children's exposure to interesting literature by reading to them frequently. Children are constantly reminded

Children begin very early to develop an interest in print. This interest
should be encouraged and developed by parents.

of the need to read and of the joy of reading because teachers read to them a great deal.

☐ Time is provided for children to read books they like. All children get an opportunity during the school day to read or to look at books that interest them.

☐ Teachers know the interests of children and take the time to suggest and expose them to books or magazines that will be motivating to them.

☐ Teachers constantly modify the instruction of reading so that children's needs are met. They never try to force the child to fit a program that has resulted in failure.

☐ Time is provided for children to share what they have read with teachers and with each other.

☐ Children are publicly recognized and rewarded for reading.

☐ Children are encouraged to write and read their own books.

☐ A variety of high-interest reading material is provided in the classroom. Teachers know the value of incidental learning.

☐ Reading lessons are taught in an interesting, varied manner. The pace of the sessions does not foster boredom.

☐ Children are constantly made to interact with print. Questions and tasks focus on helping children respond to, identify with, become involved in, learn from, and enjoy print.

Certainly, parents can motivate children to read without the assistance of teachers. Similarly, teachers can motivate children without the help of parents. Undoubtedly, however, the most effective situation is one in which parents and teachers work together to motivate children toward learning in general and toward reading in particular.

Developing and Maintaining Motivation

Teachers can use many strategies to motivate children to read. These strategies are relatively simple to institute and can easily be integrated into any instructional format. The strategies fall into two categories: working with the home environment and improving the school environment.

Working with the Home Environment Teachers can affect children's motivation toward reading by creating open and healthy communication between the home and the school. If children are to learn to read, then the efforts of the school must be reinforced at home. This is true for *all* children, but it is essential for children who are experiencing difficulty in learning to read.

Teachers often criticize parents for not becoming more involved in their children's education. Indeed, some parents do not accept enough responsibility for their children's learning, but many parents do not respond simply because they do not know specifically what to do with children; they do not understand the extent to which they should become involved in school; or they do not realize the importance of their involvement. Many more parents would become involved if teachers instituted frequent and specific communication between school and home. Such communication would add significantly to the motivation children feel toward learning and reading. A cooperative attitude between parents and teachers also reinforces in children a positive attitude toward reading.

Following are strategies that teachers can use to communicate with the home and specific suggestions that teachers can give to parents so they can help their children read.

1. At the start of the school year, send home a "Reading and Your Child" sheet that provides parents with general ideas about reading with children. This sheet can include such suggestions as the following.

> Read to your child at least ten minutes a day.
> Provide a quiet time free from TV, radio, and so on, to read to and with your child.
> Position the book so that your child can see the print.
> As you come to special words, repeated phrases, and the like, point them out for your child.
> Encourage your child to read familiar segments with you.
> Discuss the story with your child.
> Read something interesting to yourself within sight of your child each week.

2. Periodically throughout the school year, provide parents with "How-to" sheets, each addressing a specific topic such as "How to Question Your Child," "How to Help Your Child with Phonics," "How to Build Sight Vocabulary," and "How to Help Your Child Read Faster." Each sheet can contain a few clear, specific suggestions. Figure 11–1 is a sample how-to sheet. Limit these sheets to one page and give clear, useful, practical ideas. It is important that teachers give parents guidelines about helping children with phonics. Otherwise parents may resort to needless drill that has the potential to threaten the parent-child relationship and create in children avoidance behaviors about reading. Providing parents with alternatives to meaningless drill can greatly foster phonic learning.

FIGURE 11–1
Sample how-to sheet

HOW TO HELP YOUR CHILD WITH PHONICS

When you have some free time with your child, before or after meals, before bedtime, after reading, preparing meals, riding in the car, setting the table, play the following games.

1. "Starts like" game: Give me a word that starts like *step* or *boy*. Find the word in this line that starts like *Mom*.
2. "Ends like" game: Give me a word *or* find a word in this line that ends like *man*.
3. "Rhymes with" game: Give me a word or find a word in this line that rhymes with *bed*.
4. "Thinking of" game: I am thinking of a word that begins with an *m*. (Child guesses.) "It ends with an *n*." (Child guesses.) "It shines at night." Give clues until the child guesses correctly.
5. "Provide the missing word" game: Give the child a sentence or read a sentence and delete or cover the last word. "I'd better open the _____." Have the child guess any word that fits. Then give letter clues as in number 4 until the child guesses the word. Go back and say or read the entire sentence.
6. Segment words and have the child put the sounds together. For example, /b/ +/a/+/t/ = *bat*. This will help with auditory blending.

---

3. Send home monthly progress charts with children. The charts should present areas of growth, areas that need practice, and specific suggestions to parents regarding helping children at home. The information should not be elaborate, but it must be *very* specific. An example is shown in Figure 11–2.

4. With slower readers, send home weekly word practice sheets and ask parents to practice with children. You can time the words initially (phrases, sentences, and short paragraphs can also be used) and ask parents to encourage children to practice until they cut their time in half. Charts can be very simple, as the one in Figure 11–3 shows.

5. At the beginning of each new unit, send a "Unit Information Sheet" home with children. Let parents know about the unit that will be presented and give them suggestions about library books that would be helpful to read to children. This is particularly important for children who lack basic concepts or who have difficulty in comprehension. An example of an information sheet is shown in Figure 11–4.

6. Invite parents to be "parent helpers." Give them opportunities to volunteer their services for regularly scheduled, short segments of time so that they don't see the time commitment as too overwhelming. It might be helpful to seek helpers in two categories:

FIGURE 11–2
Monthly progress chart

READING PROGRESS CHART

Name: Donny Winter

Areas of Growth:

1. Recognizing the words *them, in, through, school,* and *is*
2. Using beginning sounds *br, bl, pr, pl,* and *t*
3. Attitude toward reading

Areas of Need:

1. Recognizing the words *enough, some, then, said,* and *late*
2. Pronouncing beginning letter combinations *st, sp, th,* and *gr*
3. Predicting what will happen next

Comments:

Parents, as you read with Donny this month, please practice the need areas with him. Thank you for working with Donny. I am very pleased with his progress.

FIGURE 11–3
Weekly word practice sheet

Name: Cindy Smith

Words	*Phrases*
in	in the house
the	the big man
school	go to school
went	I went home
mouse	a little mouse
we	we went to school
Time: 25 seconds	Time: 1 minute 10 seconds
Goal: 10 seconds	Goal: 30 seconds

parent helpers in the classroom and in the home. If parents choose the first option, they would come into the classroom and work with individual children or small groups on teacher-assigned tasks. If they choose the second option, they would agree to perform certain tasks with their children and send a completed checklist back to school each week. The checklist would include specific reading-related tasks. An example is shown in Figure 11–5.

7. Make parent-teacher conferences as positive, specific, and helpful as possible. Inform parents of specific areas of strength, growth, and need. Give them specific suggestions for helping their

FIGURE 11–4
Information sheet

UNIT INFORMATION SHEET

Dear Parents,

Next month we will be beginning our unit on *Ecology*. The unit will last for 3 weeks. During this time please read at least 4 of the following books to *Helen* and discuss the material with *her*. All the books are available both at the public library and from the school library.

All Upon a Stone by Jean George
Around the House that Jack Built: A Tale of Ecology by Roz Abisch
The Beaver Pond by Alvin Tresselt
The Only Earth We Have by Laurence Pringle
The Seal and the Slick by Don Freeman
Who Really Killed Cock Robin? An Ecological Mystery by Jean Craighead George

Also, on January 24, at 7 p.m., on Channel 10, National Geographic will be representing a 30-minute special on ecology. It would be helpful if you watched the program with your child.

Thank you.

Mr. Greer

---

child. Acknowledge evidence of parents' work with children and encourage further involvement.

Working with the School Environment One of the most important elements in the development of motivation toward reading is the classroom environment. Motivation and interest are not likely to occur in an environment that does not foster and encourage open communication, stimulation of language, and a variety of print options. Although there are several specific suggestions that can be made to help teachers interest children in reading, motivation depends to a large degree on the teacher's attitude, behavior, and feeling toward print. Teachers who love to read, who enjoy books, and who value reading for the sheer joy of it tend to transmit to children an interest in and a curiosity about reading and learning to read. A delight in reading is often contagious, and many children exposed to this delight "catch" the joy of reading. Perhaps the most important ingredients in a motivating reading environment are delight in and sharing of print. Certain principles are basic to a motivating, stimulating, and interesting classroom reading environment.

Principle 1: Read aloud to children daily. Part of the school day should be devoted to reading interesting, high-quality material to

FIGURE 11–5
Reading checklist for parents

PARENT HELPERS IN THE HOME: READING CHECKLIST

Name _____

Dear Parent: during this week please take the time to complete the following tasks with your child. As you do so, check off the task and please return this checklist on Monday morning, _____ (date).

Tasks	Completed	Not Done
1. Help your child learn the following sight words: *through*, *enough*, *strange*, *breakfast*, *parade*, *beautiful*.	_____	_____
2. Read and discuss the following books:		
The Terrible Thing That Happened at Our House by Marge Blaine	_____	_____
Annie and the Old One by Miska Miles	_____	_____
Maxie by Mildred Kantrowitz	_____	_____
3. Help your child to practice the following letter-sound relationships: *pr*=/pr/, *gr*=/gr/, and *sp*=/sp/.	_____	_____

Also use the ideas on the "Help Your Child with Phonics" sheet sent home last month.

Thank you for being an "In the Home" parent helper.

Miss Marks

children. Children need to hear the sound of print read by a capable adult model. The material read need not be limited to narrative stories. It can also be factual material. Children need to hear the rhythm of a variety of written language forms. They need to be exposed to material that makes them think, respond, laugh, cry, learn, change, and grow. Reading to children not only exposes them to fine printed material but also makes them realize that reading is important enough for the teacher to take the time to do consistently. It is important that teachers include books they love and those in which they have a personal investment. To expose children to a variety of high-quality material, begin with the Caldecott Award Winners and the Newbery Award Winners, which are listed in Appendixes A and B. Following are further suggestions of good read-aloud literature for the primary and intermediate grades.

Primary Grades

Why Mosquitoes Buzz in People's Ears by Vera Aardema, Dial, 1977

The Secret in the Dungeon by Fernando Krahn, Clarion, 1983

Fortunately by Remy Charlip, Parents, 1964

A Circle of Seasons by Leonard Everett, Holiday House, 1982

Strega Nona by Tomie De Paola, Prentice-Hall, 1975

Ashanti to Zulu by Eleanor Estes, Harcourt, 1944

Noisy Nora by Rosemary Wells, Dial, 1973

Chicken Soup with Rice by Maurice Sendak, Harper & Row, 1962

The Velveteen Rabbit by Margery Williams, Doubleday (undated)

When I Was Young in the Mountains by Cynthia Rylant, Dutton, 1982

Crow Boy by Taro Yashima, Viking, 1955

Hailstones and Halibut Bones by Mary O'Neil, Doubleday, 1961

You Read to Me, I'll Read to You by John Ciardi, Lippincott, 1962

Alexander and the Terrible, Horrible, No Good, Very Bad Day by Judith Viorst, Atheneum, 1974

Ira Sleeps Over by Bernard Waber, Houghton Mifflin, 1972

Rainbow Warrior's Bride by Marcus Crouch, Pelham, 1982

Avocado Baby by John Burningham, Crowell, 1982

Blizzard at the Zoo by Robert Bahr, Lothrop, Lee & Shepard, 1982

Clementine's Cactus by Ezra Jack Keats, Viking, 1982

Maria by Thea Dubelaar, Morrow, 1982

The Mousewife by Rumer Godden, Viking, 1982

Mysteriously Yours, Maggie Marmelstein by Marjorie Weinman Sharmat, Harper & Row, 1982

Upper Grades

The Foundling by Donald Carrick, Dial, 1978

Charlie and the Chocolate Factory by Roald Dahl, Knopf, 1964

Sounder by William Armstrong, Harper & Row, 1969

Five Summers by Joann Guernsey, Clarion Books, 1983

Where the Red Fern Grows by Wilson Rawls, Doubleday, 1961

The Best Christmas Pageant Ever by Barbara Robinson, Harper & Row, 1972

Charlotte's Web by E. B. White, Harper & Row, 1952

The Girl Who Cried Flowers by Jane Yolen, Crowell, 1974

Reflections on a Gift of Watermelon Pickle . . . And Other Modern Verse, compiled by Stephen Dunning, Scott, Foresman, 1966

The Wind in the Willows by Kenneth Grahame, Scribner's, 1908

Zeely by Virginia Hamilton, Macmillan, 1967

The Tempering by Gloria Skurzynski, Clarion, 1983
Witch Week by Diana Wynne Jones, Greenwillow, 1982
The Magic Dog by I. G. Edmonds, Dutton, 1982
The Lore and Legends of Flowers by Robert L. Crowell, Crowell, 1982
Fifth Grade Magic by Beatrice Gormley, Dutton, 1982
Cannily, Cannily by Simon French, Angus and Robertson (Sydney, Australia), 1981
The Road to Camlann: The Death of King Arthur by Rosemary Sutcliff, Dutton, 1982
The Sword and the Circle by Rosemary Sutcliff, Dutton, 1981
The Light Beyond the Forest by Rosemary Sutcliff, Dutton, 1980

Principle 2: Provide time for all children to read and to share books. Many classrooms across the country have instituted a "Sustained Silent Reading" period during which all individuals in a classroom read print of their choice for a set period of time (between ten and thirty minutes) (McCracken, 1978; Aulls, 1982). In addition, teachers can provide a "Browse with Books" period during which children read, look at pictures, skim through books, read together, and so on. A period should also be provided at least weekly in which children and the teacher share with the class favorite books they have read during the week. This period can also be used as an "advertisement" session in which children publicize their favorite books and try to persuade others to read them.

Principle 3: Provide a mini-library in your classroom. Part of developing an interest in books is making available a variety of interesting books. Within the classroom there should be picture books, wordless picture books, predictable pattern books, easy reading books, high interest–low vocabulary books, comic books, trade books, magazines, newspapers, content-area books, poetry books, plays, and so on. Books can be borrowed weekly from the library, teachers and children can bring in their favorite books, and parents and community merchants might be asked to donate books. Teachers can also suggest titles of books and magazines that might be added to the school library. Numerous fine book titles have been suggested in this chapter. Following is a list of extremely popular magazines for children. Many of these magazines contain material that can be used to extend children's concepts in literature and in the content areas.

Child Life (ages 7 and up)
1100 Waterway Blvd., Box 567B
Indianapolis, IN 46206
Contains activities, stories, articles. Emphasizes health, nutrition, and safety.

One way of motivating children to read is by providing them easy access to a large variety of interesting print that they can enjoy in a relaxed setting.

Cricket (ages 6–12)
Box 2670
Boulder, CO 80322
Contains stories, poems, and plays.

Dynamite (ages 8–13)
654 Count Morbida's Castle
Marion, OH 43302
Contains articles, features, humor, games, puzzles, and activities.

Ebony Junior (ages 6–12)
Johnson Publishing Co.
820 S. Michigan Ave.
Chicago, IL 60605
Contains articles, stories, and activities.

Jack and Jill Magazine (ages 7 and up)
1100 Waterway Blvd.

Box 567B
Indianapolis, IN 46206
Contains stories, games, songs, poetry, and original writing
and pictures by children.

National Geographic World (ages 8 and up)
National Geographic Society
Washington, DC 20036
Contains feature articles on social studies and science topics.
Includes posters and pull-out pages.

Ranger Rick's Nature Magazine (ages 7 and up)
National Wildlife Federation
1412 16th St. N.W.
Washington, DC 20036
Contains articles dealing primarily with animals, conservation,
and the environment. Includes photos, projects, crafts, and
games.

Scholastic Action (grades 6–9)
Scholastic Magazines
902 Sylvan Ave.
Englewood Cliffs, NJ 07632
Contains high-interest, low-readability (grades 2.0–2.9) stories,
articles, plays, poetry, and activities.

Scholastic Sprint (grades 4–6)
Scholastic Magazines
902 Sylvan Ave.
Englewood Cliffs, NJ 07632
Contains high-interest, low-readability (grades 2.0–2.9) arti-
cles, stories, plays, and games.

Stone Soup: A Magazine by Children (ages 6–12)
Box 83
Santa Cruz, CA 95063
Contains stories, poems, articles, humor, and drawings created
by children ages 6–12 for children ages 6–12.

Weekly Readers (by grade level, K–6)
Xerox Educational Publications
1250 Fairwood Ave.
P.O. Box 444
Columbus, OH 43216
Contains news and current event articles, pictures, puzzles,
games, and activities.

Summer Weekly Readers (by grade level, K–6)
(published six times during the summer)
Xerox Educational Publications
1250 Fairwood Ave.
P.O. Box 444
Columbus, OH 43216
Contains stories, articles, projects, games, and puzzles.

Principle 4: Identify children's interests. Many children become turned off to reading because the material they are asked to read is of no interest to them. If teachers are aware of children's interests, they will be able to guide children's reading into areas that will motivate them to read. One way to identify interests is to administer an interest inventory to each child at the start of the school year. This inventory can then be used to select material for children. An example of an interest inventory follows.

Interest Inventory Questions

Do you have a library card?
How often do you go to the library?
Do you like to be read to? What books do you like to have read?
Does someone read to you often at home? Who?
Do you have favorite books or stories? What are they?
How many books do you own? Where do you keep them?
What kinds of stories do you most like to have read to you?
Can you read any books by yourself? Which ones?
What is your favorite TV show? Why do you like it?
Do you have any collections? What do you collect?
Do you have any hobbies? What are they?
What sports do you like most?
What is your favorite part of the school day? What is your least favorite? Why?
Would you like to learn to read well? Why or why not?
If you could read anything you wanted to, what kinds of things would you read?
What do you not like to have read to you or to read?

Principle 5: Provide incentives for children to read. Some children become initially motivated toward reading when they are rewarded for reading. Reading competitions can be instituted in which children gain points for reading and responding to books. As they accumulate points, they earn certain privileges.

Teachers can also try "Book Karate," in which children read a certain number of books and complete tasks based on each book, thus earning "karate belts" ranging from the white belt (simplest) to the black belt (most difficult).

Another idea is to have "Readers of the Week" (or month) presentations in which two awards are presented: "Reader of the Most Books" and "Most Improved Reader." Children can be given certificates to take home.

Teachers should also orally recognize before the class children who show progress in reading.

Principle 6: Vary the reporting format. Often children become turned off to reading because each time they read they are asked to do a traditional book report. Teachers should have children report on books in a variety of ways and should often give children a choice of reporting formats. There are many alternatives to the traditional book report. Some suggestions follow.

Draw a sketch of your favorite character.
Make placemats or coasters, illustrate them with your favorite scenes, laminate them, and take them home.
Make a wall hanging of your favorite scene.
Compose a poem or a song about your favorite character.
Create a different ending for your story.
Collect pictures to depict particular scenes, mount them, and write explanations.
Write a letter to the author or publisher and give your impressions of the book.
Write a newspaper advertisement for the book.
Develop a crossword puzzle or a word-find puzzle using important words from your story.
Make a timeline illustrating the most important sequential events.
Read your book (or favorite sections) to a group of younger readers.
Prepare a "Book of the Week" display.
Make a series of bookmarks and illustrate them with favorite scenes.
Make a mobile of favorite characters and scenes.
Create a word tree with your favorite words and meanings from the book.
Create a series of riddles that would indicate places or characters from your book.
Make a jacket for your book and illustrate it with a captivating scene.

Compare and contrast two characters.

Tell the story to younger children and draw favorite scenes to illustrate the story as you tell it.

Make a map illustrating the places in your story.

Retell the story on tape.

Write an additional chapter that would extend beyond the end of the book.

Make a collection of favorite quotations from your book.

Create a good test about your book.

Decide on your favorite scene and transform it into a play.

Principle 7: Add variety to instructional sessions. It is difficult for children to be motivated toward reading when the teaching sessions lack variety, interest, interaction, and appropriate pacing. During reading instruction, teachers should use a variety of strategies to introduce, develop, assess, and follow up reading material. This text has stressed the importance of matching strategies to the demands of the material and to students' needs. Lessons should never be allowed to be slow-paced, boring, or totally predictable. Teachers should make an effort to involve all children in the material through appropriate questioning strategies.

Principle 8: Involve children in the writing process and give them opportunities to read their own and their peers' written work. It is very important that children gain exposure to writing. Writing is an effective aid to reading. When children are involved in creating written material, not only do they begin to develop a personal investment in print, but they are also significantly more able to read print. Teachers should frequently help children to write their own material. These creations may be typed or clearly written down, illustrated by the children, bound, and added to the permanent book collection in the classroom or library.

Teachers can involve children in a variety of writing experiences, such as the following.

1. Writing texts to wordless storybooks. Wordless storybooks provide children with pictures that illustrate a plot. After looking at all the pictures, discussing them, and discovering the plot, children tell the story in their own words, thus literally creating the text to go along with the pictures. The teacher's task is to generate discussion and to write the material down for children. This is a very fine way to get young children involved in writing. It also gives them an overall structure in which to create. This form of writing can be started as early as kindergarten. The stories may be typed, illustrated by the children, and used for free reading, group reading, or storytelling. Figure 11–6 is an example of a text written to Fernando Krahn's

Giant Footprints

Once a little house was in a wood. Mom, Dad and the kids went to the house for a vacation. It snowed and snowed. The next morning they looked outside and saw huge footprints.

"This is dangerous," said Dad. "I'd better get my gun."

They followed the footprints up the hill, through a forest, over the house, through the town and the footprints were still there. Soon other people followed, too. They went across the lake, on the other side of the lake, across dangerous paths and then they saw a cave. They went into the cave and there were two big one-footed things.

"Can we keep them? They are neat." said the kids.

"What will we call them?" asked the parents.

"Why, one-footed things, of course," said the kids.

So they tooks the one-footed things home and fed them cereal.

FIGURE 11–6
Wordless storybook text written by a student

wordless storybook *The Mystery of the Giant Footprints*, by a six-year-old first grader, Carl. After the teachers have written down the stories, they can reread them to the children and the children, with the teacher's help, can edit them. At this point, teachers have a perfect opportunity to discuss elements such as capitalization, punctuation, quotations, word choice, and so on. A list of wordless storybooks is presented in Appendix D.

2. Writing stories based on highly predictable pattern books. Predictable pattern books have a very obvious language pattern, like *Brown Bear, Brown Bear* (1974):

> Brown Bear, Brown Bear
> what do you see?
> I see Red Bird
> looking at me.
>
> Red Bird, Red Bird
> what do you see?
> I see Yellow Duck
> looking at me.
>
> Yellow Duck, Yellow Duck
> what do you see?
> I see Blue Horse
> looking at me.

After hearing this story read to them several times, children can be helped to imitate the pattern to write stories of their own. In this case, teachers might ask children: "What if we wanted to write our own Brown Bear story? How could we begin the story? What could we say instead of 'Brown Bear'? Could we say 'Mary, Mary' or 'John, John' or 'Plant, Plant' or 'Table, Table'?" With questions such as these, children can be led to write their own stories. With repeated exposure to this strategy, children will require less prodding and guidance from the teacher.

The stories children write can be written down or typed, illustrated, bound, and read to, with, and by children. Children who are poor readers will find that the strong patterns help their decoding. Reading predictable print also allows a great deal of incidental learning. Predictable print books should be an important part of children's reading and writing experiences. A bibliography of predictable print literature is presented in Appendix C.

3. Writing factual, informative books. Most children have a wealth of knowledge on at least óne topic. Many know a great deal about pets, dogs, cats, dinosaurs, skiing, football, cooking, video games, cars, and so on. Teachers should encourage children to dictate

My Book About Cats

Cats are animals with claws and whiskers and are very fast and <u>smart</u>. A leopard can run up to 70 m.p.h. with its polka-dot coat. It keeps it warm in the winter but cool in the summer.

From kittens to tigers, cats are very playful – playful and fierce. A lion tugs on a rope and..... Oh boy!

When a cat pulls in her claws, it means that it won't scratch. However, a cheeta can't pull their claws in.

Siamese cats do <u>not</u> speak Siamese. (They don't speak U.S.A. either) They do speak cat language (MEOW). They talk to each other. I am not saying that a lion talks to a kitten. That would be too dumb. The kitten wouldn't understand anyway.

A black panther will be a good mother and a good father, too. But you have to be careful. They are not always gentle.

A Poem

We're almost done with our little book.
I'll tell you the name of our author —
Her name is Brooke!

Now, if you liked this book about cats, you would like <u>The Little Book About Mammals</u>. These cats sure do.

FIGURE 11–7
Factual text written by a student

or write about what they know, and the children can illustrate these informational books with pictures or drawings and can share them with the class. Children can read their books to the class, their reading groups, or children in other classes. Parent volunteers, advanced students in the classroom, or children in the upper grades can be asked to assist teachers in writing material for children who are unable to do so. After the initial writing, teachers should help children edit their material. Figure 11–7 contains a factual text written by a six-year-old girl, Brooke. Children should have frequent opportunities to write books like this and to share their books with their friends and family.

4. Writing creative stories. As children gain experience with writing, they should be encouraged to write creative stories based on familiar experiences and situations or on fantasy and science fiction themes. It is important that teachers frequently read a variety of printed material to children to develop an interest in reading and to expose them to different plot options and writing styles.

5. Participating in a young authors' conference. Many schools across the country are involved in programs that encourage children to write, illustrate, and publish their own books. These books are then exhibited and shared in what is called a young authors' conference. Parents, children, teachers, and guests are invited to attend. Children who participate in this conference are on hand during the exhibition to discuss their books. Such a conference allows students who enjoy composing literature to work on a book until it is perfected and to be recognized and praised by their peers, teachers, and parents. Each participating author receives a certificate. Some schools appoint committees of teachers, parents, and students to read the books submitted to the young authors' conference and select one or two books per grade level to receive special recognition. These awards may be given at an assembly at the close of the conference.

Computers and Reading Instruction

The 1980s will undoubtedly be remembered as the first decade in which computers became a routine part of society and the school environment. Although computers have been used for instructional purposes since the start of the 1970s, their presence has been most visible during the early 1980s. Computers hold tremendous promise for providing significant instruction and motivation toward many levels of learning for children. Computers have already made a major impact on education, and many writers predict that they will be primary instructional tools in the vast majority of classrooms within a few years (Brandt, 1983; Dammeyer, 1983; Melmed, 1983). It will very soon be imperative that all teachers have at least a working knowledge of computers. In the field of reading instruction, the potential for computers is limited only by the knowledge and creativity of the individuals using them.

Types of Computer Applications

According to the literature on the use of computers in education, there are two broad categories of computer applications in reading: computer-assisted instruction (CAI) and computer-managed instruction (CMI).

CAI   Computer-assisted instruction is a process in which learners interact directly with the computer and perform lessons that are displayed on the screen. These lessons include drill and practice exercises in reading skills, such as letter identification; sight-word practice; vocabulary; phonics; word, sentence, and paragraph comprehension; and syllabication. CAI also includes tutorial programs designed for remedial readers and games used for extensions, practice, and reinforcement. As students interact with computers and perform specific lessons, their incorrect responses are identified and they are given opportunities to correct their errors. Many programs provide additional activities at the same level as the errors until children demonstrate mastery at that level. Other programs provide a specified number of chances for correction; then, if the child's response is still incorrect, the program will provide the student with the correct response. Many programs are designed to automatically include children's names in responding to their input. For example, the computer might print, "That's the right answer, Susan" or "Try again, Jeff" or "Good job, Peg." This is not only a motivating feature for children, but it also makes the instruction significantly more personal.

CMI   Computer-managed instruction refers to the use of the commuter not as an instructional tool as in CAI but as a record keeper, diagnostic tester, test scorer, and prescriber of what students should study next (O'Donnell, 1982). Students are usually given tests to take on the computer. The computer scores the tests, records the results, analyzes the results, summarizes the analysis, prescribes the level at which the child should receive instruction, and stores that information in the student's name. CMI proves extremely useful to teachers because it relieves them of a great deal of tedious and time-consuming record keeping. Teachers therefore have more time for guiding and instructing children.

Applications to Reading

Computers have major applications to reading management and instruction. The remarkable versatility of the computer makes its applications to the field of reading practically limitless. Thompson (1980), in reviewing the applications of computers to reading instruction, speaks of this versatility, pointing out the following.

1. Computers are capable of containing programs based on the entire range of reading theories. Material can reflect phonic, linguistic, or psycholinguistic perspectives.
2. Computers are capable of supporting a variety of reading content. Exercises can be provided in vocabulary development, word recognition, decoding, and comprehension.
3. Computers are capable of being used equally effectively with different types of learners. They can provide instruction, practice, remediation, and extension to gifted, average, remedial, or severely handicapped readers.
4. Computers are capable of being used in a variety of settings. They can effectively be used with individuals, pairs, small groups, or large groups.

This versatility makes the computer a most valuable asset to teachers. The amazing speed with which computers are being introduced into schools is making it imperative for all teachers to have at least a working knowledge of computers. Many people interpret this as a need for teachers to become experts in computers, and this causes some teachers to be somewhat intimidated by the rapidly progressing computer age. That interpretation is inaccurate, however. Certainly teachers must eventually become familiar with computers, but there are varying degrees of knowledge. O'Donnell (1982) defines three very helpful levels: level 1, computer awareness; level 2, computer use; and level 3, computer programming.

Level 1 At level 1, computer awareness, individuals gain a basic understanding of computers. This might involve an awareness of the role of computers in society and the impact technology is making on society. This awareness might be gained by building a personal knowledge base through discussions with interested individuals and through reading journals and periodicals that provide information relevant to computers and their use. Several such journals are specifically geared to educators:

> *Classroom Computer Learning*
> Pitman Learning, Inc.
> 19 Davis Drive
> Belmont, CA 94002

The Computing Teacher
Dept. of Computer & Information Science
University of Oregon
Eugene, OR 07403

Educational Computer
Box 535
Cupertino, CA 95015

Instructional Innovator
Association for Educational Communication & Technology
1126 16th St. N.W.
Washington, DC 20036

Micro Computers in Education
5 Chapel Hill Drive
Fairfield, CT 06432

Educational Technology
140 Sylvan Ave.
Englewood Cliffs, NJ 07632

Certainly, all teachers need to reach this level of awareness as soon as possible. One obvious step in helping teachers reach this level is for school libraries to subscribe to a number of these journals.

Level 2   At this level, computer use, a person learns actually to use the computer — to view and evaluate instructional programs, to provide drill, practice, and remediation for children, and to keep records of students' progress and needs. Though school administrations must assume the major responsibility for providing adequate in-service experiences and training for teachers in the use of computers, teachers can also take steps toward educating themselves. They can do this by reading a computer self-help book. Some of the most helpful books are those written for children. Among the best are the following.

Kids and the Apple
Kids and the VIC-20
Kids and the Atari
Prentice-Hall

Armchair Basic
McGraw-Hill

Introduction to Basic for the VIC-20
Commodore Business Machines

I Speak Basic
(Everything you need to teach students and yourself about microcomputing)
Editions for the TRS-80, Apple, and PET computers
Hayden Book Company

The Elementary Apple
Data Most

Once teachers have a basic knowledge of how to use computers, they can begin to critically preview software created for classroom use. Although there are many fine instructional programs available for the computer, not all the material is appropriate for all children. It is essential that teachers and administrators actively preview and evaluate reading material and choose appropriate material for classroom use. An increasing number of software distributors provide free catalogs of instructional material and opportunities for schools to preview material for a certain time prior to making financial commitments. A major advantage of such distributors is that they sell software of many different publishers created for some of the readily available computers. Some of these distributors are the following.

American Micro Media
Box 306
Red Hood, NY 12571

EAV (Educational Audio Visual)
Pleasantville, NY 10570

EISI (Educational Instructional Systems, Inc.)
2225 Grant Road, Suite 3
Los Altos, CA 94022

Follett Library Book Company
4506 Northwest Highway
Crystal Lake, SC 60014

K–12 Micro Media
Box 17
Valley Cottage, NY 10989

Sunburst
39 Washington Ave.
Pleasantville, NJ 10570

In addition, several professional journals, including the following, provide specific reviews of instructional software. Teachers can use such journals for initial screening of material.

Booklist
50 E. Huron St.
Chicago, IL 60611

Micro Soft Reviews
Northwest Regional Educational Lab
300 SW 6th Ave.
Portland, OR 97204

The Book Report
Box 14466
Columbus, OH 43214

Journal of Apple Courseware Review
Apple Computer, Inc.
Box 28426
San Jose, CA 95159

Digest of Software Reviews
PRO/Files
E.P.I.E. and Consumers Union
Box 620
Stony Brook, NY 11790

In analyzing and evaluating reading software, the following criteria for quality software developed by *Electronic Learning* (1981) are very useful. It suggests that quality software should

be free of technical or pedagogical errors;
take advantage of the machine's unique capabilities without substituting flash for substance;
provide positive reinforcement and at the same time help students to understand wrong answers;
include some diagnostic features;
be creative, stimulating creativity among users;
allow for easy modification by teachers; and
provide clearly written support material and activities.

Level 3   Level 3, computer programming, is the most advanced level and requires the most sophisticated training. There is a great need for classroom teachers who know instruction as well as children to become involved in the writing of computer programs for classroom use in reading instruction. Many available programs lack pedagogical credibility because they are written by individuals who are unfamiliar with how children learn reading and with appropriate teaching techniques. If some teachers become excited enough about computer-assisted instruction to gain the needed skills in computer programming, they could add significantly to the quality of reading material designed for the computer. Inability to write programs, however, should not prevent teachers from creating material. Interested teachers can work with an expert programmer and jointly develop excellent instructional software.

As teachers become progressively familiar with the use of computers, they will find that the "computer explosion" can be a highly effective, captivating, and motivating instructional tool. In addition, as teachers begin to involve themselves in evaluating instructional software and in developing such material, the effectiveness of computer-assisted instruction will significantly increase and the needs of the children in our schools will be more effectively met.

Summary

It is very important that teachers refine their competence in teaching children how to read. It is equally important that teachers develop the art of motivating children to want to read. Children's attitudes toward reading are just as important as their skill in reading. A well-balanced and effective reading program exposes children to the techniques involved in reading while it immerses children in the joy of reading and captures their interest in print. The most effective way to motivate children toward learning is for the home and school environment to work together. Teachers must work with parents and involve them in the motivation and learning of children. The school environment must generate interest in and motivation toward reading. The most valuable gifts teachers can give children are the tools to read and the desire to use those tools.

References

Aulls, M. *Developing Readers in Today's Elementary School.* Boston: Allyn and Bacon, 1982.

Brandt, R. "Doing Better with Less." *Educational Leadership*, vol. 40 (February 1983).

Brown Bear, Brown Bear, What Do You See? Bill Martin Instant Readers. New York: Holt, Rinehart and Winston, 1974.

Dammeyer, J. W. "Computer-Assisted Learning — or Financial Disaster." *Educational Leadership*, vol. 40 (February 1983).

McCracken, R. A., and M. J. McCracken. "Modeling: The Key to Sustained Silent Reading." *Reading Teacher*, 31:4 (January 1978).

Melmed, A. S. "Productivity and Technology in Education." *Educational Leadership*, vol. 40 (February 1983).

O'Donnell, H. "Computer Literacy, Part I: An Overview." *Reading Teacher*, 35:4 (January 1982).

_____. "Computer Literacy, Part II: Classroom Application." *Reading Teacher*, 35:5 (February 1982).

Thompson, B. J. "Computers in Reading: A Review of Applications and Implications." *Educational Technology*, vol. 20 (August 1980).

Appendix A
Newbery Award Books

1922   *The Story of Mankind* by Hendrik Van Loon (Liveright)

1923   *The Voyages of Doctor Dolittle* by Hugh Lofting (Lippincott)

1924   *The Dark Frigate* by Charles Boardman Hawes (Little, Brown)

1925   *Tales from Silver Lands* by Charles J. Finger (Doubleday)

1926   *Shen of the Sea* by Arthur Bowie Chrisman (Dutton)

1927   *Smoky, The Cowhorse* by Will James (Scribner's)

1928   *Gayneck, the Story of a Pigeon* by Dhan Gopal Mukerji (Dutton)

1929   *The Trumpeter of Krakow* by Eric P. Kelly (Macmillan)

1930   *Hitty, Her First Hundred Years* by Rachel Field (Macmillan)

1931   *The Cat Who Went to Heaven* by Elizabeth Coatsworth (Macmillan)

1932   *Waterless Mountain* by Laura Adams Armer (Longmans)

1933   *Young Fu of the Upper Yangtze* by Elizabeth Foreman Lewis (Holt, Rinehart and Winston)

1934   *Invincible Louisa* by Cornelia Meigs (Little, Brown)

1935   *Dobry* by Monica Shannon (Viking)

1936   *Caddie Woodlawn* by Carol Ryrie Brink (Macmillan)

1937   *Roller Skates* by Ruth Sawyer (Viking)

1938   *The White Stag* by Kate Seredy (Viking)

1939   *Thimble Summer* by Elizabeth Enright (Holt, Rinehart and Winston)

1940   *Daniel Boone* by James H. Daugherty (Viking)

1941   *Call It Courage* by Armstrong Sperry (Macmillan)

1942   *The Matchlock Gun* by Walter D. Edmonds (Dodd, Mead)

1943   *Adam of the Road* by Elizabeth Janet Gray (Viking)

1944   *Johnny Tremain* by Esther Forbes (Houghton Mifflin)

1945   *Rabbit Hill* by Robert Lawson (Viking)

1946   *Strawberry Girl* by Lois Lenski (Lippincott)
1947   *Miss Hickory* by Carolyn Sherwin Bailey (Viking)
1948   *The Twenty-One Balloons* by William Pene du Bois (Viking)
1949   *King of the Wind* by Marguerite Henry (Rand McNally)
1950   *The Door in the Wall* by Marguerite de Angeli (Doubleday)
1951   *Amos Fortune, Free Man* by Elizabeth Yates (Dutton)
1952   *Ginger Pye* by Eleanor Estes (Harcourt, Brace)
1953   *Secret of the Andes* by Ann Nolan Clark (Viking)
1954   *. . . and Now Miguel* by Joseph Krumgold (Crowell)
1955   *The Wheel on the School* by Meindert DeJong (Harper & Row)
1956   *Carry On, Mr. Bowditch* by Jean Lee Latham (Houghton Mifflin)
1957   *Miracles on Maple Hill* by Virginia Sorensen (Harcourt, Brace)
1958   *Rifles for Waite* by Harold Keith (Crowell)
1959   *The Witch of Blackbird Pond* by Elizabeth George Speare (Houghton
        Mifflin)
1960   *Onion John* by Joseph Krumgold (Crowell)
1961   *Island of the Blue Dolphins* by Scott O'Dell (Houghton Mifflin)
1962   *The Bronze Bow* by Elizabeth George Speare (Houghton Mifflin)
1963   *A Wrinkle in Time* by Madeleine L'Engle (Farrar, Straus & Giroux)
1964   *It's Like This, Cat* by Emily Neville (Harper & Row)
1965   *Shadow of a Bull* by Maia Wojciechowska (Atheneum)
1966   *I, Juan de Pareja* by Elizabeth Borten de Trevino (Farrar, Straus &
        Giroux)
1967   *Up a Road Slowly* by Irene Hunt (Follett)
1968   *From the Mixed-Up Files of Mrs. Basil E. Frankweiler* by E. L. Konigs-
        burg (Atheneum)
1969   *The High King* by Lloyd Alexander (Holt, Rinehart and Winston)
1970   *Sounder* by William H. Armstrong (Harper & Row)
1971   *Summer of the Swans* by Betsy Byars (Viking)
1972   *Mrs. Frisby and the Rats of NIMH* by Robert C. O'Brien (Atheneum)
1973   *Julie of the Wolves* by Jean Craighead George (Harper & Row)
1974   *The Slave Dancer* by Paula Fox (Bradbury)
1975   *M. C. Higgins, the Great* by Virginia Hamilton (Macmillan)
1976   *The Grey King* by Susan Cooper (Atheneum)
1977   *Roll of Thunder, Hear My Cry* by Mildred D. Taylor (Dial)
1978   *Bridge to Terabithia* by Katherine Paterson (Crowell)
1979   *The Westing Game* by Ellen Raskin (Dutton)
1980   *A Gathering of Days* by Joan W. Blos (Scribner's)
1981   *Jacob Have I Loved* by Katherine Paterson (Crowell)
1982   *On Market Street* by Arnold Lobel (Greenwillow)

Appendix B
Caldecott Award Winners

1938   *Animals of the Bible,* illustrated by Dorothy O. Lathrop (Lippincott)

1939   *Mei Li* by Thomas Handforth (Doubleday)

1940   *Abraham Lincoln* by Ingri d'Aulaire and Edgar Parin d'Aulaire (Doubleday)

1941   *They Were Strong and Good* by Robert Lawson (Viking)

1942   *Make Way for Ducklings* by Robert McCloskey (Viking)

1943   *The Little House* by Virginia Lee Burton (Houghton Mifflin)

1944   *Many Moons* by James Thurber, illustrated by Louis Slobodkin (Harcourt, Brace)

1945   *Prayer for a Child* by Rachel Field, illustrated by Elizabeth Orton Jones (Macmillan)

1946   *The Rooster Crows* by Maud Petersham and Miska Petersham (Macmillan)

1947   *The Little Island* by Golden MacDonald, illustrated by Leonard Weisgard (Doubleday)

1948   *White Snow, Bright Snow* by Alvin Tresselt, illustrated by Roger Duvoisin (Lothrop)

1949   *The Big Snow* by Berta Hader and Elmer Hader (Macmillan)

1950   *Song of the Swallows* by Leo Politi (Scribner's)

1951   *The Egg Tree* by Katherine Milhous (Scribner's)

1952   *Finders Keepers* by Will (William Lipkind), illustrated by Nicolas (Nicolas Mordvinoff) (Harcourt, Brace)

1953   *The Biggest Bear* by Lynd Ward (Houghton Mifflin)

1954   *Madeline's Rescue* by Ludwig Bemelmans (Viking)

1955   *Cinderella* by Charles Perrault, illustrated by Marcia Brown (Scribner's)
1956   *Frog Went A-Courtin'* by John Langstaff, illustrated by Feodor Rojankovsky (Harcourt, Brace)
1957   *A Tree Is Nice* by Janice May Udry, illustrated by Marc Simont (Harper & Row)
1958   *Time of Wonder* by Robert McCloskey (Viking)
1959   *Chanticleer and the Fox*, written and illustrated by Barbara Cooney (Crowell)
1960   *Nine Days to Christmas* by Marie Hall Ets and Aurora Labastida (Viking)
1961   *Baboushka and the Three Kings* by Ruth Robbins, illustrated by Nicholas Sidjakov (Parnassus)
1962   *Once a Mouse* by Marcia Brown (Scribner's)
1963   *The Snowy Day* by Ezra Jack Keats (Viking)
1964   *Where the Wild Things Are* by Maurice Sendak (Harper & Row)
1965   *May I Bring a Friend?* by Beatrice Schenk de Regniers, illustrated by Beni Montresor (Atheneum)
1966   *Always Room for One More* by Sorche Nic Leodhas, illustrated by Nonny Hogrogian (Holt, Rinehart and Winston)
1967   *Sam, Bangs, and Moonshine* by Evaline Ness (Holt, Rinehart and Winston)
1968   *Drummer Hoff* by Barbara Emberley, illustrated by Ed Emberley (Prentice-Hall)
1969   *The Fool of the World and the Flying Ship* by Arthur Ransome, illustrated by Uri Shulevitz (Farrar, Straus & Giroux)
1970   *Sylvester and the Magic Pebble* by William Steig (Windmill Books)
1971   *A Story — A Story* by Gail E. Haley (Atheneum)
1972   *One Fine Day* by Nonny Hogrogian (Macmillan)
1973   *The Funny Little Woman* by Arlene Mosel, illustrated by Blair Lent (Dutton)
1974   *Duffy and the Devil* by Harve Zemach, illustrated by Marge Zemach (Farrar, Straus & Giroux)
1975   *Arrow to the Sun,* adapted and illustrated by Gerald McDermott (Viking)
1976   *Why Mosquitoes Buzz in People's Ears* by Verna Aardema, illustrated by Leo and Diane Dillon (Dial)
1977   *Ashanti to Zulu: African Traditions* by Margaret Musgrove, illustrated by Leo and Diane Dillon (Dial)
1978   *Noah's Ark* by Peter Spier (Doubleday)
1979   *The Girl Who Loved Wild Horses* by Paul Goble (Bradbury)
1980   *Ox-Cart Man* by Donald Hall, illustrated by Barbara Cooney (Viking)
1981   *Fables* by Arnold Lobel (Harper & Row)
1982   *Jumanji* by Chris Van Allsburg (Houghton Mifflin)

Appendix C
Predictable Pattern Books

Aliki. *Go Tell Aunt Rhody.* New York: Macmillan, 1974.

———. *My Five Senses.* New York: Crowell, 1962.

Balian, Lorna. *Where in the World Is Henry?* Scarsdale, N.Y.: Bradbury, 1972.

Barohas, Sarah E. *I Was Walking down the Road.* New York: Scholastic, 1975.

Baum, Arline, and Joseph Baum. *One Bright Monday Morning.* New York: Random House, 1962.

Becker, John. *Seven Little Rabbits.* New York: Scholastic, 1973.

Beckman, Kaj. *Lisa Cannot Sleep.* New York: Franklin Watts, 1969.

Bonne, Rose, and Alan Mills. *I Know an Old Lady.* New York: Rand McNally, 1961.

Brand, Oscar. *When I First Came to This Land.* New York: Putnam's, 1974.

Brandenberg, Franz. *I Once Knew a Man.* New York: Macmillan, 1970.

Brown, Marcia. *The Three Billy Goats Gruff.* New York: Harcourt, Brace, 1957.

Brown, Margaret Wise. *Four Fur Feet.* New York: William R. Scott, 1961.

———. *Home for a Bunny.* Racine, Wisc.: Golden Press, 1956.

Carle, Eric. *The Mixed-Up Chameleon.* New York: Crowell, 1975

———. *The Very Hungry Caterpillar.* Cleveland, Ohio: Collins World, 1969.

Charlip, Remy. *Fortunately.* New York: Parents' Magazine Press, 1964.

———. *What Good Luck! What Bad Luck!* New York: Scholastic, 1969.

Cook, Bernadine. *The Little Fish That Got Away.* Reading, Mass.: Addison-Wesley, 1976.

de Regniers, Beatrice Schenk. *Catch a Little Fox.* New York: Seabury, 1970.

———. *The Day Everybody Cried.* New York: Viking, 1967.

Domanska, Janina. *If All the Seas Were One Sea.* New York: Macmillan, 1971.

Ets, Marie Hall. *Elephant in a Well.* New York: Viking, 1972.

————. *Play with Me.* New York: Viking, 1955.

Galdone, Paul. *Henny Penny.* New York: Scholastic, 1968.

————. *The Little Red Hen.* New York: Scholastic, 1973.

————. *The Three Bears.* New York: Scholastic, 1972.

————. *The Three Billy Goats Gruff.* New York: Seabury, 1973.

————. *The Three Little Pigs.* New York: Seabury, 1970.

Hutchins, Pat. *Good-Night Owl.* New York: Macmillan, 1972.

Keats, Ezra Jack. *Over in the Meadow.* New York: Scholastic, 1971.

Kraus, Robert. *Whose Mouse Are You?* New York: Collier, 1970.

Lobel, Arnold. *A Treeful of Pigs.* New York: Greenwillow, 1979.

Mack, Stan. *10 Bears in My Bed.* New York: Pantheon, 1974.

Martin, Bill. *Brown Bear, Brown Bear.* New York: Holt, Rinehart and Winston, 1970.

Mayer, Mercer. *If I Had . . . .* New York: Dial, 1968.

————. *Just for You.* New York: Golden Press, 1975.

Memling, Carl. *Ten Little Animals.* Racine, Wisc.: Golden Press, 1961.

Peppe, Rodney. *The House That Jack Built.* New York: Delacorte, 1970.

Preston, Edna Mitchell. *Where Did My Mother Go?* New York: Four Winds Press, 1978.

Sendak, Maurice. *Where the Wild Things Are.* New York: Scholastic, 1963.

Shulevitz, Uri. *One Monday Morning.* New York: Scribner's, 1967.

Tolstoy, Alexei. *The Great Big Enormous Turnip.* New York: Franklin Watts, 1968.

Welber, Robert. *Goodbye, Hello.* New York: Pantheon, 1974.

Zaid, Barry. *Chicken Little.* New York: Random House, n.d.

Zemach, Harve. *The Judge.* New York: Farrar, Straus & Giroux, 1969.

Zemach, Margot. *Hush, Little Baby.* New York: Dutton, 1976.

————. *The Teeny Tiny Woman.* New York: Scholastic, 1965.

Zolotow, Charlotte. *Do You Know What I'll Do?* New York: Harper & Row, 1958.

Appendix D
Wordless Storybooks

Alexander, Martha. *Bobo's Dream.* New York: Dial, 1970.

———. *Out, Out, Out.* New York: Dial, 1970.

Anderson, Laurie. *The Package.* Columbus, Ohio: Bobbs-Merrill, 1971.

Anno, Mitsumasa. *Dr. Anno's Magical Midnight Circus.* New York: Weatherhill, 1972.

———. *Topsey Turvies.* New York: Weatherhill, 1970.

Ardizzone, Edward. *The Wrong Side of the Bed.* New York: Doubleday, 1970.

Aruego, Jose. *Look What I Can Do.* New York: Scribner's, 1971.

Asch, Frank. *The Blue Balloon.* New York: McGraw-Hill, 1972.

———. *In the Eye of the Teddy.* New York: Harper & Row, 1973.

Barton, Byron. *Elephant.* New York: Seabury, 1971.

Billout, Guy. *The Number 24.* New York: Dial, 1973.

Bolliger-Savelli, Antinella. *The Knitted Cat.* New York: Macmillan, 1972.

Carle, Eric. *Do You Want to Be My Friend?* New York: Crowell, 1971.

———. *I See a Song.* New York: Crowell, 1973.

———. *The Very Long Tail.* New York: Crowell, 1972.

Carrick, Donald. *Drip Drop.* New York: Macmillan, 1973.

Fromm, Lilo. *Muffel and Plums.* New York: Macmillan, 1973.

Goodall, John S. *Kelly, Dot, and Esmeralda.* New York: Atheneum, 1972.

———. *Shrewbettina's Birthday.* New York: Harcourt Brace Jovanovich, 1970.

Hoban, Tana. *Look Again.* New York: Macmillan, 1971.

Hogrogian, Nonny. *Apples.* New York: Macmillan, 1972.

Hutchins, Pat. *Changes Changes.* New York: Macmillan, 1971.

Krahn, Fernando. *A Flying Saucer Full of Spaghetti.* New York: Dutton, 1970.

————. *How Santa Claus Had a Long and Difficult Journey Delivering His Presents.* New York: Delacorte, 1970.

————. *Journeys of Sebastian.* New York: Delacorte, 1968.

Keats, Ezra Jack. *Skates.* New York: Franklyn Watts, 1973.

Lisker, Sonia. *The Attic Witch.* New York: Four Winds, 1973.

Mayer, Mercer. *A Boy, a Dog, and a Frog.* New York: Dial, 1967.

————. *Bubble Bubble.* New York: Parents' Magazine Press, 1973.

————. *Frog on His Own.* New York: Dial, 1973.

————. *Frog Where Are You?* New York: Dial, 1969.

Olschewski, Alfred. *Winterbird.* Boston: Houghton Mifflin, 1969.

Reich, Hanns. *Laughing Camera for Children.* New York: Hill and Wang, 1970.

Ringi, Kjeli. *The Magic Stick.* New York: Harper & Row, 1968.

————. *The Winner.* New York: Harper & Row, 1969.

Simmons, Ellie. *Cat.* New York: David McKay, 1968.

————. *Dog.* New York: David McKay, 1967.

————. *Family.* New York: David McKay, 1970.

————. *Wheels.* New York: David McKay, 1969.

Spier, Peter. *Noah's Ark.* New York: Doubleday, 1978.

Ueno, Noriko. *Elephant Buttons.* New York: Harper & Row, 1973.

Ungerer, Tomi. *One, Two, Three.* New York: Harper & Row, 1964.

————. *One, Two, Where's My Shoe?* New York: Harper & Row, 1964.

Ward, Lynd. *The Silver Pony.* New York: Houghton Mifflin, 1973.

Index